It's Just the Normal Noises

The New American Canon: The Iowa Series in
Contemporary Literature and Culture

Samuel Cohen, Series Editor

IT'S JUST THE NORMAL NOISES

Marcus, Guralnick, *No Depression*, and

the Mystery of Americana Music

Timothy Gray

University of Iowa Press, Iowa City

University of Iowa Press, Iowa City 52242
Copyright © 2017 by the University of Iowa Press
www.uipress.uiowa.edu
Printed in the United States of America

Design by Ashley Muehlbauer

The University of Iowa Press is a member of Green Press Initiative
and is committed to preserving natural resources.

An early version of "Hip Americana: The Cultural Criticism of Greil
Marcus" appeared in Prospects, Volume 27 (2002), 611–39. Copyright
2002 by Cambridge University Press. Reprinted with permission.

Printed on acid-free paper

Library of Congress Cataloging-in-Publication Data

Names: Gray, Timothy, 1964–
Title: It's just the normal noises : Marcus, Guralnick, *No Depression*,
and the mystery of Americana music / Timothy Gray.
Description: Iowa City : University of Iowa Press, [2017] | Series: New
American Canon | Includes bibliographical references and index.
Identifiers: LCCN 2016042839 | ISBN 978-1-60938-488-3 (pbk) |
ISBN 978-1-60938-489-0 (ebk)
Subjects: LCSH: Musical criticism—United States. | Popular music—
United States—History and criticism. | Americana (Music)—History
and criticism. | Marcus, Greil—Criticism and interpretation. |
Guralnick, Peter—Criticism and interpretation. | No Depression.
Classification: LCC ML3785 .G73 2017 | DDC 781.640973—dc23
LC record available at https://lccn.loc.gov/2016042839

For Maria, Alexander, and Charlotte

Contents

Acknowledgments

This is a book about music writing, but it's inspired by decades of informal conversations I've shared around kitchen tables and on bar stools in Boston and San Francisco, in my dad's car, in high school Spanish class (sorry, Mr. Allen), and on a dilapidated screened-in porch on Berkshire Street in Rochester, New York. *It's Just the Normal Noises* is the harmony; these folks provided the melody: Alyson Bardsley, John Barnett, Christopher Betts, Jason Bott, Greg Campbell, Chris Cummings, Bill Drumm, Irene Gammon, Harold Gray, Scott Gray, Dave Hebb, Tommy Klemperer, Bill Loveland, Lew Silverman, Dava Silvia, Ann Stedronsky, Alan Sun, Kevin Tile, Tim Wager, and Kathleen Winter. For her love and encouragement, I thank Carolyn Gray. Thanks, Joe Parsons, for believing in this project from its inception. Much gratitude to the University of Iowa Press folks, especially Elisabeth Chretien, Catherine Cocks, Sam Cohen (the series editor), Susan Hill Newton, and Allison Means. Kudos to my excellent copy editor, Faith Marcovecchio. Thanks to Brian Campolattaro, Rob Ruth, and Steve Sikking. And to Don Barnett, Grace Barnett, James Barnett, Beth Cummings, Caroline Cummings, Crosby Cummings, Matthew Cummings, Susan Dunne-Lederhaas, Cherylanne Gray, Megan Gray, and Melissa Gray. To my home base—Maria Barnett, Alexander Gray, Charlotte Gray—you keep getting dedications, so you must be doing something right. Keep on rocking in the free world.

Introduction

Although I am writing a book about the written word, I begin with sound. I was awakened to the world by the music of my parents' voices and by the din of my immediate surroundings, which on the eastern shore of Maryland was gentle: breezes on the riverside, waterfowl on the wing. Reading was still a long time off, as was writing. That's just the usual course of development.

Likewise, the sound of the radio sparked my interest in pop music years before I picked up *Rolling Stone* or Greil Marcus's *Mystery Train*. Gary Puckett and the Union Gap had a string of hits when I was four years old, and even then, I remember thinking all their songs sounded the same, brassy and schmaltzy (like those of the Buckinghams), but perfect for the car radio. Later, I got hooked on New Year's Eve countdowns on WABC New York, which kept me up long after my bedtime, thanks to a single earplug I jacked into my Toot-A-Loop radio. I tracked the chart position of Elton John singles and heard that the Hues Corporation scored the #1 song of 1974 with "Rock the Boat." I learned about mimesis when Bob Seger put out a pair of singles ("Night Moves" and "Mainstreet") that traced my little town's cultural geography, from the woods out beyond the cornfields to the gritty heart of downtown with its dive bars and "losers." During this time, my father served as advisor to a tiny college radio station, WKCS, which had a signal range of about a square mile. For me, that hardly mattered. The station got the same promotional copies and posters the bigger stations got (an oversized photo of Billy Preston posed in front of a jukebox on *Everybody Likes Some Kind of Music* was my favorite). I marveled at the studio turntables, control boards, and microphones. When I attended college myself, the campus radio station was my first stop, and it was there, on WFNM Lancaster, that I hosted an evening jazz show. I still had the Phil Upchurch and McCoy Tyner albums I had borrowed from WKCS.

Radio pioneers who ruled the airwaves long before my time (John R. on WLAC Nashville, Jimmy "Early" Byrd on WILD Boston, Dewey Phillips on WHBQ Memphis) did for other listeners what soul deejays on WDKX Rochester and purveyors of indie rock on WMBR Cambridge did for me: facilitate a more spacious and inclusive vision of America. Growing up in Minnesota, Bob Dylan was inspired by genre-busting southern radio programs drifting up the Mississippi River valley after nightfall. Phil Walden defied his Georgia parents and listened to black radio long before becoming the manager of Otis Redding. Black and white, rich and poor, northerner and southerner put aside their differences in the magical space radio created. In later years, Dylan himself was prompted to take a turn as deejay, hosting a show on satellite radio and informing a new generation about the mysteries of Americana. B. B. King, Peter Wolf, and Waylon Jennings actually launched their careers from the jock's box. For these reasons and others, radio will always be the sound salvation, however satirical Elvis Costello seemed when biting the hand that fed him ("Radio Radio"). The Velvet Underground, the Replacements, the Kinks, and even the Carpenters offered encomiums to radio in songs they placed there. This may sound quaint in the age of Spotify, but it's true.

Eventually, I became a literature professor, drawn to books. Writing on rock and roll has not only fueled my interest in music, it has also broadened my knowledge of American culture and selfhood. Admittedly, I find some rock writing purely entertaining. I still recall one-liners from Parke Puterbaugh about Van Halen's 1982 album *Diver Down* (hearing David Lee Roth sing covers of 1960s hits, he said, was like listening to someone read cue cards). I remember Karen Schoemer's review of Fleetwood Mac's 1997 reunion concert (she said Stevie Nicks's lyrics for "Landslide" resembled a young girl's journal poetry). And I salute whoever described sedate fans of Belle and Sebastian and rowdy fans of the Dropkick Murphys eyeballing each other during an awkward twin bill. Other rock writing I appreciated for its intellectual heft. *The Rolling Stone Illustrated History of Rock and Roll* (1976) was my de facto history text when I was a teen. Through this source, I discovered Greil Marcus's *Mystery Train: Images of America in Rock 'n' Roll Music*, a rock book that was ambitious and socially conscious; it made me rethink my ideas of American culture. Enraptured, I gravitated toward the longer arguments rock journalists like Marcus put forth in books, and over time I thought that an extended meditation on rock and roll writers might make a good book of its own.

It's Just the Normal Noises aims to be more than the sum of its parts. For fans of popular music and devotees of American studies, I hope to add a creative dimension to the interdisciplinary interests we share. Instead of offering specialized analysis, I'd like this book to resemble the rock albums I return to, full of diverse tracks that range in mood and, together, tell a story. If (in an old-fashioned way) an album remains a statement of where an artist finds him- or herself at a given moment, it's only natural that a writer considering these albums reflect a change of perspective every four or five years. It's Just the Normal Noises spent a bit more time percolating than my other books, and thus it has a looser structure. Writing, like life, is always in motion. As Bob Dylan surmised in 1965, the best writing "happens with a collage of experiences which somebody can actually know by instinct what's right and wrong for him to do. Where he doesn't have to feel guilty about anything" (quoted in Cott 2006, 38). Dylan said that in the midst of a wildly creative period during which he put out four game-changing albums. But truthfully, feeling secure about one's writing can make one less prolific. As Alex Chilton remarked, "Only about 1975 did I really become self-confident about my abilities, which coincides with the time when I began to write far fewer pieces of music" (Gordon 2001, 210). Like Chilton, I think I write less these days because I am more confident about what I want to say, and about what I don't.

Like a lot of the music it considers, It's Just the Normal Noises embodies a sense of restlessness, though maybe that's attributable to age. Toward the end of When That Rough God Goes Riding, his book about Van Morrison, Greil Marcus describes a typical moment in late middle age when "the world as it presents itself in advertisements, talk, technology, dress, movies, music, money, and perhaps most of all manners, the way in which people walk down the street, the way they say hello or goodbye or don't bother to do either, becomes an affront to one's entire existence" (2010a, 168). These words certainly describe the irascible Morrison, and to some degree they reflect my frustration with academia, though mostly I'm looking to accentuate the positive.[1]

I realized halfway through the writing of Urban Pastoral (2010), my book on the New York School of poets and painters, that I was part of my own disappearing act where scholarly writing was concerned, abandoning traditional literary criticism for more imaginative modes. I thought about my recreational reading and began to consider the music writers who had shaped my vision of America. I wanted to return the love. In *Urban Pastoral*, I emphasized the work/life balance of creative people, and soon I noticed some rock writers doing the same. Reviewing an album Patti Smith released in 1988 after a decade spent with her family in Michigan, Robert Palmer wrote, quite approvingly, that *Dream of Life* sounded like music nurtured over time rather than product put out to adhere to a schedule (2009, 310). I respected Smith's choice, and loved that Palmer saw its positive effect on her art. Similarly, I learned that in his informative and warmhearted books, Peter Guralnick forged empathetic bonds with the roots musicians whose careers he chronicled, remaining attentive to their daily concerns, connecting these with his own. For Guralnick, writing *Sweet Soul Music* was colored by "the odd process of self-revelation" (1999, 329). I liked that he wasn't afraid to record his own desires and insecurities alongside those of the musicians. Reading his work, I felt as though my own mission had been articulated. If I couldn't match the talent of Smith, Palmer, or Guralnick, I could at least take courage from them, more conscious than ever of life's daily drama and of good writing's role within it.

At the same time, I knew that salient cultural issues suffused the life stories of musical artists. Music can function as an escape from the outside world or as an explanation of that world. Listeners identify with the music's message and shape their social understandings accordingly. Marcus and Guralnick, titans of rock criticism, tap this fluid dichotomy, considering the personal appeal of roots music alongside national ideals of democracy and selfhood. In very different ways, Marcus and Guralnick enter a conversation the music has already opened up. Inevitably, that conversation involves personal crises, or what literary scholar Martha Banta calls "failure and success in America," the title of her 1979 book. Country songwriter Charlie Rich's down-home exegesis on humility and resignation, "Life's Little Ups and Downs," is exemplary in this regard, as are, in other contexts, *No Depression* magazine's empathetic coverage of Hurricane Katrina and Kurt Cobain's laconic performance on MTV of the Nirvana song "Dumb." These tales of success and failure punctuate chapters 2, 3, and 4 in *It's Just the Normal Noises*. Earnest as each is, irony cuts through most of them. Musicians strive for success, but they are most successful singing about disappointment. It's no mistake that Marcus's "Presliad" (about Elvis, in *Mystery Train*) and Guralnick's "The Death of the Dream" (about the fall of

Stax Records, in *Sweet Soul Music*), arguably the two best essays ever written about rock music, are each based on heartbreaking failure.[2]

Not surprisingly, it was when rock music suffered growing pains in the 1970s that the first substantial books about the subject got written, extending the "think pieces" rock periodicals had begun publishing. For many, rock had become airless and claustrophobic: too satisfied. In retrospect, we know that punk came along to revitalize rock, as the Blues Revival and the British Invasion had a decade earlier. But a cast of talented music writers did their part as well, challenging rock to live up to its potential while urging listeners to consider musical gems they had overlooked. Patti Smith remembers the early 1970s as "a time when the vocation of a music journalist could be an elevated pursuit … I modeled myself after Baudelaire, who wrote some of the great idiosyncratic critiques of nineteenth-century art and literature" (2010, 178). Experimental writers tried longer forms, breaking through the confines of deadline journalism to revisit rock's original promise, and the nation's. They assured readers that good music still existed, even as naysayers rang out rock's death knell.

But growing pains persisted. In the 2000s, a heckler shouted to Dean Wareham, the front man of Luna, "Don't let your middle age go to waste!" (Wareham 2009, 308), putting a new spin on the indie rock anthem Wareham once performed with Galaxie 500, "Don't Let Our Youth Go to Waste" (which, in turn, was not just a cover but a total transformation of an old Jonathan Richman song). Waste looks quite different from the perspective of middle age, especially if you're still involved in a culture hooked on youthfulness, or if you remain fixated on a historical period when being wasted seemed so much more romantic. Rock stars are famous for dying at age twenty-seven.[3] But those who make it beyond that date face irrelevance. As Dana Spiotta notes in *Stone Arabia*, her novel about a rock and roll has-been, "the saddest obituaries are the premature but not uncommon middle-aged 'young' people, say between thirty-five and fifty" (2011b, 84): roughly my own age as I composed this book. When Bob Seger revealed the plight of Sweet Sixteen-turned-thirty-one in his 1977 single "Rock and Roll Never Forgets," he didn't consider what would happen when Sweet Sixteen turned fifty. Given the chance, most middle-aged musicians and writers would choose thirty-one in a heartbeat, remembering it as a time when youth was still in bloom, when vitality and experience seemed evenly balanced. On the back end of middle age, by contrast, the trappings of success (security, status, career) lead people to swap adventure for authority. In such cases, vibrancy and truth go missing.

Like musicians, rock journalists have a hard time carrying their work forward as they age. They have to be flexible in a changing economy, leaving or entering mainstream outlets as circumstances dictate. Former *No Depression* co-editor Grant Alden negotiated a separate peace when he left the industry town of Nashville and moved to Morehead, Kentucky. Today, he tries to live a sustainable life in an out-of-the-way location, blogging on the *No Depression* website, reporting unapologetically on life "in these middle years, in this small town." Rock writers who got their start earlier, such as Marcus, Guralnick, Bill Friskics-Warren, Anthony DeCurtis, and Holly George-Warren, may have enjoyed stellar reputations, but they saw lucrative journalism assignments disappear with the rise of the Internet. In addition to publishing more books, these writers have entered the academy on a part- or full-time basis to help pay the bills. I honor their versatility and integrity.[4]

Whenever rock commentators adopt an academic apparatus in an awkward quest for intellectual relevance, the rock community is there to bring them back to earth. "Let the rock critics read Adorno and Althusser," Dean Wareham once said. "I will study Pops Staples and the Chocolate Watchband" (2009, 108). Ann Powers and Carrie Brownstein, among the best writers on indie rock, both left graduate school at Berkeley to pursue their true calling. It is indeed a virtue, Richard Goldstein said, to move beyond "Ph.Dylanology" and the "Rolling Tenure Review" (quoted in Dettmar 2009, 160). Similar complaints about academic music writing got expressed by some Memphis natives who disbanded a folklore panel at the National Endowment for the Arts because of its pretentious take on Skip James's music. "We figured there was not enough known about class and gender and racism in general for any comment to be made about the aesthetics or the meaning of the music," musician Randall Lyon claimed. "Other than enjoying it as a human fucking being" (quoted in Gordon 2001, 153). My choice of words might be different, but my sentiment is largely the same.

In sum, I don't want academia to become for me what Vegas became for touring musicians, a steady but soul-deadening gig. That's why I wrote this book at this time. After discovering books on youth subcultures by Ann Powers and Donna Gaines, I realized that I share Spiotta's preoccupation in *Stone Arabia*, which is "how anyone copes with aging and reconciling what you thought you'd be with what you end up being" (Spiotta 2011, interview with Alex Shepherd). To facilitate that coping, I think of Tom Waits, who said, "Time is not a line, or a road where you get further away from things. It's all exponential. Everything that you experienced at eighteen is still with you" (quoted in Hoskyns 2009, 434). I seek the wacky atmosphere Robert Gordon identifies in his hometown of Memphis, where "nothing ever happens but the impossible" (2001, 41–57). To appreciate the independent-minded writers composing stories about independent-minded musicians, I think of what Tom Wilson said about producing Dylan's 1965 album *Bringing It All Back Home*: "You have to be as free on this side of the glass as he is out there" (quoted in Henthoff 2006, 17). And I think of what Greil Marcus said about Pauline Kael's *I Lost It at the Movies*: "I want to feel as free as she must have felt when she wrote that" (quoted in Reynolds 2012, part 1).

And so, chasing freedom, I have decided to indulge my curiosity about American roots music, heeding Dylan, who on his *Theme Time Radio Hour* reminded listeners, "Whatever music you love, it didn't come from nowhere" (quoted in Polito 2009, 151). The deep mystery Dylan plumbs in his best songs shapes a cultural category known as Americana, which is the best umbrella term I can provide for the music I consider in the first three chapters of *It's Just the Normal Noises*. Back in the 1920s, there was a column called "Americana" in H. L. Mencken's *The American Mercury* (McNally 2014, 172). In 1971, Don DeLillo named a novel after the term, and four decades later, Ray Davies (memoir) and Chimamanda Ngozi Adichie (fiction) did the same, the latter adding an "h." As a concept, Americana remains vague, albeit alluring. Americana is what the Solemn Old Judge deemed the Grand Ole Opry to be back in 1927: "nothing but realism, down to earth for the earthy" (Guralnick 1989, 50). It is the "primordial America" that Barney Hoskyns locates in Tom Waits's music, shaped by the aura of what people leave behind, like bicycles and shoes, but constantly return to in their minds, emblematic of a simpler America one senses near campfires, by railroad tracks (2006, 288, 290, 423–24). Americana is the lonesome train whistle Waits heard while growing up in Whittier, California (10), the same whistle young Dick Nixon heard when he lay awake at night and dreamed of future success (Ambrose 2014, 26). Americana excavates national history to unearth artifacts infused with aura: antique weather vanes, vintage trains, and tattered *Farmers' Almanacs*. It honors the symbols Greil

Marcus included on the title page of *Mystery Train*: Indians, a banjo, a gospel shouter, Civil War soldiers, Elvis.[5] Americana can be either deep or kitschy, or both at the same time.

Nostalgia and revisionism are crucial to most versions of Americana. The good old days seem good, even if they weren't, because time plays tricks on you. Marcus taps the temporal promise of Americana when he espies in Bob Dylan's aptly titled comeback album *Time Out of Mind* (1997) "the reappearance of the forgotten past in an empty present" (2010, 212). Similarly, Jon Pareles, in a review of Robert Plant and Alison Krauss's roots album *Raising Sand* (2007), says that T Bone Burnett's production results in a "terra incognita somewhere between swamp and mountain, memories and eternity." With Americana, we may feel that we have approached the heart of the heart of the country. But we also feel that we don't know an exact location or specific time frame, which suits most folks just fine. If there's any security that emerges from indeterminacy or any focus to be found in haziness, Americana manages to tap it. It has what Dylan says it has: "a broad grasp of the country, its conditions" (2005, 26)

In the realm of music, Americana is beholden to a "mythic origin" (Pecknold 2008, 28), tied to folks as varied as Stephen Foster, the Carter Family, and Blind Lemon Jefferson. Yet as a music format, Americana dates back only to 1995, when Rob Bleetstein and Jon Grimson devised an Americana chart for the trade industry paper *The Gavin Report*. Bleetstein has said that he originally wanted to call the chart Crucial Country but accepted the advice of Grimson, who suggested the name Americana (and ended up trademarking it). Thereafter, Americana was, for lack of a better word, "branded." As Grant Alden, co-editor of *No Depression*, liked to say, "brands are for cattle," although as former president of the Americana Music Association, he knew the power of marketing as well as anyone (Alden 2010).

Prior to *The Gavin Report*'s imprimatur, the Americana movement was sparked by Uncle Tupelo's debut album, released in 1990, and by the belated appearance of Dylan's 1983 blues chestnut, "Blind Willie McTell," on *Bootleg Series Volumes 1–3*, issued in 1991 (which wasn't merely "the year punk broke").[6] Rick Rubin's 1994 rescue of Johnny Cash on *American Recordings* made waves, as did Smithsonian Folkways' 1997 reissue of Harry Smith's *Anthology of American Folk Music* (1952) on a six-CD set. Dylan's *Time Out of Mind* (1997) solidified this return to old-time roots, as did albums put out by rockers who had rediscovered Smith's eclectic anthology (see *The Harry Smith Connection* tribute album from

1998, as well as David Johansen and the Harry Smiths' eponymous album from 2000).[7] Solidifying the Americana revival was the release of the Coen Brothers film *O Brother, Where Art Thou?* (2000) and its award-winning soundtrack, which put old-timey acoustic string music on the radar for a younger audience. Shortly thereafter, Nick Spitzer launched his excellent NPR program *American Routes*, providing entertaining musicology for newcomers and experts alike. By 2010, the Grammy Awards had formed a separate category for Americana music, and so many members of Generation X had adopted a back-to-basics lifestyle that a major publishing house issued *United States of Americana*, a far-ranging account of roots-based values and practices: backyard chicken farming, beard grooming, crafting, and amateur musicianship.

In time, as the trend leveled out, complaints about commercial and cultural appropriation replaced paeans to folksy wisdom. An academic collection edited in 2008 by Pamela Fox and Barbara Ching was especially perceptive. Contributors broke down the marketing strategy and political power plays hiding behind all the myths and symbols. But as much as I appreciated the corrective insight of *Old Roots, New Routes: The Cultural Politics of Alt.Country Music*, neither its opinions nor its style fits my current purpose. Erudition is evident, and the cautionary tales are carefully developed, but on the whole there is little joy expressed, and not enough soul. I prefer a different mode of American studies, one that matches the music styles I love.

Trippers and askers surround me. When I finished *Old Roots, New Routes*, a nagging question emerged. Am I a fanboy? The moniker got tossed around in derogatory ways in Fox and Ching's volume, and at academic conferences. Was I lacking in rigor? Was I delusional? Immature? Then I saw that Peter Guralnick had a section in an early book titled "A Fan's Notes," and I felt like I had good company. Guralnick talked unabashedly about how honored he was to be in Howlin' Wolf's presence, even if the self-absorbed performer remained oblivious (1989, 280). Similarly, in profiles on Charlie Rich, Guralnick positioned himself "as both a friend and as a journalist" (145). He confessed to the "adulatory" writing he had done on Waylon Jennings (215–16), and he breathlessly celebrated Elvis Presley's 1968 Comeback Special in the *Rolling Stone Illustrated History of Rock and Roll*, calling it "one of the great moments in rock" (1992, 33).

Even the relatively circumspect Greil Marcus has confessed to being a "shameless fan" of Elvis (2015, 141n). Elsewhere, Marcus said that "becoming a Bob Dylan fan made me a writer," calling his door-stopper compilation of Dylan pieces "an attempt to remain a part of the conversation that Bob Dylan's work has always created around itself" (2010, xvii). As Marcus told Simon Reynolds in 2012, "One of the great things about fandom is, we all love stuff and often love the same stuff, but we do it for our own different reasons. We get different sorts of satisfactions. But the satisfactions are close enough that we can talk about it, or want to know what someone else thinks" (quoted in Reynolds, 2012, part 2). *No Depression* editors Peter Blackstock and Grant Alden called themselves fanboys, thumbing their noses at detractors like Fox and Ching while managing to put out a first-rate publication. Blackstock and Alden featured artists they liked and then sat back to gauge the reactions of readers. It was, in its own way, an intellectual maneuver. Fandom is, at base, a challenge: a line drawn in the sand. As Marcus says:

> For Nik Cohn to say that "The Book of Love" by the Monotones meant more to him than all of *Blonde on Blonde*—that's a serious intellectual argument, that's a challenge. That forced me to think. Because I was like, "No no no, *Blonde on Blonde* means more to me than anything. But I love 'The Book of Love' too, so what is he saying?" And that really made me think about what matters, and about how much can happen in three minutes, as opposed to what can happen in an hour and a half. And maybe a lot more can happen in three minutes. It took me aback, in a way that I just loved. (Marcus, quoted in Reynolds, 2012, part 4)

Still, the cynics swarm, rejecting subjective interjections and lampooning Americana's quest for authenticity in a postmodern age. Sarah Thornton maintains in her book *Club Cultures* that "authenticity is to music what happy endings are to Hollywood cinema—the reassuring reward for suspending disbelief" (1996, 26). Jon Smith, whose attitude is typical of *Old Roots, New Routes*, cites Thornton (and other prominent British cultural materialists) to discredit as puerile an alternative country movement he has "grown out of" (2008, 62). Also tapping southern studies scholarship, Smith sets out to puncture alternative country's fanboy fantasies: "By associating the South with the authentic, cotton-pickin' past and 'the nation' (including Canada as the ultimate progressive 'North' and the source of much alt.country) with youth culture and the future, country/alt.country rhetoric tends to lend country music an aura of maturity it does not especially deserve while simultaneously both valorizing and infantilizing alt.country in terms necessarily similar to those used … to valorize and infantilize Generation X" (53).

Against Smith (and the scholars he cites) I hold no grudge. But readers should know that mine is not a story of "growing up and out of alt.country." Neither can I dismiss outright the rock and roll fun that led me to this project. As the Mekons liked to shout from the stage: "Do you want to be part of the crime, or do you want to be part of the punishment?" (Marcus 2015a, 10). If the authenticity of roots rock is constantly questioned, I can at least try to be my authentic self, granting others (musicians, writers, readers) the same leeway. There are echoes here of debates that wafted through American studies programs a few decades ago. In one camp were scholars who employed anecdotal evidence and creative writing as they explored national meaning. In the other camp were scholars who attacked these writers for their "unscientific method," the way they favored appreciation over intellectual conceptualization. Clearly, I side with the first camp, while honoring the reservations expressed by the second camp.

Readers will discover that the rock writers I admire underscore the human aspect of the cultures they study. In musicians' homes or on their tour buses, academic jargon doesn't count for much, and explains even less. Challenging situations arise and are met head-on. Peter Guralnick says that on a trip down South his questions as to the whereabouts of Robert Pete Williams were met with utter incredulity by black locals (1999a, 126). Finding Mr. Williams at his home, Guralnick acted naturally; he neither objectified nor condescended to the musician. According to Guralnick, Williams "beamed proudly as we shook hands all around and told us—as if that had been the point of our whole visit—that we could tell our friends back home that we had had a real country supper" (148–49). A similar dynamic held sway when Guralnick drank lemonade at the home of Jerry Lee Lewis, who joked with the teetotaler journalist about spiking his drink with vodka (177). Another time, Guralnick ventured into Johnny Jenkins's tough city neighborhood only to be confronted by the retired guitarist, who was working on his car: "What does a white motherfucker like you want to find out?" Guralnick honestly stated his intentions and found that amazing access was granted. People liked telling their stories, he learned, so long as you were respectful.

A good music writer is not afraid to go against the grain. It is why, in *Delta Blues*, Ted Gioia restores to blues researchers the quirky humanity bled out of them by revisionist historians. It is why Guralnick says that "whatever else they have been, the Stones have always proved the best advertisement for American black music outside of the music itself" (1999a, 28). It is why feminist journalists such as Ellen Willis and Lisa Robinson found themselves championing the Stones, against their better judgment.[8] And it is why, contrary to expectations, I prefer Uncle Tupelo's performance of "Moonshiner" to most other versions of the Appalachian folk classic.

Some critics denigrate Uncle Tupelo's Jay Farrar for being the son of a bookstore owner rather than an authentic hillbilly. Truth is, Farrar's family came from rural Missouri, and he grew up in Belleville, Illinois, where his parents saturated the house with roots music (Simkin 2008, 208). Whatever desperation Farrar heard in traditional folk music he applied to life in the forgotten towns of southwestern Illinois. By "writing and talking about a non-descript place in such specific terms," Greg Kot maintains, Farrar and Uncle Tupelo "also ennobled it in some strange way," (2004, 101). The so-called dean of the American rock critics, Robert Christgau, begs to differ, criticizing Farrar for "mourning an American past too atmospheric to translate into mere words" (quoted in Kot, 103). But I come from a corner of rural America similar to Farrar's, and I know that sometimes "atmosphere" was the only thing we had to hold on to. For me, Uncle Tupelo's "Moonshiner" shows Generation Xers in quest of authenticity, cutting through the crap, searching for a truer sound. And if it's true that I was a twenty-something working a bookstore graveyard shift when I first heard Farrar belt out the Uncle Tupelo version on a tape deck, that shouldn't make my reaction any less relevant; it just makes it unfashionable in certain circles.

Because I am a fan of indie music, my thinking has to be equally independent, simply to keep pace. I make a beeline toward writers doing the same, whatever genre of music they address. Roots matter. Publishing a book about Nirvana at its zenith, Michael Azerrad underscored the integrity of the band's music, reminding readers of the original Northwest soundscape. Nirvana was a multiplatinum cash cow, but it wasn't always that way, and not everyone who bought Nirvana's records was jumping on a bandwagon. For Azerrad, "the investigative zeal required in order to make one's way through the morass of independent music was in effect a rebuke of herd consumerism … Independent music required independent thinking, all the way from the artists who made the music to the entrepreneurs who sold it, to the people who bought it" (2001, 4). Sara Marcus says something similar in her study of the Riot Grrrl movement, claiming that anyone, at any time, can create a scene and make art that matters: "Do it in paint, in plaster, with drums and harp, with words and dance. Start your own scene with your friends, rooted in the particulars of your own lives and what gets you riled up. Craft a mythology around it. Be grandiose; be overblown; do it all the way and then keep going" (2010, 329–30). Such independence led to publication and distribution of 'zines through which Riot Grrrls depicted themselves as they wished, keeping outsiders at bay, maintaining their grass roots.

It's something to root for, and to shoot for. As Grant Alden said of *No Depression*: "Did I think the magazine was going to be something? Yes, I did. Did I want to act like that when we started it? No. Because I wanted it to be organic—from the community that it sought to serve … You talk, in college, about how you want to live your life. And then you go and you compromise for the rest of your life. I just don't compromise very well" (2006). I am fairly confident that Alden's message reverberates throughout *It's Just the Normal Noises*.

Granted, the indie life is not always easy. Azerrad's *Our Band Could Be Your Life* abounds with examples of bands that got tired of sleeping alongside their gear in Econoline vans night after night. Plaintively expressing that road weariness in "Whiskey Bottle," Jay Farrar of Uncle Tupelo sang of unhappiness in a "three-hour-away town." Indie labels were chronically late in royalty payments. Concert tee shirt sales determined what the band got to eat that night. Fanzines folded after a few issues due to lack of funds. Looking back, Dean Wareham says, "There was no such thing as being proud to be indie. There was simply no other option at the time." Wareham heard *Rolling Stone* call his outfit, Luna, "the world's greatest rock-and-roll band no one's heard of" (2009, 180). Bemused by this appraisal, Wareham held true to his vision, accepting success on his own terms. "We didn't set the world on fire," Wareham says of his various bands, "but it feels good to think that the people are still listening to a little album that you made with your friends back in 1989 fifteen years later, halfway around the world, as the sun comes up. Can that be my legacy?" (288).

My ambitions pretty much mirror Wareham's. *It's Just the Normal Noises* salutes spirited writers who bring contemporary American music alive. My book is certainly not a comprehensive study of rock journalism, which has transformed itself constantly from the early days of *Crawdaddy!* and *Rolling Stone* in the mid-1960s to the emergence of *Spin* and *Vibe* a couple decades later to the crush of blogs and social media outlets available today. On the contrary, my book is framed, in part, as memoir. I am not a musicologist, nor am I a music critic. If you have heard me play guitar, you know I am not a musician. But I am a student of American culture, and rock writers have helped me understand the nation and my place within it. As Greil Marcus has put it, circuitously and mysteriously, when discussing Bob Dylan, "America is the life's work of the American artist because he is doomed to be an American" (2010, 24). That said, here is my life's work.

Across four chapters, I investigate the impact of rock writers across various lines of inquiry: Greil Marcus on cultural studies; Peter Guralnick on biography; *No Depression* magazine on fan-based community; and a host of creative writers on indie rock's expressions of failure and loneliness. Marcus and Guralnick are rightly acknowledged as legends. They were there on the ground floor of rock journalism in the 1960s and have produced many influential books. Marcus's *Mystery Train*, originally published in 1975 and currently in its sixth edition, remains the touchstone for serious rock and roll writing, a companion for music lovers across the land.[9] In Marcus's hands, rock and blues performers become mythic figures, archetypes, in the nation's complicated narrative. Guralnick's books are impassioned without being naïve. His masterful *Sweet Soul Music* (originally published in 1986) is a case in point. Guralnick delights in daily scenes—like Sam and Dave shooting craps in the Stax studio as David Porter and Isaac Hayes compose the songs they will record—but in the end his book presents soul music in a larger context, as "an education in an aspect of Americana and a facet of American business" (Guralnick 1999, 1). If rock culture is a Baby Boomer legacy, Marcus and Guralnick are its keepers.

The writers featured in the second half of *It's Just the Normal Noises* are not as well known. But by investigating how rock has meshed into subgenres such as alternative country or hardcore punk, they have tracked new and vibrant modes of belonging. Although I discovered it more than halfway through its print run, *No Depression* magazine was a godsend to me, not only for its coverage of alt-country music but also for its wide-angle view of our nation. I was raised in rural America, but I have spent my adult years in cosmopolitan settings. *No Depression* didn't so much bridge that geographical divide as it helped me rediscover my roots. I like punk rock attitudes. I like small towns bordered by open fields and crossed by railroad tracks. I have known both.

Why can't I enjoy both simultaneously? The enthusiasts of alternative country at *No Depression* told me I could.

Reading the memoirists and novelists featured in chapter 4 elicited another strong response. In these pages we see the anguish of teenagers denied acceptance by mainstream society. We also witness their resolve as they form communities based on shared musical interests. I investigate this subject from a variety of angles, tapping the work of multiple writers working in different genres. In this chapter, it's less about format and more about flow. Multiple texts speak to one another. For me, reading memoirs by the wise and wistful city-dwellers Patti Smith and Ann Powers shed light on the sociological study of troubled suburban heavy metal kids penned by Donna Gaines. Reading Charles Cross's biography of Kurt Cobain and Holly George-Warren's biography of Alex Chilton helped me understand the loneliness lingering on the margins of fame. Comparing contemporary novels by Dana Spiotta and Eleanor Henderson convinced me that a teenager's immersion in music can teach him more than his parents would ever dare discuss. Operating in a more subjective register than the journalists discussed in previous chapters, the writers featured in chapter 4 trace emotional scars music has the power to heal.

Beyond the scope of music and music writing, my book is a study of generational contrasts. As someone who was born in June 1964, Freedom Summer, I straddle a well-known generational divide, but I mostly claim allegiance with Generation X. I identify with *Easy Rider*, but only because it signifies the end of a dream. It is a sad story I love coming back to. I got caught up in the romance of Woodstock when I saw the film in 1979 and when I trekked to the Bethel site in 1989 (spotting Michael Lang, who smiled at me). But I had heard about Altamont, too. Sadly, the "common imagination" Marcus identified in Dylan's mid-1960s songs was not, for Gen X, our commonality, or our truth, however much we liked Dylan's mercurial persona. Nope, we teens of the 1970s missed out on the love, as Victoria Williams sang in "Summer of Drugs." And yet our ironic sensibility has been oversold. We like the snide side of Dylan, as the Boomers did, but we really latched on to the vulnerability evident on 1975's *Blood on the Tracks* (see the poignant essay by Carrie Brownstein in the *Cambridge Companion to Bob Dylan*). We also relate to Big Star, an early 1970s band that never quite made it. We prefer Alex Chilton's "Do You Wanna Dance" to the Bobby Freeman/Beach Boys hit of the same name (great as it is) because Chilton is better at acknowledging our collective hurt.

Times change, sometimes too fast. Left out of my study is a newer generation of writers, the Millennials. With their high-tech savvy, they have roots and tastes very different from mine. I have also refrained from extended analysis of talented British writers such as Jon Savage and the brilliant Simon Reynolds, preferring to focus on homegrown American themes. And I regret not granting separate chapters to other commentators on American rock: Lester Bangs, Ellen Willis, Stanley Booth, and Nick Tosches, to name a few. But you have to draw the line. Last call always rolls around, and it's best to have as much fun as you can until it does.

It may sound brave, or it may sound dumb, but fun is at the heart of *It's Just the Normal Noises*. If I tend to exemplify rather than theorize, as the old "myth-symbol" scholars were accused of doing, consider yourself forewarned. But songs don't theorize, and writing that theorizes too heavy-handedly about rock songs risks missing their very essence. Besides, fun can lead to wisdom, as Marcus and Guralnick have separately opined. And subjectivity rules, okay? Like Marcus, I see that what once looked like personal questions I was asking of myself are actually questions America is asking of me through roots rock music. I am therefore taking stock of several things at once, and revealing something of myself in the process. Tracking her rock star brother's long demise, novelist Dana Spiotta's middle-aged character Denise Kranis says, "Now that I was older, and actually had a life story, I didn't feel like telling it or hearing it" (2011b, 68). I'm not sure whether her sentiment holds true for me, or for most people, who tend to be effusive if not always linear or inherently logical when considering their life journeys.[10] But I do know that many of the stories I've cherished and the life lessons I've learned fill the pages of this book. Perhaps you'll find a bit of your American experience as well.

★ 1 ★

Hip Americana: The Cultural Criticism of Greil Marcus

In 1976, as many in our nation were celebrating the Bicentennial and listening to AM radio schlock like "Afternoon Delight," I persuaded my father to buy me an oversized paperback I had been perusing at the mall. The book was the *Rolling Stone Illustrated History of Rock and Roll*, a landmark collaboration edited by Jim Miller. Throughout my teenage years, I pored over its photographs, memorized its discography sections, and took instruction and courage from its lively, opinionated writing. Looking back at the *Illustrated History*, I find that its list of contributors reads like a who's who of rock criticism. Peter Guralnick, Robert Christgau, Lester Bangs, Robert Palmer, Jon Landau, and Dave Marsh are just a few who went on to make their names as critics, musicologists, and biographers. On this occasion they managed to weave the separate strands of rhythm and blues, folk, country, and rock into a cohesive tapestry.

Arriving when it did, on the cusp of punk and during the onslaught of disco, the *Illustrated History* signaled the end of rock's "classic" phase. While canonical status might seem anathema to rock, with its maverick posturing and emphasis on novelty, we should not underestimate any subculture's desire for legitimacy and respect (see Hebdige 1979). This is where another of the *Illustrated History*'s contributors, Greil Marcus, enters the picture. For the past fifty years, he has situated rock and roll deep in the American grain, equating it with great literature. As a student at Berkeley during the Free

Speech Movement, as editor and columnist for periodicals such as *Rolling Stone, Artforum, Interview,* and *Salon,* and as professor of American studies at Princeton, Berkeley, Minnesota, and the New School, Marcus has moved easily between the hallowed halls of academia and the concert halls of the rock world.[1] His cultural criticism takes its cue from the breadth of his experiences and is facilitated by his effort to break down disciplinary barriers that have prevented partisan thinkers from recognizing the countercultural spirit at the heart of the American dream.

In much of his writing, Marcus invokes the spirit of something I am calling "hip Americana," a hybrid concept that helps bridge the divide between academic discourse and popular entertainments. At first glance, any effort to combine the hip (denoting whatever is trendy, subversive, and ephemeral) and Americana (a time-tested repository of folk aesthetics, beliefs, and values) would seem destined for failure. After all, once the hip is defined, it tends to lose its allure, whereas Americana becomes increasingly coherent to the degree one pauses over and worships its timeless store of riches. What both camps secretly share, however, is a bedrock belief in their ability to summon a theoretical safety zone, a place where signified relations are comprehensible and chaos is temporarily held in check. According to Andrew Ross, hipness marks an "inherent style of doing things [that is] inscrutable beyond any organized hermeneutics of meaning" (99–100). Of course, boundaries inevitably emerge to make whatever is inherent and unorganized recognizable to those in the know. For the American hipster of the 1950s, Ross explains, these boundaries took the shape of a contested racial imaginary. Marcus amends Ross's schematic insofar as he links the hip with a more improbable imaginary register: America's "usable past." Unlike Norman Mailer, who in "The White Negro" (1957) emphasized the existential hipster's rejection of history, Marcus argues that cutting-edge musicians of the 1950s and 1960s such as John Lee Hooker and Bob Dylan tapped our nation's legacy by rooting themselves in a forgotten folk aesthetic, a "vernacular national culture" (2015a, 212). Paying homage to the past, and to the artists and theorists who have brought its lessons to bear on the present, Marcus renounces Mailer's existential detachment in favor of an impassioned American "weirdness," a quality he says is as basic to Puritan jeremiads as it is to blues and folk traditions. In the "old, weird America" (1997, 89), where beauty is wrung from terror, hipsters and traditionalists have more in common than they care to admit.

Marcus's writings on popular music have made him an important participant in an ongoing conversation about historiography and cultural identity in post-modern America, particularly about the dashed dreams and broken promises of the 1960s. A brief whiff of utopianism at the end of that turbulent decade turned to disappointment and disillusionment in the 1970s, which in turn led to a recuperative and almost obsessive interest in "culture" in the 1980s and 1990s, especially within the emergent fields of New Historicism and cultural studies. Although Marcus is acquainted with these academic categories and trends, he asserts that the most influential considerations of history and culture in this era came from musicians. In the 1960s, a host of rock, folk, and soul music "prophets" reminded Americans that their nation continually compromised its principles of freedom and equality. These performers knew that in order to resist disposses-sion of their own rights, they would have to embrace American ideals as never before: hence the unlikely appearance of patriotism in the counterculture. In *Easy Rider* (1969), Captain America paints the American flag on his chopper's teardrop gas tank and sports its image on the back of his leather motorcycle jacket as an open dare to anyone refusing his right to full citizenship. Marcus has taken a similar stand. Focusing his intellectual energies on underground movements that are surprisingly aboveboard in their national allegiances and passions, he has offered a fascinating history of postmodern America.

Marcus is best known as the author of *Mystery Train* (originally published in 1975), a book he wrote after dropping out of the doctoral program in Ameri-can political thought at UC Berkeley. While not quite the first, it is arguably the most passionate chronicle of rock music ever written.[2] *Mystery Train* places the music of Robert Johnson, the Band, Sly Stone, Randy Newman, and Elvis Presley within a pantheon of classic American texts. As he fleshes out his thesis, Marcus bridges the divide between the popular mind of the 1950s and 1960s and the high literature of the previous century's "Ameri-can Renaissance." He also reconsiders the cultural tensions that challenged foundational democratic tenets of freedom and inclusiveness in each era. As it happened, democratic crisis filled the air as Marcus was putting the finishing touches on his first book. The author's note in *Mystery Train* is dated August 9, 1974: the very day Nixon resigned the presidency. Even as Marcus sought "a recognition of unities in the American imagination that already exist" (xiii), he stood before an America that was no longer all that it seemed.[3] With the imminent fall of Saigon, the onset of stagflation, and a general feeling of malaise, the national experiment teetered uneasily, as though over a void. If the lonesome train whistle that inspired the young Nixon to dream about the presidency still blew across the dark fields of the republic, it would have to be given new meaning. In *Mystery Train*, Marcus made that whistle speak to another silent majority, one that called a boy from Tupelo their king. He could not have known that Elvis would meet his own demise three years later, on August 16, the day Robert Johnson died in 1938 and just a day before Jimi Hendrix unfurled his "For Whom the Bell Tolls" version of the "Star-Spangled Banner" at Woodstock in 1969. Whether the timing is paradigmatic or merely coincidental is hard to say, but as Marcus once stated, "Coincidences make metaphors, and metaphors make culture" (2000b, 190). Somewhat less disputable is the fact that Elvis experienced the same ambitious rise and fall, the same proclivity for comeback and redemption and colossal disappointment that led Bob Dole, awash in tears at Nixon's funeral, to mutter, "How American."

In its theory and scope, *Mystery Train* is indebted to the "myth-symbol" school of American studies made popular by Perry Miller, Leo Marx, Leslie Fiedler, Henry Nash Smith, and other writers who, having weathered the national crises of the 1930s and 1940s, ascended in the academy shortly after World War II.[4] Heavily reliant upon concepts like archetype and paradigm, the myth-symbol scholars sought to uncover a deep structure in American culture that they believed to be relatively uniform and timeless. By the early 1970s, when Marcus sat down to write *Mystery Train*, the myth-symbol approach had become largely obsolete in academic circles, its central arguments altered by the advent of multiculturalism and New Historicism in America and by a range of post-structural theories from Europe. Why, then, did Marcus return so frequently to D. H. Lawrence's *Studies in Classic American Literature* and Leslie Fiedler's *Love and Death in the American Novel* when writing about 1950s and 1960s rock? Why would a progressive voice of the counterculture seek refuge in traditional methodology that prized historical continuity above all else? Should *Mystery Train* be regarded as a postmodern vehicle, up to date in its mingling of high and low culture, or as the caboose of late modernism, the last trace of an outdated vanguard disappearing around the bend? To begin answering these questions, we must examine the educational models Marcus encountered at Berkeley in the 1960s.

When Marcus was an undergraduate, the American academy was in a period of transition. At Berkeley, students involved in the Free Speech Movement and the Vietnam Day Committee said they would no longer abide by the conformist agenda of university president Clark Kerr's "multiversity." In fact, Berkeley was the proving ground for what later became known as New Historicism. Abandoning hierarchical varieties of formalism and humanism for interdisciplinary models that preached inclusiveness and political awareness, New Historicists studied populations or events that have been routinely overlooked or otherwise slighted by traditional methods of historiography. In the 1960s, New Historicism was not yet a recognizable quantity. Even so, neither professors nor students could have doubted that a new social context in the streets was challenging the status of assigned canonical texts as well as the theoretical and pedagogical models that paid them homage. According to Stephen Greenblatt, a leading voice of New Historicism in the American academy, the proponents of reform often took drastic measures to advance their case:

> When I arrived at Berkeley in 1969 ... the campus was redolent of tear gas. Everything was in an uproar; all routines were disrupted; nothing could be taken for granted. Classes still met, at least sporadically, but the lecture platform would often be appropriated, with or without the professor's permission, by protestors, and seminar discussions would veer wildly from, say, Ben Jonson's metrics to the undeclared war over Cambodia. Many students and at least some faculty were calling for the "reconstitution" of the university—though no one knew quite what "reconstitution" was—so that even ordinary classes had an air of provisionality. It was, in its way, sublime. (1990, 4)[5]

When I interviewed him at Princeton, Marcus confirmed Greenblatt's recollections. He remembered that while he was a student at Berkeley, the walls of ivory tower academia were tumbling down, and the artificial separation of intellectual life and everyday life no longer seemed to hold. "Whatever you studied in class had analogues outside class that were in your face ... that brought the texts you read to life," he recalled. "It was a world that was politically alive and unmade outside the classroom while you were reading and trying to put a world together" (2000a, conversation). As Marcus explained elsewhere, "Everything was at stake and, in one way or another, everyone took part … Your own history was lying in pieces on the ground, and you had the choice of picking up the pieces or passing them by. Nothing was trivial, nothing incidental. Everything connected to a totality, and the totality was how you wanted to live, as a subject or as an object of history" (1990, 444).

Notwithstanding the attractions of the New Left and a nascent New Historicism, Marcus found that the old myth-symbol scholars still had a lot to offer. Most of these scholars were partisans of the Old Left, outdated and even fusty in their populist pronouncements, but hardly the worst enemy a progressive thinker might imagine. Henry Nash Smith articulated their democratic values when he praised "collective representations rather than the work of a single mind" (1950, v). Although postmodern theorists distrusted their humanism and reliance on deep structures, some revisionists admitted that myth-symbol scholars enabled an inclusive brand of cultural analysis. For Robert Berkhofer, American studies "was in its classic period already a leader in the trend" of breaking down boundaries between popular and elite culture, and of calling into question literary and artistic canons in need of an overhaul, or at least adding to them (1999, 284). Marcus must have come to a similar recognition, for he has adopted several characteristics of myth-symbol scholarship, a few of which are worthy of review.

The first characteristic is the "framing anecdote." In their effort to make their complex analyses accessible to first-generation college students in the 1950s, myth-symbol scholars would often begin their books with a personal story. Perry Miller's *Errand into the Wilderness* contains a famous example, as the author describes working on an oil tanker in Africa during his extended hiatus from the University of Chicago: "It was given to me, disconsolate on the edge of a jungle in central Africa, to have thrust upon me the mission of expounding what I took to be the innermost propulsion of the United States, while supervising, in that barbaric tropic, the unloading of drums of case oil flowing out of the inexhaustible wilderness of America" (1964, viii). This "jungle epiphany," Miller goes on to explain, spurred him to continue his education and specialize in the study of early America, itself a frontier of the imperial imagination. Few who picked up Miller's study of the New England Puritans could have expected to read about his experience in the African jungle, but the passage cited above proves that the impulse to write criticism is often profoundly personal and can lead an author through some strange avenues of the memory.[6]

Marcus's approach to rock journalism is not so different. When he writes about hearing the Beatles or the Velvet Underground for the first time (1992a, 212–13; 2000b, 68), or when he describes how his discovery of a Robert Johnson LP in a Berkeley record shop not only helped him deal with the trauma he witnessed at Altamont but also led him to renounce rock music for a short period (1995, 141–54; Goldberg 2000), he is employing the same anecdotal imperative, and tying it to social purpose. "Papa Was a Rolling Stone" was not simply a song Marcus happened to hear on the radio; it was a defining moment in the nation's collective consciousness:

> Imagine—or simply remember—the chill of driving easily through the night, and then hearing, casually at first, then with interest, and then with compulsion, the three bass patterns, repeated endlessly, somewhere between the sound of the heart and the judge's gavel, that open "Papa Was a Rolling Stone." The toughest blues guitar you ever heard in years cracks through the building music like a curse; the singer starts in.
>
> More than one person I knew pulled off the road and sat waiting, shivering, as the song crept out of the box and filled up the night. (2015, 75)

Here, Marcus pays tribute to an experience many Americans shared, even if they never actually pulled off the road one night in 1972. The shift to present tense verbs betrays an immediacy that is there even in the retelling. An anecdote like this works so well on our imagination because it updates an older symbolic registry and makes it seem relevant, almost palpable. Few radio listeners knew about Stagger Lee, but Marcus figures they might recognize the archetypal "bad man" once his book gave them the proper coordinates in popular culture: Robert Johnson, Sly Stone, *Super Fly*, even the latter-day Temptations.[7]

Often, Marcus asks that his "Great Story" argument be taken on faith. For this reason, *Mystery Train* is vulnerable to the same kind of criticism Alan Trachtenberg levied on Smith's myth-symbol classic, *Virgin Land*: "Its informing theory nowhere gets a theoretical exposition: the book prefers to exemplify rather than theorize" (quoted in Kuklick 1999, 71). Indeed, the thesis of *Mystery Train* hinges on a diverse array of musical and literary documents that "evoke like crazy" (Marcus 2015, 121). The passage below is typical; Marcus seizes upon a heady cultural moment (the blaxploitation craze in 1972) and employs a second-person address to persuade his reader to share in a mysterious "verge" of common American experience. By so doing, he places that reader in a cultural theater of his own making:

> When a single like the O'Jays' "Back Stabbers" rams home the result of years of shifting black consciousness and takes over the charts, it creates a cultural moment shared by a good part of the country, shoving a particular sensibility through all sorts of ordinary barriers that grow up between audiences. The passion and clarity of the song can connect a black pimp, whose life it was virtually meant to define, to a middle-class white kid, who just digs the beat and will find his or her place in the lyrics soon enough. When a movie like *The Godfather* becomes the national pastime, you can feel, as you sit for perhaps the first time in a theater half black and half white, that for better or for worse America's fantasies are at last becoming common property; that artists and audiences have come to a verge, that the stakes of American life have been raised. (103)

Marcus occasionally apologizes for the anecdotal asides that steer his thinking, but he ends up reiterating the communal aspects of his rock and roll fantasy. Like those in the political arena who charted a course for American liberalism during the Cold War, he searches for consensus at every turn, even as he tries to maintain his gadfly image.

For Marcus, consensus in Cold War America stemmed from shared fanaticism, which as it turns out is another characteristic of myth-symbol scholarship.[8] This is probably why Elvis looms so large in his imagination, and in ours. As "the King," Elvis became the mythic presence that diverse groups of people, rednecks as well as rockers (with African Americans remaining a relatively unexplored exception), could turn to for symbolic meaning and cultural cohesion.[9] "Presley's career almost has the scope to take America in," Marcus explains in "Presliad," the majestic chapter that brings *Mystery Train* to a close. He follows this grand pronouncement with a list of the singer's virtues and vices, employing the vocabulary of rock journalism but mimicking the hokey phrasing of Nixon's "Bring Us Together" stump speeches:

> The cultural range of [Presley's] music has expanded to the point where it includes not only the hits of the day, but also patriotic recitals, pure country gospel, and really dirty blues; reviews of his concerts, by usually credible writers, sometimes resemble Biblical accounts of heavenly mir-

acles. Elvis has emerged as a great *artist*, a great *rocker*, a great *purveyor of shlock*, a great *heart throb*, a great *bore*, a great *symbol of potency*, a great *ham*, a great *nice person*, and, yes, a great American. (113)

Returning to his anecdotal style later in the chapter, Marcus pauses to remember an interview he conducted with former teen idols Brian Hyland and Bobby Vee at a 1973 deejay convention. After a few drinks and some banter about the fleeting nature of fame, talk turns to Elvis and "suddenly the whole tone of the conversation is different. Professional cool drops away and we are all shameless fans" (141n). Lester Bangs famously paid homage to Elvis's magnetic presence in a *Village Voice* piece published two weeks after Presley's death:

> If love is truly going out of fashion, which I do not believe, then along with our nurtured indifference to each other will be an even more contemptuous indifference to each other's objects of reverence. I thought it was Iggy Stooge, you thought it was Joni Mitchell or whoever else seemed to speak for your own private, entirely circumscribed situation's many pains and few ecstasies. We will continue to fragment in this manner, because solipsism holds all the cards at present; it is a king whose domain engulfs even Elvis's. But I can guarantee you one thing: we will never agree on anything as we agreed on Elvis. So I won't bother saying goodbye to his corpse. I will say goodbye to you. (1988, 216)

So strong is our attraction to Presley, Marcus argues in *Dead Elvis* (1991) and in the regularly expanded "Notes and Discographies" section of *Mystery Train*, that it sometimes verges on fascism, as deranged "Elvis imitators" like Jim Jones and David Koresh and bands like Elvis Hitler have eerily demonstrated (Marcus, 2015, 355n). Marcus takes a more democratic tack in *Double Trouble: Bill Clinton and Elvis Presley in a Land of No Alternatives* (2000), which likens America's first Baby Boomer president to "the young Elvis" (whose visage appeared on a postage stamp that was itself put to a vote during the 1992 campaign), the Elvis who embodied the ultimate American dream, that of the small-town boy made good.[10] Like those who supported Clinton through his many tribulations, Marcus cannot help but adore the charismatic man-child who holds fast to the competing dreams of subversion and consensus, rebellion and adulation. Nor can he help but notice that the spate of Elvis sightings magically disappeared from supermarket tabloids once Clinton took office (175).[11]

In truth, Clinton is one of many Elvises; they range from the ridiculous (Steve Jones, ex-husband of Clinton nemesis Paula Jones, in the Jim Jarmusch film *Mystery Train*) to the intellectually sublime (Isidore Isou, the handsome leading man of the Lettrist movement in postwar France) (Marcus 1991, 192, 196–97; 1990, 249). Clinton just happened to be the deadest ringer of them all, the one who "revealed America to itself, and in so doing made the country a bigger place than it ever was before"; the one "who for the months of his impeachment sat in the White House as a specter of shame and defiance, daring Americans to believe that they were better than he was" (Marcus 2000b, 230). Above all, Clinton was the one whose big dreams and flawed presidency reaffirmed the old William Carlos Williams maxim, cited repeatedly by Peter Guralnick whenever he writes about Elvis, that the "pure products of America go crazy" (1985, 53) as they seek the unbounded opportunity their nation promises but rarely delivers, or ends up delivering in the strangest of ways.

Marcus's discussions of success and failure in America are colored by his complex attitude towards irony, a taboo subject for the myth-symbol scholars but a litmus test for the postmodern thinker. In *Mystery Train*, Marcus takes after myth-symbol mentors like Lawrence and Fiedler, who manage to be irreverent without being cynical or distant toward their subject matter. Myth-symbol scholars take jabs at American authors, but only when those writers fail to embrace a gloriously flawed American ideal: a surface-level morality undercut by fleshly desire and general duplicity. In *Studies in Classic American Literature*, Lawrence chastises an overly moralistic Ben Franklin for the "barbed wire contraption" of American success that Poor Richard "rigged up" (14), while praising Herman Melville for exposing the "doom [that] is in America. The doom of our white day" (160). It is this impending sense of doom, this futile grasping for "some unfulfilled, perhaps unrealized purpose" that Americans rally around in the name of freedom (6). One is not a true American, in Lawrence's estimation, unless one embraces this unrealized purpose fully, without any trace of irony. Marcus mentions that Americans today prefer Elvis's flawed idealism—his "shout of freedom"—to Lawrence's paternalistic lectures on the subject (2015, 154). Still, we might wonder why he bothered pairing Presley and Lawrence at all. Well, for starters, both were rebels who possessed a deep love for America. Both were censored for unprecedented displays of sexuality. After precocious starts, both died young, in their mid-forties. Most important, neither was particularly ironic. Each man wore his faults on his sleeve, called them his strengths, and asked to be accepted on those terms. Though they were regarded as subversive, neither man sought to undermine the American dream once he invoked it. The medley "An American Trilogy" (a combination of "Dixie," "Battle Hymn of the Republic," and "All My Trials") that Elvis included in Vegas shows can be taken as camp, but there is no evidence to suggest the singer took it as such.

In a 1975 review, Marcus lambasted a pair of blockbusters—Robert Altman's film *Nashville* and E. L. Doctorow's novel *Ragtime*—as misguided attempts to encompass the big American picture through irony, implicitly pitting these texts against another document of Americana released that year, his own *Mystery Train*. As Marcus saw it, Altman and Doctorow suffered from a "cold" and insular attitude. They refused to implicate themselves in the stories they told, whereas someone like Scott Fitzgerald poured himself completely into his fiction. "There are times when saying no is [merely] to say yes to one's audience," Marcus declares, and by 1975, "a stylish work that proclaims the failure of civilization—of America, to be precise—has become the artistic equivalent of the sucker punch" (1995, 89). Marcus shares Lawrence's suspicion that too much twentieth-century literature is "pretty empty of any feeling, and proud of it" (Lawrence 1964, 1).

Marcus launched similar attacks in his rock criticism, lamenting that arty New York punks privileged irony over purity, "irony being understood as just one more way of not having to mean what you said" (1992, 599).[12] He prefers L.A. bands like X for sharing with noir novelist Raymond Chandler an "essential commitment to the story being told," despite their "finally-got-smart coldness" and "readiness for violence" (1993, 133, 134), or Elvis Costello and the Attractions for "boiling off the irony" inherent in Nick Lowe's post-hippie joke song "(What's So Funny 'Bout) Peace Love and Understanding" (357).[13] Similarly, in *Mystery Train* Marcus praises Fitzgerald and Chuck Berry for refusing to put the slightest irony into *The Great Gatsby* and "Back in the USA," and for submitting their characters so willingly to failure, which in America is regarded not merely as a sign of weakness but as "a kind of betrayal, of a mass of shadowy, shared hopes" (2015, 18).[14]

At times, Marcus's search for elemental truth hints at American exceptionalism. As an automobile advertisement once bragged, it's hard to be humble when you hail from "the nation that invented rock and roll." Some who deplore American hegemony in political or economic arenas nonetheless find themselves laughing at Eurodisco, or at French concert audiences when they clap along to the Velvet Underground's "Heroin" as though it were the "Beer Barrel Polka." Maybe it is because they secretly agree with the pronouncement put forth by Lawrence and echoed by Marcus in *Invisible Republic* (154) that classic American writers were naturally extreme whereas European modernists were merely "*trying* to be extreme" (Lawrence 1964, viii). Cultural bias cuts both ways, of course, and Marcus is not blind to the irony that arises in other situations. He knew, for instance, that many Europeans who were fans of Bob Dylan or Randy Newman liked to believe these artists were anti-American, when this was far from being the case. Marcus delights in describing the confusion French students felt when Dylan hung an enormous American flag behind his amplifiers during a 1966 tour (2015, 251). But Marcus saw that Americans were just as apt to misread lyrics, a tendency that came to a head in the Reagan years, when many who heard Newman's "I Love L.A." and Bruce Springsteen's "Born in the U.S.A" mistook a courageous "no" for a parochial or jingoistic "yes" (2015, 308; 1993, 267–71).[15]

Just as Altamont led him to take a break from listening to rock, the election of Reagan, a president summoning American myths and symbols for radically different purposes, prompted Marcus to take leave of familiar subject matter and embark on an extended tour of the European avant-garde, from Dada to situationism to punk. "Sometimes you have to go somewhere else, in thought if not in body," Marcus told me at Princeton, explaining his decision to abandon American themes throughout much of the 1980s. As he said elsewhere, "I hated what [Reagan] did to this country and I hated what he stood for. And I couldn't bear to look at the country—to seriously, intellectually, grapple with it, critically—in those years" (quoted in Reynolds 2012, part 3). *Lipstick Traces*, first published in 1989 and the end product of his sojourn into alternative European traditions, might seem irrelevant to a discussion of American roots music. Actually, this intellectually ambitious book maps out the historicist routes Marcus would travel when he returned to American themes in the 1990s. Investigating silences and erasures, he discovered unacknowledged histories that secretly shape the official history of a nation or a tradition.

As is his wont, Marcus approached European intellectual history through popular music. He begins *Lipstick Traces* with a long chapter titled "The Last Sex Pistols Concert" and works backward in time, paying tribute to an array of dissenters in the process. Marcus argues that the "collective vehemence" expressed in Sex Pistols songs such as "Anarchy in the U.K." and "God Save the Queen" unleashed a "potlatch of yeses and noes that sounded like a conversation in which everything was at stake" (437–38). Since the latter song, banned by the BBC for its subversive lyrics, nonetheless hit the top of the U.K. pop charts as a blank title, Marcus knew that he had found a fit example of silenced history, an interstitial gap, an open secret that confounded traditional conceptions of nationhood and plebian identity. The new music was not nihilistic exactly, but it was "pretty vacant" (to summon another Pistols single), and it was this vacancy that punks claimed as their birthright. Punk music was more theoretically aware than commonly thought, but it was hardly pretentious, or even ambitious. Punk preferred to wallow in the destruction of the transitional moment, Britain's so-called Ice Age, strumming power chords in the dark until the moment passed.

Punks wore their love of historical gaps on their sleeves (quite literally, if one considers their torn clothing) and in their flesh (safety pins became body-piercing devices). To reiterate his own love of gaps, Sex Pistols singer Johnny Rotten halted in the "untitled" song that rocketed to the top of the national charts. "God Save the Queen / We mean it, man / God *save*" [end of line], he shrieked facetiously, implying all the while that nothing whatsoever in Britain was worthy of salvation, except maybe one thing. "God save history," Rotten continued, careening through the band's rollicking diatribe. "God save your mad parade / Lord God have mercy, all crimes are paid / When there's no future, there cannot be sin." This foreclosure of the future came with an unexpected twist: British punks were simultaneously cursing their nation and relieving it of its debts. Johnny Rotten wanted to look back into the past and see what he and other Britons had worked and paid for. "Every youth movement presents itself as a loan to the future, and tries to call in its lien in advance," Marcus explains, extending Rotten's monetary metaphor, "but when there is no future all loans are cancelled" (1990, 11). Punk was not a form of history exactly, but neither was it simply a musical genre. It was, above all, a language of possibility. "All that remain are wishes without language," Marcus surmises after listening to "God Save the Queen" for the umpteenth time; "all that remains is unmade history, which is to say the possibility of poetry" (308).[16] Like their avant-garde forebears, punk rockers seized the opportunity "to create ephemeral events that would serve judgment on whatever came next" (82), infiltrating an official history that, up to that point, had been written by out-of-touch intellectuals and authorized by an entrenched set of political leaders.

Holding his admission ticket to other "ephemeral events," Marcus spends the rest of *Lipstick Traces* delving into various subversive European movements—Dada, Lettrism, and situationism—from which punk music took its impudent spirit. Johnny Rotten had likely not uttered the word "dada" since he was two years old, Marcus is forced to admit at one juncture (200), but the theoretical impulse of his music was largely the same: "it had no idea what it was prophesying, and its strength was it didn't care" (238). By serving judgment on sanctioned varieties of European modernism, Dadaists and situationists scripted a parallel or "secret" history of the twentieth century. The Sex Pistols acted similarly when they confronted an overinflated rock culture and an ineffective British political system in the mid-1970s.

The bold interventionism must have prompted Marcus to reconsider his myth-symbol approach. Whereas the classic American studies paradigm Marcus embraced iconography and cohesion, the avant-garde movements stressed iconoclasm and discord. Their contrary attitude is epitomized by a 1952 Lettrist International leaflet attacking Charlie Chaplin, a boring symbol of American cinema to whom the Lettrists wished a "quick death," and by a follow-up letter sent to the left-wing daily *Combat* asserting that "the most urgent expression of freedom is the destruction of idols, especially when they claim to represent freedom" (quoted in Marcus 1990, 341, 343). Nothing could have strayed further from the archetypal language of *Mystery Train*.

Marcus's methodological shift became even more apparent in the 1990s, once he brought the concept of a "secret history" to bear on his study of American popular culture. Taking up the mantle of New Historicism, he explored suspicious absences in American history and listened to the silenced voices that haunt the nation in its most vulnerable moments. Glimpsed from this perspective, *Mystery Train* sometimes seems like a retreat into a mythical American past, and *Invisible Republic: Bob Dylan's Basement Tapes* (1997) a more pertinent study of the historical hiccups affecting the way Americans think about their destiny.

Invisible Republic is a chaotic book, and a brilliant one. Marcus explores *The Basement Tapes*, a series of impromptu performances Dylan recorded with the Band in the basement of Big Pink, their barnlike bungalow in upstate New York, as he recuperated from a 1966 motorcycle accident. More than just a knockoff experiment, these sessions became for Marcus a "map" or "laboratory" of a troubled America. During the summer of 1967—a Summer of Love or a long, hot summer, depending upon whether you happened to live in San Francisco or Detroit—Dylan and the Band spelled out their own affection and violence by dipping into a forgotten folk aesthetic, one codified, Marcus maintains, by Harry Smith's *Anthology of American Folk Music*. Appearing in 1952, at the height of McCarthyism, Smith's leftist document was conceived as a "legal bootleg," an open secret whose songs chronicled the violent travails, hard luck, spiteful envy, and unflagging optimism of the "old, weird America" (Marcus 1997, 89). Fifteen years after Smith's compilation was released in a Catskills retreat far removed from Haight-Ashbury, Vietnam, and urban blight, Dylan and his mates wove the *Anthology*'s murder ballads and folk lyrics into their own spontaneous compositions, until time and nation seemed to stand still. The basement of Big Pink "was an *omphalos*," Marcus posits, "and the days spent within it a point around which the American past and future slowly turned" (69). As these musicians "held palavers with a community of ghosts" (86), they crafted music relevant to current crises of the day, yet indebted to folk legends of days gone by. "The stronger the songs get, the older they feel," Marcus marvels at one point. "This uncertain feeling, deepening into vertigo, is present throughout the music: the sense that the past is rushing forward, about to sweep all the conceits of the present away for good, to take away all its knowledge, deprive its deeds of value, as if the past holds chits on the present and is ready to call them in" (83–84). Although Marcus does not come right out and say it, the Dylan he describes in *Invisible Republic* is a modern-day Rip Van Winkle, mired in Cold War culture but preferring to sleep, perchance to dream of a more tolerant and equitable America.

When Marcus claims that Dylan's basement recordings rank among "the most intense outbreaks of modernism or of the whole Gothic-romantic traverse of American self-regard" (xi), he is employing the language of the myth-symbol scholars to make *The Basement Tapes* seem canonical and writers like Poe and Faulkner seem hip. In this fashion, it would appear that he is simply extending the argument he made in *Mystery Train*. On other occasions, though, he pushes forward to examine historical silences and deconstruct the surface reality of any given moment. To describe the atmosphere at Big Pink, Marcus summons the theater metaphor he used to talk about the O'Jays in *Mystery Train*. But it becomes apparent rather quickly that the basement theater will not accommodate the kind of consensus Marcus located on prior occasions:

> The music suggests one of those queer theaters-in-the-round built and soon demolished in the 1970s, where a circular platform actually moved as a band played, the musicians catching only a glimpse of faces as they circled past the audience, the audience catching distorted fragments of the sound the band was making as the band approached and for a moment hearing the music whole, then turning as if they could see what they were ceasing to hear, the sound dimming and leaving an echo as the musicians disappeared around the bend. In the basement theater, nothing was exactly clear and nothing was obviously wide open. There were doors all around the room, a door for every worry or imagining; all you had to do was find the key. Each time a new key opened a door, America opened up into both the future and the past—and it is perhaps only a progressive notion of time that leads one to presume that when Dylan spoke of an America that was wide open, he meant open to what was to come, not to what had been, open to the question of who or what Americans might become, not to the question of who or where they came from. There is no nostalgia in the basement recordings; they are too cold, pained, or ridiculous for that. The mechanics of time in the music are not comforting. In the basement the past is alive to the degree that the future is open, when one can believe that the country remains unfinished, even unmade; when the future is foreclosed, the past is dead. How the future depends on the past is more mysterious. (70)

The lost-in-the-funhouse architecture of this theater, with its carousel stage and its doors leading to different historical moments, would seem to pose a severe challenge to the actor who wants to summon a usable past. The atmosphere suggests disconnect rather than communion or continuity. A hipster prophet like Dylan can talk effectively about the American past only when he gets his countrymen to see that their national experiment is far from complete. Patriots who take a "love it or leave it" approach, or everyday Americans who subscribe to the status quo, will never hear the angry and forlorn voices rising up from the past to complicate citizenship in our own day and point a way to a more equitable future. The songs Dylan performs in the basement will remain largely inaudible and their images of the republic invisible so long as

Americans comb the present time for positive signs of consensus. At their best, *The Basement Tapes* urge Americans to deconstruct the official chronology they have been handed, to escape the symbolic structures that, especially in 1967, no longer seemed relevant.

Marcus's analysis of *The Basement Tapes* resembles the "reversible connecting factor" championed by situationist leader Guy Debord, an avant-garde hero championed in *Lipstick Traces*. For Debord, a principle of negation always exists within the dominant structures that constitute the "society of the spectacle." If the social spectacle in postwar France was built on symbols, as Debord claimed it was, "then a demolition of [those] symbols was the surest way to reveal the invisible terrain on which people actually lived" (Marcus 1990, 141). If we translate this back to an American context, we can see Marcus owning up to a new challenge. In *Mystery Train*, he tried to situate rock in the pantheon of Americana, with its "ultimate images" (22). Two decades later, taking his cue not only from Dylan and Harry Smith but also from Debord and other European intellectuals who "believed in the ruins," Marcus demolishes the symbolic spectacle of his own nation so that he might discover amid its rubble an Invisible Republic, the type of place Americans "actually lived."[17]

In Paris and London, Marcus discovered while researching *Lipstick Traces*, Debord and Alexander Trocchi devised a "psychogeography," a way of looking at a city that summoned forth the nearly impenetrable secrets lurking there. "They looked for new streets, which meant the oldest streets, as if the streets they thought they knew were judging their unreadiness to understand the secrets the streets contained" (1990, 363). Invoking *détournement*, a playful form of reversibility and effacement, these situationists managed to "create a city of possibilities in the heart of the city of the spectacle" (364), employing cognitive mapping decades before Fredric Jameson spoke of its dialectical efficacy (1991, 54). In *Invisible Republic*, Marcus surmises that this kind of cognitive mapping was occurring in America even before Dylan and the Band holed up in the basement. Harry Smith's *Anthology of American Folk Music* broke ground for a newly imagined national community, a town Marcus calls "Smithville," much as Tom Slater, the F. O. Matthiessen figure in Mark Merlis's novel *American Studies*, assembled a pantheon of literary figures to create "a little country of his own" (Merlis quoted in Marcus 1997, 91). By themselves, the songs Smith collected were obscure and isolated commentaries on American life. Once he cobbled them together, though, Smith was able to orchestrate a village choir of disaffected and politically powerful voices reaching across traditional barriers of time and space. According to musicologist Robert Cantwell,

> We should recognize that the *Folkways Anthology of American Folk Music* achieves its end aurally—working as a kind of solvent on the fixed definitions of continuous rational space, with its visual-tactile gradient, and transforming it into an altogether dynamic, discontinuous, and irrational space: a multifarious, simultaneous universe, all of its differentiations uncertain, its boundaries permeable and its forms protean, the ephemeral world whose perceptual surface we must continually penetrate to construct a palpable reality, one that always partakes of our own experience. (1996, 237–38)

The Basement Tapes are infused with the same magic. Filled with freaks and convicts, daredevils and dime-store mystics, the individual tracks Dylan recorded gain momentum once they are placed alongside one another. "Like the records Smith collected," Marcus argues, "the known and unknown basement tapes together make a town—a town that is also a country, an imagined America with a past and a future, neither of which seems quite as imaginary as any act taking place in the present of the songs" (1997, 128). The stakes of these story cycles are higher than one might think. "Politics are buried deep in stories of individuals who make up a nation only when their stories are heard together," Marcus mused after listening to the hardscrabble tales on *Nebraska*, Bruce Springsteen's masterful, if sorely underappreciated, Reagan-era jeremiad. "But if we can hear their stories as a single, whole story, they can't" (1993, 236–37).[18]

Above all, Dylan and the Band sought a space where time stood still. In 1967, this was no mean feat. Protests against the Vietnam War were raging. Cities were burning. Rock was chock-full of experimentation and social consciousness. Interestingly, Dylan decided at this moment go underground, not in any effort to abandon America but as a way to rediscover its core values. In this characteristically passionate excerpt from *Invisible Republic*, Marcus sets the scene:

> In 1967 the orderly assumptions and good-natured disruptions that in the 1950s bordered real life were melting down in riot and war; the civil rights movement, the great wave of belief in a republic fulfilling its own promises, disappeared into the Summer of Love, into the undertow of

belief in a world where everyone was his or her own Christ. "When anything was possible," Dylan said. When was it, to his mind, in his voice, that America began to go into the past, changing shape from flesh to ghost?

It's not a personal question. The republic itself asks it; you simply answer. Just as every schooled American carries a sense of the country's beginning as event, so too does every such American harbor a sense of national ending, less as a historical event than as a fading away, a forgetting, a common loss of memory experienced all at once in a single heart: a great public event locked up in the silence of the solitary. For any American it is a defining moment; no promise is so precious as in the moment one knows it can never be kept, that now it belongs to the past. In 1967, in the basement of Big Pink, this event was in the air, the peculiar air of that particular room, as history's dare to the pioneer, the Puritan's dare to the future. The past hadn't claimed the future, but the past was alive with temptation and portent, a kingdom anyone could rule. (1997, 68–69)

Although the historical memories Dylan summoned in 1967 were "alive with temptation and portent," they would nonetheless have to be pushed aside for another time. *The Basement Tapes* were available only on bootlegs until 1975, just as the classic rock era was coming to a close and *Mystery Train* was putting its imprimatur on rock's canonical status. In the minds of many, including Alan Liu, a prominent New Historicist, this eight-year period marks a time of failed revolution.[19] By the 1970s, Marcus noticed, rockers were no longer talking about "risk," but rather "survival" (1990, 46; 1993, 57), which in the brave new world of major label deals and stadium shows meant turning a blind eye to 1960s values (cf. Goodman 1997). Later, the 1960s came to represent a "myth of wholeness," a pop lingua franca that for the young people who missed the decade the first time around but flocked to see a film like *The Doors* instead of contemporary fare like *Pump Up the Volume* is both a beacon and a burden, something they "feel as an absence, like the itch of a limb amputated before they were born" (2000b, 19).

Dylan spotted this trend in advance. Blessed (or cursed) with the preternatural insight of Natty Bumppo (Marcus 2000b, 56; 2010, 168), Dylan imagined what the 1960s would look like several years down the road, indicting the myth of that decade at the very moment it was getting constructed, the very moment the nation was getting *deconstructed*. Dylan made an unlikely prophet, yet there he was, chastising his countrymen for their wrongheadedness. American prophets had pointed a way to go, he laments in "Tears of Rage," but the populace thought it was just a place to stand. Plunging headlong into a historical gap of his own making, the rock star who headed underground discovered that he was able to commune with a folk culture that most Americans, rednecks on the right as well as rockers on the left, had recklessly abandoned in a combustible atmosphere of war, solipsism, and greed. In 1965, when Dylan "went electric," people pricked up their ears. "More than thirty years ago, when a world now most often spoken of as an error of history was taking shape and form," Marcus muses on the first page of *Invisible Republic*, "Bob Dylan seemed less to occupy a turning point in cultural space and time than to be that turning point. As if culture would turn according to his wishes or even his whim; the fact was, for a long moment it did" (ix). In 1967, that moment was extended as rock fans tried to fathom just what was happening in an upstate New York basement.

Marcus's description of Dylan's "long moment" in American popular culture harks back to his earlier discussion about the "founding crime" of situationism. In *Lipstick Traces*, he had this to say about Michel Mourre's co-optation of the altar during a mass at Notre-Dame in 1950: "Notre-Dame made a breach in stopped time, opening a route to 'play and public life' … For the moment of poetic adventure not only opened up the possibility of creating events and their languages. It also brought 'all the unsettled debts of history back into play,' and in this case they were enough" (311). Segue to Johnny Rotten, draping himself in the Union Jack and bringing historical debts to bear on a "pretty vacant" Britain experiencing unemployment and racial tensions. In each case, a self-proclaimed rebel pauses for a moment, looks to the past, and wraps himself in the trappings of the prevailing ideology, not merely as an excuse to stir up trouble but as a means of tearing open the fabric of his troubled nation, in the hopes of celebrating the spirit still lurking there.[20]

For lovers of Americana, too, the spirit of a nation is revealed when its citizens challenge the import of time-honored traditions, usually on a particular date, taking stock of their own situation in the process. In Britain, the Sex Pistols used the Silver Jubilee of Queen Elizabeth II as the occasion to release "God Save the Queen," making their indictment of monarchy infinitely more topical. In America, writers such as Henry David Thoreau and Frederick Douglass voiced their most vehement complaints on the Fourth of July, and for good reason, since this is our day of national promise. It is no mistake, Marcus argues, that in the "The Coo Coo Bird," a folk-lyric about a man who builds a log cabin at the top of a hill so that he can look down upon his neighbor (condescendingly, but perhaps also lovingly), the Fourth of July emerges as the day the parasitic, nest-robbing bird finally hollers. For Marcus, this little folk-lyric is a "a narrative of American willfulness and fatedness, a narrative implied but altogether missing, replaced instead by hints and gestures, code words and winks, a whole music of secret handshakes" (1997, 119–20). The same impulse spurred Smith, "near the end of his life, as shaman in residence at the Naropa Institute in Boulder, Colorado, to record every sound he encountered in the course of a Fourth of July, from speech to fireworks to crickets" (92). If we would all just open our ears and listen, Smith's example suggests, we might learn that the sounds of the present contain the lessons of the past, and that these sounds continue to ring across the skies of America, in an atmosphere that is mysterious, even prophetic, but hardly rarefied.[21]

"*Listen.*" Dylan utters this single word just before he launches into his initial taping of "Tears of Rage," the mournful song that takes Independence Day as its frame of reference (Marcus 1997, 204). As Marcus listens to Dylan's tale about the faithlessness that pervades family life and eventually distorts national character, he is moved to mention another American prophet whose mournful legacy is always close at hand:

> In the shame and guilt that all but possess Dylan's singing in the first recording of the song, in the singer's despair over his failure to pass on the ethics of place and loyalty, you can see Lincoln's face as it appears in bronze busts all through *The Manchurian Candidate*, more mute and saddened in each successive scene, forced to bear witness to plots to destroy the republic Lincoln preserved. (1995, 206–7)

Lincoln is one of many Americans from the past who haunt the nation when it fails to live up to its initial promise. Marcus expanded on this theme in a 1997 lecture, which he later published in the *Threepenny Review* ("Four Moments of Prophecy"), then used as the basis for an American studies course ("Prophecy and the American Voice"), then expanded into a book (*The Shape of Things to Come*). Once again, Marcus tracks the combination of desire and dread shaping American thinking for centuries. As early as 1630, John Winthrop proclaimed the "wish and the need for utopia in the American story" (Marcus 1998, 15). It remained for Winthrop's descendants—Lincoln, Martin Luther King Jr., and Allen Ginsberg—to shepherd this idealist vision through terrible times when all appeared lost. If Lincoln's second inaugural address, a gloomy, war-weary prophecy that took its cue from the Book of Amos, "spoke of a debt to be paid in blood," as Marcus claims, then *The Manchurian Candidate* (1962)—whose haunting busts of Lincoln "prefigured the state of mind that would accompany the assassinations that followed it" (Marcus 1995, 204)—showed that by the time the 1960s rolled around, those debts had not yet been paid.[22] One year after *The Manchurian Candidate* came to theaters, in front of the Lincoln Memorial, Martin Luther King Jr. laid the chits on the table one more time:

> In a sense we've come to our nation's capital to cash a check. When the architects of our Republic wrote the magnificent words of the Constitution and the Declaration of Independence, they were signing a promissory note—to which every American was to fall heir. America has given the Negro people a bad check, a check that has come back marked 'Insufficient funds.' (quoted in Marcus 1998, 17)

By 1966, the year of Dylan's motorcycle accident, the nation appeared to be out of checks altogether. It was during these dark days that a "homosexual dope-fiend Om-chanting poet who liked to wear an Uncle Sam hat" (Marcus 1998, 18) took a trip in the middle of the United States and uttered the fourth prophecy, probably the most compelling prophecy in the annals of hip Americana. In "Wichita Vortex Sutra," Allen Ginsberg moves across the broad sweep of Kansas prairie at night, not unlike Walt Whitman in "The Sleepers," processing a series of signifiers he sees through the windshield (billboard messages, radio signal towers) or hears on the car radio (weather reports, body counts, Holy Roller gospel shouting), trying to understand his nation's involvement in the Vietnam War. "I call all powers of imagination / to my side in this auto to make Prophecy," Ginsberg chants ominously. "I lift my voice aloud, / make Mantra of American language now, / I here declare the end of the War!" (1984, 406, 407). As deluded as Ginsberg may have appeared to the majority of Americans in 1966, Marcus maintains that he was in fact prophetic, citing the poet's 1994 performance of "Wichita Vortex Sutra" (with Philip Glass and other avant-garde New York musicians) as evidence. "McNamara made a 'bad guess'"—a refrain in the original poem—rang truer than ever in 1994, since Robert McNamara was about to release *In Retrospect*, a memoir in which he admitted to terrible mistakes regarding Vietnam. Remarkably, it appears as though a Beat poet on a harum-scarum journey through the Midwest knew better than the Johnson administration that America was betraying its initial promise, and that one day it would pay for those mistakes. Finally, "on stage in 1994, the war does end," and Marcus sees that the countercultural prophet has come to a peaceful resolution:

> Or maybe the right way to put it is to say that the voice discovered in the poem has catapulted the poet out of his time, as if he knew that, some-day, he could stand in public, having outlived almost all of those whose names would move through the poem … that someday he would stand in public and look back, and bring the past forward, as if his prophecy were not of the future, but of the future shape of the past. (1998, 19)

What Ginsberg knew in 1966 was not so different from what Harry Smith knew in 1952, or what Bob Dylan knew in 1967: there exists in the very heart of the American landscape an assembly of voices that can speak cogently and prophetically to the crises plaguing our nation. One merely has to fight through the cacophony of the present moment to claim citizenship, no matter what others might think about one's status as an American, and those older voices will come through loud and clear.

Ginsberg's lesson was not lost on Bruce Springsteen, who commented extensively on "Wichita Vortex Sutra" when he accompanied Marcus to a class at Princeton. As Marcus told an old buddy, rock journalist Dave Marsh, in a letter sent a few days after Springsteen's visit,

> [Bruce] pressed especially the notion of Ginsberg coming to Kansas as a presumptive outsider, a Jewish New York left wing dope fiend intel-lectual queer (in Bruce's words, "a gay man"), coming to a place where it could be presumed he did not belong and wasn't welcome, and insisting in the poem, on the page in 1966 and in his performance in 1994, that he did belong, that this place at the very heart of the country … was as much his place as anyone else's or any other place. Bruce insisted on the generosity of spirit in the poem and the performance, the love for country it expressed even in, or especially in, its most critical and

sardonic moments. He could not have been better prepared—although it's not as if he hasn't been thinking about the questions the poem raises for years, or as if he hasn't covered much of the same territory, from a not altogether different point of view, in "Nebraska" and any number of other places. (2000)

Marcus does not say whether he regards Springsteen as a prophet, but it is clear that he admires his willingness to wrestle with the complicated notion of American identity. During the Reagan years, while Marcus was off on his European sojourn, Springsteen was at home in America, staking his claims as a citizen, reading Flannery O'Connor and writing the acoustic ballads that filled *Nebraska*. Although he has suffered the misfortune of having his lyrics misread, by Ronald Reagan in his stump speeches and by countless others around their stereo sets and radios, Springsteen has recognized and extended the reach of Americana. For decades, he has updated his nation's folk legacy and made prophecy in unlikely places, whether in the Midwest or in New Jersey (which on *Nebraska* serves as a stand-in for the Midwest), joining a select group of Americans who believe that a rebellious attitude and a deep love of country are anything but mutually exclusive.

The American ideal that Marcus's prophets summon is imperfect, and in many ways the legacy they bequeath to us is unrealizable. But as citizens of this land we are free to stake our own claims, and in the process discover something bigger than ourselves, as Marcus suggests we should:

> We go back, with these prophecies, as if in a time machine—and find, as all time travelers find, that we can change nothing. We can only relive the prophecies once made as they were never fully lived, except in those moments of prophecy. Hearing them all at once, though—on the home ground that, in the present moment, almost always shrinks to the petty borders of our everyday envies and vanities—we can get a glimpse of how vast the sweep of the nation really is, or from the beginning meant to be. (1998, 19)

Marcus's work on prophecy took on new resonance after the 9/11 attacks, when American exceptionalism became an even more loaded topic, and again after the election of Barack Obama, since the "check" Martin Luther King mentioned in the 1963 March on Washington seemed finally to have been cashed. In the first decade of the twenty-first century, Marcus assayed, there existed "a sense of portent and doom," an "urge of the nation, in the shape of a certain kind of American hero, to pass judgment on itself" (2006a, 8).

The extension of that argument, *Shape of Things to Come: Prophecy and the American Voice* (2006), could have been a great book. The 9/11 tragedy and the military involvement in Iraq and Afghanistan provided Marcus additional opportunity to unpack an American crisis. Indeed, Marcus has called *The Shape of Things to Come* his Bush book, much as *Mystery Train* was his Nixon book and *Lipstick Traces* his Reagan book (Reynolds 2012, part 3). His premise remains the same: "More than any other place on earth, America can be attacked through its symbols because it is made up" (Marcus 2006a, 10). Always in America there has existed a promise, a betrayal of that promise, and a prophet who held the nation accountable for that betrayal. Sadly, Marcus's concentration on film, television, and fiction, rather than music, leaves his writing without an anchor. In *Shape*, connections among texts seem random or forced, and the overall argument too subjective to be representative of the American temperament Marcus endeavors to describe.

Although it is not titled as such, the "Four Moments of Prophecy" essay is situated in *The Shape of Things to Come* immediately after a meditative fugue on the 9/11 attacks, in actuality a cranky concatenation of voices followed by Marcus's invocation of a traditional American "covenant." The implication is of chickens coming home to roost: haunting visages of Winthrop, Lincoln, King, and Ginsberg silently admonish Bush-era warmongers from various corners of American history. Without stating it outright, Marcus conveys his belief that the September 2001 tragedy had been preordained, and that the examples offered by the four American prophets constitute for all citizens "a drama of foreboding" (2006a, 17). Old Testament references abound in a nation that is alternately blessed and doomed, and ultimately found wanting.

Unfortunately, successive chapters on Philip Roth's late-1990s novels, Bill Pullman's and Sheryl Lee's film and television acting roles, and even David Thomas's esoteric avant-punk music fail to deliver on Marcus's promise, and by extension, the nation's promise. I like that Marcus has been inspired over the years by Pauline Kael, David Thomson, and Larzer Ziff, but the role of film critic and literary critic doesn't suit his particular style, which like a guitar riff requires an additional musical line. Granted, bands like Heavens to Betsy and Talking Heads make cameo appearances, but mostly as a touchstone for film noir. Marcus's brief references to novels by Richard Price and John Kaye shed light on the character of James Earl Ray and other assassins of American prophets. But his extended analyses of the facial expressions of B-list actors do not advance my understanding of American prophecy very much. In *Mystery Train* and *Invisible Republic*, citations of non-musical texts shed light on the songs and albums at the heart of those books. In *Lipstick Traces*, citations of European avant-garde art and situationist politics were convincingly cast as the long foreground to punk rock. But that seamless weave is largely missing in *The Shape of Things to Come*. Its arguments about the American dream shaped in the seminar room, the book misses having the chaos of rock and roll at its core.

On the plus side, Marcus was continuing his dialogue with Bob Dylan. The appearance of *Like a Rolling Stone: Bob Dylan at the Crossroads* (first published in 2005) and *Bob Dylan by Greil Marcus: Writings 1968–2010* (2010) not only showed Marcus getting his groove back but also bookended a prolific period in Dylan studies. Updated Dylan books arrived from old hands like Clinton Heylin and Michael Gray, and new studies were published by a diverse crop of Dylanologists, including professors Sean Wilentz (Princeton), David Pichaske (Southwest Minnesota State), and David Yaffe (Syracuse). *The Cambridge Companion to Bob Dylan*, edited by Kevin Dettmar (Pomona College), further cemented the songwriter's academic credibility.

It's with Dylan more than any other rock artist that D. H. Lawrence's maxim from *Studies in Classic American Literature*—"Never trust the artist, trust the tale"—proves useful. Dylan has always been a chameleon, be it in interviews or in songs, and most journalists, Marcus excluded, have fallen into his traps. By devoting an entire book to *Highway 61 Revisited*, Marcus pushes Lawrence's idea into interesting territory, raising the purportedly outdated (but once hotly contested) question of whether an album represented a major statement from a musician.[23] *Like a Rolling Stone: Bob Dylan at the Crossroads* is good as far as it goes, but it lacks the cultural heft of *Invisible Republic*, where Dylan's more obscure songs emerge powerfully within a discussion of other firebrand prophets. *Like a Rolling Stone* is a solid song-by-song analysis of (arguably) the most influential album in rock history, but it isn't an intellectual investigation of America.

Far more intriguing is the compendium of Dylan writings Marcus published in 2010. With writings spanning four decades, *Bob Dylan by Greil Marcus* is sustained by the manifold mysteries Dylan's art has inspired, and by a sense of playfulness and discovery. Marcus does not play the stolid role he saw Robert Shelton playing in his disappointing Dylan biography: that of "village explainer" (Marcus 2015a, 130). No, he wanted immediacy and engagement. Time after time, it's a question embedded in one of Marcus's record reviews or concert reviews that stands out: "Can we trust this guy?" Marcus asks after hearing "Watching the River Flow" (2010, 33); "Who is this man? Where did he come from?" he asks in the wake of *The Last Waltz* performance (83); "Didn't he once have a way with words?" he asks in response to the atrocious *Empire Burlesque* (121); and most famously, back in 1970 he asks, in an excoriating review of *Self Portrait*, "What is this shit?" (7). The musician and the music writer possess a relationship so intertwined that such questions aren't merely rhetorical. There's a sense of expectation, need, even betrayal behind a lot of them.

Dylan's unexpected rise from the ashes in the 1990s occasioned Marcus's most affecting pieces. It's fitting that Dylan's official release of "Blind Willie McTell" (1991) and his under-the-radar return to folk and blues covers on *Good as I Been to You* (1992) and *World Gone Wrong* (1993) coincided with Marcus's ongoing research on Dylan's *Basement Tapes* and Harry Smith's *Anthology of American Folk Music*. By tapping once again into the old, weird America via a range of folk songs, Dylan regained his footing and, eventually, with the Grammy-winning album *Time Out of Mind* (1997), his popularity.

Marcus's essay "Dylan as Historian," originally published in 1991 and included in his 2010 compendium (155–61), links "Blind Willie McTell" with Richard "Rabbit" Brown's "James Alley Blues," a track from 1927 featured on Harry Smith's *Anthology* back in 1952 and covered by a very young Bob Dylan in Bonnie Beecher's Minneapolis apartment in 1961. The way Marcus talks about Dylan's late-period masterpiece is a tribute to Americana, however resistant to definition that term may be: "Bob Dylan's 'Blind Willie McTell' moves in a circle of images—tent meetings of itinerant holiness preachers, antebellum plantations, the slave driver's lash, chain gangs, painted women, drunken rakes—and it calls up many more" (2010, 155). Calling up our nation's old images and mysteries, getting listeners to question their murky origins and murkier beliefs: that, for me, is what Americana is all about. And according to Marcus, it's what Dylan knows best. "'Blind Willie McTell' makes it clear that his greatest talent is for bringing home the past, giving it flesh" (157). Comparing "Blind Willie McTell" with folk standards like "St. James Infirmary" and

"James Alley Blues," Marcus presents an unbroken circle of belonging to this land. Readers not only hear of a spirit that possessed New Orleans bluesman Rabbit Brown, but of the spirit affecting the young Minnesotan who played Brown's song for his bohemian friends. This feedback loop of Americana is indeed a gift: a "preternatural, bottomless strangeness, seemingly the voice of another world, right here, where you live, the prosaic dissolved by a faraway ominousness, a sense of the uncanny, an insistence on paradox and curse" (160).

Dylan's solo acoustic album *Good as I Been to You*, released in November 1992 on the very day Bill Clinton was elected president, and *World Gone Wrong* (1993), also solo acoustic, are brilliant folk albums. We should remember that they preceded *American Recordings*, a series of albums Johnny Cash recorded with producer Rick Rubin that reinvigorated Cash's own career and solidified the Americana movement in mainstream consciousness. Recorded lo-fi in Dylan's Malibu garage, *Good as I Been to You* and *World Gone Wrong* sold modestly. But Marcus promoted the cyclical genius of these acoustic works, praising Dylan for "inhabiting the first-person narrative" of folk classics "as if he lived them twice" (167). The gift was repaid. With these cover versions, as with "Blind Willie McTell," Dylan sent Marcus, still reeling from the Reagan era, back to the broad sweep of American history. Marcus listens to Dylan's spare acoustic recordings and, using his favored second-person address, serves up a blueprint for *Invisible Republic*, published four years down the line:

> You hear the old songs resolve themselves into a single story: variations on the tale of innocents setting out on long journeys into the unknown and the terrible betrayals they find when they reach their destinations. It's only after a time, when the melancholy and bitterness seem too great for one voice, that you hear them as history, as more than one man's plight. Finally, all of the story is shared, the singer only its mouthpiece, medium for private miseries within the great sweep of disaster; these songs are as much yours as anyone else's. As for the guile, the slyness, the pleasing cynicism of the singer's voice, he gets to keep that—leaving you to wonder why, at just this moment in time, one person who has in stray moments seen as clearly as Natty Bumppo is offering *this* story as a version of American legacy. (2010, 167–68)

Throughout *Bob Dylan by Greil Marcus*, the critic trails the musician across his many peaks and valleys. Sure, Dylan may have succumbed to limits "fixed in advance" (93), but he also shouldered debts the nation refused to pay (120, 158, 162). The constant cat-and-mouse games in Marcus's writings on Dylan are remarkable for not having been derived from any interview or personal interaction. Instead, readers find two pop culture intellectuals trying harder than anyone else in their generation to tap a foundational understanding of the American experience through rock writing (albeit in different genres). That both men are renowned for their over-the-top style makes them a perfect match; they are like certain cartoon characters, each the foil for the other, except that nearly every utterance is underscored, however slyly, with gravitas.

Marcus's slim books on Van Morrison and the Doors, complex artists in their own right, were far simpler in their approach. "There are a zillion books about the Doors but none of them are about their music," Marcus told Simon Reynolds a year after his book on the band appeared. "I just wanted to listen to the songs. I think it's a good idea for a book: a book about listening to somebody's songs" (quoted in Reynolds 2012, part 4). If Marcus's comment is about as disarming as anything Dylan ever uttered to his interviewers, it nonetheless describes his finished product. *The Doors: A Lifetime of Listening to Five Mean Years* (2011) was written in a month, whereas books like *Mystery Train* and *Lipstick Traces* had each taken nine years. I finished *The Doors* in four hours. I enjoyed it, but didn't think much about it afterwards. I respect Marcus's decision "just to listen." I do it myself. But there existed here the potential for something more.

In *The History of Rock 'n' Roll in Ten Songs* (2014), Marcus hits upon a winning balance. The book's title is both a joke and a dare, the ten songs constituting a mix tape with a big bet to place. Prominent in Marcus's argument are the pop cycles that bring notable songs back to public consciousness, whether that is due to remakes by other artists or to historical events that rekindle the original version's message.[24] Knowing full well that he could have selected ten songs issued by the Sun label in the 1950s, ten records from female punk bands in the 1990s, or ten soul singles released in 1963, Marcus identifies his topic as "the moment when something appears as if out of nowhere, when a work of art carries within itself the thrill of invention, of discovery, that is worth listening for ... In rock 'n' roll, this is a moment that, in historical time, is repeated again and again, until, as a culture, it defines the art itself" (2014, 11). History in pop music is elastic. Pete Townshend realized that it was the explosive "event" of a rock song (12) and Neil Young the "reckless abandon" of such songs (23) that mattered far more than the date the song was actually written. Indeed, Young has said that rock and roll seemed somehow to have invented earlier genres like country and blues on account of what it said, and how powerfully it said so (23). Likewise, for Marcus rote chronology of rock history takes a backseat to "rediscoveries of a certain spirit, a leap into style, a step out of time" (12). Four decades after *Mystery Train*, the timeless aura invoked in myth and symbol scholarship still matters.

The ten songs Marcus selects exist on their own plane, regardless of who wrote them, who performed them, or when or where they did so.[25] Two chapters stand out. One concerns "Transmission," sung in 1979 by Joy Division and re-created for two movies about the band in 2007 and 2010. The other concerns "Money (That's What I Want)" and "Money Changes Everything," songs covered by a host of artists across many pop cycles, from 1959 to 2005. As British post-punks (perhaps uber-punks), Joy Division had the temerity in "Transmission" to suggest that listening to the radio was a suicidal gesture (33). The message was conveyed by singer Ian Curtis, who had the gall to name his band after a Nazi group responsible for the rape of Jewish women, and the rashness to commit suicide on eve of his band's first American tour. Curtis never saw the money from a big tour or massive radio play, but "Transmission" indicates that wasn't his aim. Meanwhile, Barrett Strong and Tom Gray (of the Brains) composed songs about the necessity of making money, or perhaps the heartbreaking reality of that necessity, only to see producers or other artists receive financial rewards and acclaim. How American.

In Marcus's hands, rock music's relationship with the market is not treated as an anomaly or an unseemly sideshow, but rather as the primary reason popular art exists. The potential of being heard, and of having others pay for the privilege of hearing what you say, is for Marcus at the core of the American experience. In the following passage, Marcus makes the writers and performers of rock songs sound like Ralph Waldo Emerson's exemplars of "Self-Reliance":

> The music—and the market, the audience that it once revealed and created—was a challenge to whoever had the nerve to try to make it. The ear of the new audience was fickle, teenagers knowing nothing of where the music came from and caring less, and why should they care? It was new, it was different, and that was what they wanted … You had to find something new. You had to listen to everything on the market

and try to understand what wasn't there—and what wasn't there was you. So you asked yourself, as people have been asking themselves ever since, what's different about me? How am I different from everybody else—and why am I different? Yes, you invent yourself to the point of stupidity, you give yourself a ridiculous name, you appear in public in absurd clothes, you sing songs based on nursery rhymes or jokes or catchphrases or advertising slogans, and you do it for money, renown, to lift yourself up, to escape the life you were born to, to escape the poverty, the racism, the killing strictures of a life that you were raised to accept as fate, to make yourself a new person not only in the eyes of the world, but finally in your own eyes too. (2014, 17–18)

For Peter Hook, bassist for Joy Division, self-expression through music was about "the drive to play. Just to be heard" (quoted in Marcus 2014, 39). Alternatively, for Barrett Strong, Tom Gray, Cyndi Lauper, and the various other American musicians Marcus features in *History*, the prospect of commercial success governs the quest for an original identity. Even if "Money (That's What I Want)" was on an intellectual level "the metaphorical representation of the out-of-control technological forces of modern society grinding the individual down to nothing"—as a very young and admittedly pretentious Marcus supposedly told friends back in 1964 after listening to the Beatles version for hours on end—the song was for Barrett Strong or John Lennon a way of getting back at the system. It was also a way of getting out of West Point, Mississippi, or Liverpool, England, and of getting over with an audience who adored rock musicians for their resolve in the face of long odds. Granted, we are talking about pop songs on the radio. But Marcus insists these songs have a serious cultural stake. When Cyndi Lauper lent her Queens accent to the tossed off "yeah" in her cover of "Money Changes Everything," she joined the Shangri-Las and other outer borough girls in making a pop song's desperate drama that much more real. However arty she might seem, Lauper knew that money did, in fact, change everything, and she knew it in a way that elite tastemakers never would.

It's interesting that Marcus ends the chapters on "Transmission" and the "Money" songs with references to movies. What Marcus didn't do so well in *The Shape of Things to Come* he does astonishingly well here, probably because music criticism takes the lead and the film citations are there merely to add color. But what color! The bitter cynicism of "Transmission" is matched by what Marcus sees in the film versions of Graham Greene's *Brighton Rock*. In the 1964 film adaptation of Greene's novel, the small-time outlaw Pinkie records a 45 rpm record for Rose, who believes, falsely, that he loves her. "What you want me to say is … I love you," Pinkie says into the microphone before affecting a perfect snarl. "Well, I don't. I hate you … I hate everything about you. You make me sick. Goddamn you little bitch, why don't you go back to where you came from and leave me alone forever?" (2014, 52). For Marcus, Pinkie's recording is "the first punk record." It's the spirit Ian Curtis internalized. After Pinkie is killed, Rose gets a chance to listen to the recording in a home for unwed or abandoned mothers-to-be. Another girl gets a record player, and at night Rose brings it close to her bed to play Pinkie's 45. "But the grooves are cheap," Marcus explains, and "the needle sticks. *'I love you.' 'I love you.' 'I love you.' 'I love you.'*—the record won't play beyond those words. Those words are all she'll ever hear, but her son will hear the music" (53). Making this connection, Marcus adds another dimension to Joy Division's "Transmission," suggesting that the transmission of earlier rebel energies, seen in Greene's novel and in the film, fueled the punk rock movement that came to fruition in the 1970s. Basically, Marcus recasts the argument he made in *Lipstick Traces*, citing a particular song and opening out to a range of references the song urges us to consider.

Likewise, the message of "Money (That's What I Want)" grows more powerful once Marcus pairs it with a scene from a film, in this case the 2012 release *Killing Them Softly*. Listening to Barack Obama's 2008 victory speech on TV while meeting with a mob fixer to collect his payday, a hit man played by actor Brad Pitt casts a wary eye at the screen. Pitt has heard Obama's sentiments expressed countless times by political orators, and still he doesn't believe a word he's hearing. As he did when citing *Brighton Rock*, Marcus ends his commentary on a pop song with a snippet of dialogue from a film to flesh out the song's importance. After roundly dismissing Obama's naïve belief in national unity and linking it to the disingenuous rhetoric once used by slaveholder Thomas Jefferson,

> [Pitt] points up to the TV, his voice quieting even more. "This guy wants to tell me we're living in a community? Don't make me *laugh*. I'm living in *America*, and in America you're on your own. America's not a country.

It's just a business. Now *fuckin'* pay me." Then the screen goes blank and on the soundtrack Barrett Strong takes the story from there. (2014, 194)

Here, and throughout *History*, Marcus gives the pop song the last word. Songs are the tales we tell; they stand as literature and as politics, reflecting the needs and desires of our nation.

In *Real Life Rock: The Complete Top Ten Columns, 1986–2014*, Marcus provides a flowchart of this dynamic, reprinting his "Real Life Top Ten" columns, which were launched at the *Village Voice* and which can now be found online at *Pitchfork*. Wading through three decades of Marcus's likes (the Mekons, Sleater-Kinney) and dislikes (Patti Smith, Lucinda Williams), we find that American prophecy is not always writ large; it gets communicated piecemeal, in three-minute installments heard on the radio. Americana, the basic feel of our national belonging, gets articulated by artists as diverse as Snakefarm, whose cover of "Frankie and Johnny" proves "the song had room in it" (2015a, 186); to Dion and PJ Harvey, "beholden to wide-open spaces" and "terrain the songs claim" (425, 446); to young California traditionalist Frank Fairfield, in whose songs "the whole country comes into view, glimpsed as if over a ridge: a place of discovery, joy, despair, defeat" (455–56). There's an intimate tone to the columns. Reading them is like hearing your best friend talking about the music he has just discovered. At the same time, we find the emphasis on nationhood Marcus has shared since *Mystery Train*. In his recent edited works, too, Marcus has spoken of the "room," "motion," and "range" of the American experience, "where what is at issue is speech, in many forms" (Marcus and Sollors 2009, xxiv).

Marcus has always been drawn to the "vast sweep" of American history, even when he has delved into the smaller and more unusual spaces occupied by the subculture. Focusing on the debts brought forth by the silenced past, and on the violent eruptions they occasion, he has shown that he is familiar with the new varieties of historicism flourishing in the academy. Yet he has dismissed the notion that we are the victims of any given historical moment. As a "shameless fan" of rock and literature, and of popular culture in general, he does not doubt the potential of everyday people to "make prophecy," to steer the course of history as it happens. As a critic, Marcus has not shied away from the ambition he noticed in David Thomson's provocative film criticism, claiming rock songs not just for music history but for American history

(2015a, 438). While his unconventional methodology might be disconcerting for some, it has been refreshingly liberating for others, especially for those who always wanted to embrace our nation's mythology and symbolism, but wondered whether it was cool to do so. By hitching a ride on an older train of thought and updating it for our times, Greil Marcus has become one of our most provocative cultural critics.

★ 2 ★

"Life's Little Ups and Downs": Peter Guralnick and Roots Biography

In graduate school, I regularly cast aside advice from professors and wallowed in what's known, pejoratively, as the "biographical fallacy." As budding post-structural critics, we were encouraged to frame discussion of literary texts with an array of theories and to regard authorial intent as a fiction. Indie to the core, I balked, risking the retrograde label by preferring to know something about my favorite writers' routines, their friendships and affairs, the triumphs and failures fueling their art in order to get as close as possible to moments of creation. Personal histories of the Beat Generation and copies of *American Poetry Review* became favored resources. I had to go far beyond the seminar room to track them down. My favorite column in *APR* featured the working spaces of poets; it answered questions my peers deemed gratuitous. What did poets' desks look like? What time of day did they write? What vistas did their windows afford? Did pictures of heroes line their walls? For me, those questions weren't gratuitous at all.

I have retained this curiosity about artistic creation, and have become more creative myself in the process. Researching visual art for *Urban Pastoral*, my book on the New York School, I sought descriptions of studio spaces, finding these crucial to any analysis I might offer. I liked knowing that painters got their smocks dirty, smelled of turpentine, and wrestled with hangovers or personal hang-ups as they pursued a truer art. To write the way I wanted, I had to inhabit their spaces, at least in my mind. Jane Freilicher's *The Painting Table*, with its portrayal of scattered brushes, tubes of oils, and cans of paint thinner, is as inspirational for me as it is for poet John Ashbery, in whose apartment the painting hangs. It represents the daily experiences of creative people: the work behind the artwork, if you will.

Writing a chapter on Peter Guralnick, America's preeminent roots rock biographer, makes me equally impassioned about the working lives of creative people. When biography illuminates the process of making art, it becomes another kind of art. Showcasing his empathy and narrative grace, Guralnick's books explain in sophisticated terms the personal stakes of songwriting and performance. Compared to Greil Marcus, Guralnick provides a telescoped view of Americana. In his biographies, the individual soul and the nation seem equally mysterious and impenetrable because they are inextricably linked and fraught with danger. Judging by certain strands of literature, music, and film—Jack Kerouac's road novels, Peter Fonda and Dennis Hopper's *Easy Rider*, Hüsker Dü's *Zen Arcade*, Sonic Youth's *Daydream Nation*, Jim Jarmusch's *Mystery Train*, Arcade Fire's *The Suburbs*—individuals who go searching for America have a hard time of it. Whether it's on the open highway or in the walled-in suburbs, characters learn that there's no discernable reason for national belonging other than their own obsessions, peculiar desires they've let surface, often to deflect competing versions of America rushing past them or hemming them in. And that's just within the artworks, behind which lie the artists who face their own obsessions about America.

For biographers, negotiating the divide between art and artist can be tricky, especially when a subject resists all inquiries. Consider *Low Side of the Road*, Barney Hoskyns's biography of Tom Waits, dismissed as second rate by the *New York Times* because of its unauthorized status. That's unfortunate. *Low Side of the Road* is informative not only about the life and career of Tom Waits but also about the challenges Hoskyns faced when Waits and associates refrained from cooperating, so circumscribed were they by the "circle of trust" the eccentric musician and Kathleen Brennan (his wife and co-writer) erected around themselves. Consider, too, Richard Holmes, whose landmark study *Footsteps: Adventures of a Romantic Biographer* opened a portal on the genre, communicating not only the thrill of the chase but also the roadblocks Holmes encountered reconstructing the lives of nineteenth-century writers. Hoskyns faced a different challenge: a living subject who seems close, yet so distant. If Romantic poets were the rock stars of their day, think of how our own celebrity culture would treat them. Had they been similarly hounded, would Lord Byron or Percy Shelley have adopted the veil of mystery worn by Tom Waits or Bob Dylan, Neil Young or Joni Mitchell, to name just a few of rock's mercurial, hard-to-access subjects? What about John Keats, an ambitious Romantic poet who never saw much fame in his brief life? We'll never know. What's clear is that Hoskyns, more than Holmes, found himself up against the artist's veil. It's poignant and cautionary to find Hoskyns playing "stage-door Johnny," waiting fruitlessly in the rain near Waits's tour bus for his subject to appear and talk (Hoskyns 2009, 495, 500–1).[1]

At other junctures on rock's magical mystery tour, access has been granted to select journalists. Whether they were fellow travelers on tour or flies on the studio wall during the recording of a seminal album, these lucky scribes have provided intimate portraits of our rock and roll heroes. Think of Stanley Booth accompanying the Rolling Stones on their incendiary 1969 tour, Chris Salewicz hanging out with the Clash in London, or Sam Shepard chronicling Bob Dylan's Rolling Thunder Revue. Of course, a dissolution of boundaries can result in bias, messiness, and unwanted drama. Jimmy McDonough interviewed Neil Young multiple times over the course of a decade for *Shakey: Neil Young's Biography*, only to receive a profanity-laced jumble of recollections. His "all-access" book got worse when he endeavored to match Young word for word. There are also musicians who grant access only to demand the story be constructed on their terms. David Yaffe tells me that he benefits from the lengthy interviews he secures with Joni Mitchell, but that he's constantly aware of what this access implicitly warrants.

In his Waits biography, Hoskyns emphasizes the protective mindset of "obtuse geniuses," recalling the rebuffs he suffered in previous contacts with misunderstood musical heroes:

> "I don't know anyone on earth that I really consider understands me as a human being whatsoever," [Alex] Chilton, co-founder of the immortal Big Star, told me. "While I have nothing against you personally, for you to write about me would be the best way for me to begin to have something against you." As for Lewis Taylor, after I wrote a piece in June 2007 proclaiming his *Lost Album* one of the greatest ever made, I received at least two e-mails from the man ordering me to take it down. To quote Jeff Tweedy, "Is that the thanks I get for loving you?" (xxi)

We see here how wary artists can get when pressed to reveal secrets of their creative process or the details of their private life. Who can blame them? Regardless, most musicians are obliged at some juncture, in some fashion, to accede to the marketplace where they've chosen to place their art if they want to maintain their profile and guarantee profitability. It's a weird symbiosis. Journalists circle like hawks, pens in their talons, and adoring fans want to know as much as possible about their heroes. Artists hoping to avoid becoming last year's flavor of the month surrender to the media so that they can go on creating. Bob Dylan and Tom Waits coordinate rounds of interviews whenever an album is released. These interviews appear in mainstream periodicals and enjoy a second life in books. Even Alex Chilton relented from time to time. His laconic interviews on WLIR radio in 1974 and on MTV's *120 Minutes* in 1985 are gems of rare price. Chilton also granted Holly George-Warren access to his materials before his unexpected death in 2010. Speaking on You Tube's *Rock Book Show*, George-Warren told host Kimberly Austin that Chilton was quite conversational with musicians and journalists so long as they were sufficiently under the radar. When George-Warren met Chilton in North Carolina in the 1980s, she was a punk rocker and he was a scuffling underground hero. A bond got formed then and there (see chapter 4). Professional journalists lacking indie credibility never stood the same chance, as Hoskyns learned the hard way.

Waits summarizes this cat-and-mouse dynamic in his song "What's He Building?" a title Hoskyns should have adopted for his biography. "A prying busybody tries to imagine what his eccentric neighbor is up to in his uninviting abode," Hoskyns says of the track (xxi–xxii). The life of a cantankerous, misunderstood genius is more or less obscured, but the public's relentless search for clues gets full coverage. Waits keeps repeating the song's title, his voice rising with intrigue, as he parrots the nosey outsiders fascinated with his music. In an interview Hoskyns conducted with Waits in 1999, before access was cut off, the songwriter lays it on the line: "We seem to be compelled to perceive our neighbors through the keyhole. There's always someone in the neighborhood—the Boo Radley, the village idiot—and you see that he drives this yellow station wagon without a windshield, and he has chickens in his backyard and doesn't get home till 3 a.m., and he says he's from Florida but the license plate says Indiana … so, you know, 'I don't trust him.' It's really a disturbed creative process" (Waits quoted in Hoskyns 2009, 424). A decade later, Hoskyns has become the song's frustrated stalker. He waits by a window, forlorn, peering in, gauging the off-limits genius of Tom Waits, hoping he won't reduce the musician to the sum of his life experiences (xvi).[2]

When I finished *Low Side of the Road*, I asked myself what Peter Guralnick would have done if put in Hoskyns's place. As far as I can tell, the situation has never arisen. Like Bob Woodward in political circles, Guralnick has emerged as the ultimate insider, talking to the right people, assembling narrative strands, and forging an interesting whole. Guralnick began his career as a profiler of American roots musicians, following performers out on the road like an embedded journalist, composing synopses of their shows and of their lives. Guralnick is *right there* with the artists he covers. He doesn't track down a story as much as open himself up to it, facilitated by his sense of craft, picked up in literary circles. In *Feel Like Going Home* (originally published 1971) and *Lost Highway* (originally published in 1979), imagination, character development, and an attention to setting help to carry Guralnick's writing beyond the norm of rock journalism. Details about musicians' everyday lives lead to broader discussions about the state of the nation, or some small corner of it. At first it seems inconsequential that Robert Pete Williams awaits the installation of telephone lines in rural Louisiana, or that Williams has promised the writer a "real country supper" (1999a, 125, 148–49). Then it doesn't. With such details, Guralnick makes palpable the gulf between communities rich and poor, white and black, northern and southern, urban and rural. He provides context for the "re-discoveries" undertaken by white blues enthusiasts in the 1960s, and in turn explains the culture shock rural blacks experienced when asked to perform before middle-class white audiences at the Newport Folk Festival and on the college circuit. Seizing on such disparities while emphasizing process over product, personality over celebrity, Guralnick underscores the incredulity of southern blues musicians when they discovered their "authenticity" was in vogue. For Robert Pete Williams, music is what he does; there's no other life. Unlike other writers who came along during the blues revival, Guralnick refuses to build a myth or steal Williams's presence. The musician takes the lead.[3]

To write his definitive biographies of Elvis Presley and Sam Cooke, Guralnick had to get inside the lives of subjects he never met, tracking down their friends and associates, sitting down for rounds of interviews, scouring obscure periodicals of yesteryear, visiting places the musicians lived and recorded. In the author's note to *Last Train to Memphis: The Rise of Elvis Presley* (1994), Guralnick cites Richard Holmes, highlighting the "pursuit" biographers undertake as they capture the fleetingness of another's life. You never quite catch the life of a subject lost to the past, Holmes admits, "but maybe, if you were lucky, you might write about the pursuit of that fleeting figure in such a way as to bring it alive in the present" (quoted in Guralnick 1994, xi). Dogged research, attention to detail, and respect for historical fact are the basic tools of the biographer. But so too is a creative spirit, an openness and empathy toward biographical subjects that Guralnick shares with Holmes. Laying bare the facts about Presley and Cooke would be one thing, Guralnick realized, but to *reveal* their stories, to bring them fully alive in the present, he needed to employ the strategies and techniques of a novelist, taking a "leap of faith" whenever circumstances dictated (1999, xiii). Fortunately, his shift toward the creative didn't involve too much of a stretch.[4]

In the 1960s and early 1970s, as Marcus studied American political thought at Berkeley, Guralnick studied literature and taught classics at Boston University. He also wrote fiction, publishing two story collections in the 1960s and a novel, *Nighthawk Blues*, some years later. A background in fiction provided Guralnick a useful lens on character. He not only recognizes but also feels deeply the tribulations country music songwriter Charlie Rich referred to as "life's little ups and downs." The biographer knows that musicians on a public stage are defined by harrowing events closed off to celebrity watchers, that their art is shaped by close-to-home traumas occurring ineluctably in real time. In "Life's Little Ups and Downs" or "Sittin' and Thinkin'," Rich's private problems get translated into masterpieces of songwriting. Guralnick unearths the facts behind the fiction, identifying with songwriters in ways most critics cannot.

When *Feel Like Going Home* was published in 1971, Guralnick was working on a novel. After completing a string of articles for *Rolling Stone*, he thought he had said goodbye to music journalism. His friend Jim Miller lured him back with a column, "Jackie Wilson Said," which appeared in Boston's *Real Paper*. Miller's suggestion that he do a piece on Waylon Jennings spurred Guralnick to consider the soulfulness of country music, expanding his repertoire in Americana and exposing him to a wider range of storytelling in song. *Lost Highway*, which contains the Jennings profile, is the perfect complement to *Feel Like Going Home*. If Guralnick's first book on music consisted of blues profiles with a sprinkling of country and hillbilly history, here, eight years later, was that roots rock mix in inverse proportion. Through it all, Guralnick foregrounded his creative approach. The emotional pull of fictional characters that led him to write short stories was evident in the colorful musicians he was meeting. "I *believed* in the people I was writing about and their art," he declared at the start of *Lost Highway* (2).

When Guralnick was writing his early profiles, objectivity was not his chief concern. It still isn't. "I want to be open without reservation for any story that can be told, to write without judgment," he told me. "I feel the major part of a story is identifying with the storyteller" (2011, 12/5 interview). If he finds a different Charlie Rich in 1970, 1973, and 1976, that's because Rich's life story changes each time (1989, 151, 156). Sun Records head Sam Phillips said that Rich was the only one of his discoveries with the talent to rival Elvis, but that the singer's failed negotiations with fame were uniquely his own. Billboard charts cannot reveal that. Guralnick, more than any other roots rock writer, can.

Guralnick benefited from hanging around musicians, and from seeing how they hang out. Telling in this regard is the anecdote launching his biography of Presley. The author recalls driving down McLemore Avenue in Memphis accompanied by one of the singer's childhood friends, who told the writer what Elvis was like when he was just a kid hanging out at the local soda fountain: in other words, who he was before he was *Elvis Presley*. Looking back at this moment, seizing upon the humble image of Elvis at the fountain, the biographer decides then and there "to keep the story in real time, to allow the characters to freely breathe their own air" (1994, xii).[5] Likewise, Guralnick told me he learned quite a bit when he was taken around southern cities by Donnie Fritts and William Bell, seeing the places famous musicians once haunted and meeting the not-so-famous folks those musicians inspired, disappointed, or otherwise affected (2011, 12/5 interview).

Guralnick's narrative pacing obliges readers to engage musical legacies day by day, or at least month by month. Reading *Last Train to Memphis* and *Careless Love: The Unmaking of Elvis Presley* (1999), I got caught up in moments the mythmakers overlooked, puzzling over the singer's obsessions and choices, half wishing there was a New York movie audience on hand to shout advice ("Don't do it, Elvis!"), even though the country boy's failings were inevitable, the mythic figure being so very human. The real-time aspect of Guralnick's biographies makes each decision seem crucial. Influenced not only by novelists but also by political biographers such as Arthur Schlesinger and David

McCullough, Guralnick explains that "one must respect not just the story but the way in which it develops" (1999, xiv). Guralnick doesn't place Presley's story within a cultural matrix, as Marcus does in *Mystery Train*. Instead, he borrows techniques from realist fiction, constructing a stage then letting Elvis pace that stage, acting out his personal drama, as blind to his future as the rest of us are to our own.

"No ideas but in things." William Carlos Williams, a modernist poet, inspired Guralnick with that phrase (2010, 8/14 interview). Countering Marcus's baroque effusions, Guralnick inveighs against "sweeping cultural pronouncements" (1989, 13). So that while his portraits of Otis Redding or Sam Cooke offer an incisive look at the mid-century South, the focus is always on the musicians themselves. Whereas Marcus's symbolic analyses of classic rock strike Bob Dylan as overly intellectual and Robbie Robertson as "beautiful but dangerous work" (quoted in Hoskyns 2006, 243, 438n), Guralnick is too busy chronicling everyday life to cook up a cultural studies stew. There's one version of Americana you get when you hear Marcus lecture at the Walker Art Center about the "myth of the open road" (Marcus 2010, 133–47) and quite another when you hear Guralnick recount his time on the road with Hank Williams Jr., traveling on the tour bus alongside the performer, pinup pictures, playing cards, and tape decks. Guralnick has an easier time than Marcus of communicating the down-and-dirty world of roots performers, providing candid snapshots, and distilling the imaginative impulses so crucial to performance.[6] Guralnick also eschews the sensationalism hampering other rock biographers. He avoids the muckraking approach of Albert Goldman and the over-the-top posturing of Jimmy McDonough, who may have aimed to match Nick Tosches's colorful approach but ended up sounding crass.

Guralnick is too even-keeled for that, too precise. "It's ten-thirty, and Bobby 'Blue' Bland is just going to work," he writes in *Lost Highway*. Importantly, Guralnick realizes that he, too, is just going to work, and loving every minute of it. In fact, it was at a Bobby Bland show at Boston's Sugar Shack in the early 1970s that Guralnick decided to abandon teaching and write stories about musicians as truthfully as possible. Waiting for a post-show rehearsal of Bland's horn section convinced him that, like journalist Murray Kempton, he was happiest "going around," getting stories firsthand from musicians while they worked, squabbled, and uttered their special language (1989, 2). Audiences saw stars; Guralnick saw professionals. He wanted to be a professional, too (1999b, 398).

Guralnick learned that professionalism isn't always glamorous. In *Feel Like Going Home* and *Lost Highway*, we see performers sweating under lights, tripping over cables, piling into tour buses. That's what work is. Yet it never dampens the excitement, empathy, and human appeal of Guralnick's prose. When Bland reveals that he has been an alcoholic for eighteen years, Guralnick shifts to the second-person to register the impact of what's been said: "You look a little askance, surprised at this casual revelation." When Bland stares blankly at a group of LPs after being asked by a radio interviewer to select a favorite for airplay, Guralnick lets slide the fact that Bland can't read, preferring to let the awkward scene speak for itself (1989, 73–74). Whenever he does offer an interpretation, Guralnick stops to consider whether it is fair to his subject. In his depiction of Waylon Jennings, he says, "You get the feeling that in another life he might have been a buccaneer. And yet you sense somehow that this is an oversimplification … You look for the intelligence, the dedication, and the vulnerability beneath the hard-bitten façade" (206–7). Another time, he explains his occasional slides into second-person confession: "It's not easy meeting your idols … Somehow a backstage glimpse, however sympathetic, disqualifies you a little as a fan" (1999a, 241). Yet what a marvel it is, after so many miles logged, so many reels of tape and notebooks filled, that his fandom remains intact.

Of *Lost Highway*, Guralnick says, "I was trying to pass along not a dry assessment but a passion" (1989, 2). Instead of running down a story, he'd rather "enter into it" and thus "capture a different emotion" (2011, 12/5 interview). A "what am I doing here?" enthusiasm emerges regularly, sometimes literally, in his books. "What *am* I doing here?" Guralnick asks upon meeting Merle Haggard, who was caught between a divorce from Bonnie Owens and a marriage to Leona Williams, both background singers, the former having agreed to serve as the latter's bridesmaid. "I am genuinely distressed to meet one of my true heroes under these circumstances" (1989, 235). "I never wanted to be a critic," he announces at the beginning of *Lost Highway*, striving to maintain the "passionate naivete I felt essential to the proper love of rock 'n' roll" (1). Without hesitation, Guralnick regards Haggard, Bobby Bland, and Howlin' Wolf as "geniuses," not simply as subjects (83, 235, 280). Sam Phillips, too: "I realized as he talked that he was speaking to every fantasy that I had ever heard about him … I had a glimmer for the first time in a long time of the unlikely notion that history is not necessarily an accident, that the self-willed individual can affect his environment, and his times, in ways that we cannot even calculate" (328, 329).

Guralnick's emphasis on individual talent leads him to distrust "critical canons" and theoretical buttonholing. As he states in *Lost Highway*, criticism "should expand, not narrow horizons, but it cannot do that if one artist is continually being played off against another, if achievement is measured not on its own terms but against some arbitrary, unreal standard, if the critic does not listen with his or her ears (and emotions) rather than some abstract ideological commitment" (13). Witness here Guralnick's fundamental difference from Marcus. Guralnick wants to understand the daily conditions under which artists live and work. To seize upon details, to see "chipped paint on the doorknob" (1999, xiii), is to appreciate the creative process before critical and historical impositions become an issue. "Thomas Jefferson and Benjamin Franklin did not sit around a table and say 'Isn't it great living in the past?'" David McCullough says. Accordingly, Guralnick recognized that someone like Elvis Presley or Sam Cooke should not be considered purely in monolithic terms, or solely as icons, in his lengthy studies (1999, xiv).[7]

The contrast between Guralnick and Marcus is illustrative of larger trends in roots rock writing. Although Marcus has published books on individual artists, he has never written a biography. Below, however, Marcus discusses the type of biography he prefers, citing James Gavin's *Deep in a Dream*, a biography of trumpeter Chet Baker:

> Except in the rare cases of those strange creatures who, like T. E. Lawrence, create themselves to such a degree that it becomes nearly impossible to imagine that they ever experienced a trivial or even workaday moment, the dramatic sweep we find in novels or movies is not really the stuff of anyone's life. No matter how the writer may try to have it otherwise, most biographies are simply one thing after another. The life of a junkie is not just one thing after another, it is the *same* one thing after another—and yet there is not a page in *Deep in a Dream* that is not engaging, alive, demanding a response from a reader whether that be a matter of horror or awe, making the reader almost complicit in whatever comes next, even when, with the story less that of a musician who used heroin to play than that of a junkie who played to get heroin, it seems certain that nothing can. (2011)[8]

We can see Marcus's respect for the biographer's art, but also his distance from it, particularly his wariness about mundane details. He respects what someone like Gavin or Guralnick does, but can't imagine he himself would have the patience to abandon macrocosm for microcosm, seminar room for tour bus. A key question emerges. Can Guralnick, so invested with the daily "stuff" of his subjects' lives, slug with the same intellectual power as Marcus, who with his looping prose style and broad historicist reach always seems to be swinging for the fences?

Elvis provides a good test case. In an early assignment for the *Boston Phoenix*, Guralnick wrote about Elvis's 1967 singles, championing the roots sound the King was rediscovering. During the heyday of psychedelic rock, Elvis was viewed as terribly uncool. But Guralnick positioned Presley (and himself) ahead of the curve, heralding in his new singles a back-to-basics approach that hip rock groups like the Byrds, the Band, and the Flying Burrito Brothers would soon adopt. But then, every discourse has its gold standard. Guralnick recalls that when he was growing up "What do you think of Elvis Presley?" was the "first business of social exchange, and your answer defined you politically, morally, sociologically" (1999a, 17). In 1967, that answer was still loaded, except few were asking the question anymore. "U.S. Male" got some airplay, but not much, and it paled in comparison to the colossal gamble played out before millions the following year: Elvis's Christmas Special. "I don't think anyone who watched the TV show will ever forget the sheer tension of the moment," Guralnick emotes, "the brief instant in which Elvis's and our passions, or fears, our illusions, were nakedly exposed" (1989, 139). From a rock historian's point of view, the TV special marked a juncture at which roots-based rock and roll, showcased on a Hollywood soundstage, was going to enjoy a second life or else fade away for good. Just as the deaths of Buddy Holly and Otis Redding forced rock and soul to envision new horizons, the appearance of a lean, leather-clad, and surprisingly vibrant Elvis returning from obscurity to sing the blues prompted the Love Generation to wake up from its stupor, to face the visceral impulse giving rise to rock and roll in the first place. If the TV special was marked by confrontation and "tension," as Guralnick claims, it's because rock and roll was laying down a challenge to rock, Elvis telling elite Boomer youth to leave the incense and peppermints at home, to take the flowers out of their hair and put on their blue suede shoes. Elvis was also reminding himself of a basic lesson. At the beginning of *Careless Love*, Guralnick says that a good biographer must "cast aside the burden of accumulation and rely on instinct alone" (xiii). This is what Elvis did in 1968, giving full expression to "If I Can Dream," making people believe its liberal sentiment, even in an *annus horribilis*. "For the first time in a long time he didn't bother to hide the fact that he truly cared" (310), Guralnick says, before returning the love: "I don't know if I can convey how truly thrilling a moment it really was" (323).[9]

The rock star's triumph of instinct couldn't last forever, and it didn't. On the TV screen, the movie screen, or the stages of Vegas, rock's transition from an expressive performance to an intensely mediated spectacle shaped by producers was inevitable. Because he was the first rocker to fall into this trap, Elvis's example looms large. As Guralnick says, "Nowhere is the adage that America seeks heroes not for their qualities but for their marketability more brutally illustrated than in the case of Elvis, whom success first gutted, then abandoned to a twenty-year state of suspended animation" (1989, 4). Given his penchant for following musicians behind the scenes, it's surprising to learn that Guralnick saw Elvis perform only once, at the Boston Garden in 1973. The King's stage show had devolved by that point into a series of ad-libs and karate chops, and his waxy complexion resembled that of a mannequin or an embalmed corpse, but the euphoria of experiencing rock and roll through Elvis remained undeniable. It didn't matter that the man himself was inaccessible. Through the Vegas years, Guralnick insists, we were all still "fans," and if we watched Elvis fail, we at least identified with the type of failure that is an undeniable component of the American dream. "Don't feel sorry for him," Guralnick wrote shortly before the King's death. "For Elvis was merely a prisoner of the same fantasies as we. What he wanted he got. What he didn't, he deliberately threw away" (1989, 140). Here, Guralnick sounds like Marcus exploring the mythological aspects of American tragedy ("throw away" is Marcus's pet phrase when he's calibrating success and failure). Yet in *Last Train to Memphis* and *Careless Love* the biographer pushes further than the cultural critic to determine the deep-seated causes and ravaging psychological costs of this pop icon's rise and fall.

Notably absent in Guralnick's work is Marcus's emphasis on metaphor as "possibility," or "insight into the myths we carry" (Marcus 2010, 26). To the contrary, Guralnick once told me that "detail establishes the metaphor," as in a novel's plot, so you're "not stuck in the same place forever, writing in a jewel-like fashion" (2010, 8/14 interview). Guralnick calls this his "inside-out approach," his attempt to "stay inside the game." He writes a 1,300-page account gleaned from hundreds of personal interviews and arcane primary sources, his critical judgment suspended in the face of facts, whereas Marcus writes a fifty-page essay in *Mystery Train* notable for its impressionistic, grandiloquent style. Marcus's "Presliad," heralds the classical ambitions of rock culture, focusing on the epic tragedy of its fallen King. It's a great piece of roots rock writing, quite possibly the best ever. But Guralnick seems to have viewed it warily. "I wanted to rescue Elvis from the dreary bondage of myth," he says in *Last Train to Memphis*, "Presliad" presumably in his crosshairs (xiii). Marcus himself etched their differences in this anecdote:

> Last fall in Nashville, Guralnick and I shared a literary forum. I've known Guralnick for thirty years, and I felt he sold himself short when he stated his credo: "My approach to writing is the same as my approach to coaching baseball. I tell the kids, 'Don't speculate. Stay inside the game.'" My approach is the opposite—speculate; get outside the game—and I think that to find a person who so completely entered the souls of others as Elvis Presley did, you have to do that. (2000b, 203)[10]

Of course, when both writers are so good at what they do, I don't feel as though I need to choose sides.

Guralnick's expressed aim in his Presley biography is to "suggest the dimensions of a world, the world in which Elvis Presley had grown up, the world which had shaped him and which he in turn had unwittingly shaped, with all the homeliness and beauty that everyday life entails" (1994, xii). To accomplish this, he places on *Last Train*'s flyleaf a map of Memphis in 1954. Readers can see the housing projects where Elvis spent his adolescence and the streets where he drove an electric company truck. With the map, Guralnick reminds us there was "no way Elvis could have missed Beale Street" (2010, 10/14 interview), the epicenter of black culture in the mid-South.[11] Positioning the singer in his environment, Guralnick makes Elvis larger by making him small, and thereby more relatable to the masses.[12] Even in *Careless Love*, the volume that recounts the King's long decline, readers come to appreciate Elvis as a human being, wincing when his foibles and obsessions dilute his talent, but wondering too whether any hometown momma's boy could have withstood celebrity's spotlight with his sanity intact. I find it telling that on the flyleaf of

Careless Love, Guralnick provides two photographs of Graceland, the mansion that became the first symbol of rock star status and then, inevitably, a prison. Some writers might concentrate on Graceland's symbolism and ignore the singer inside the gilded cage. Not Guralnick. In *Careless Love*, readers find Elvis suffering disappointment but reveling in little victories his fans didn't see and his handlers didn't really care about. The karate kicks Presley introduced in his stage act and the racquetball courts he built behind Graceland may have perplexed fans and critics, and in time they became the stuff of comedy routines goofing on Elvis. Guralnick shows why these diversions meant something to the man, why Elvis the person was willing to follow his bliss and engage in activities not expected of Elvis the performer.[13]

Going further than Marcus did in "Presliad" or *Dead Elvis*, Guralnick wrests simple truths from the competing clutches of cynical criticism and obsequious flattery. The slightest detail, like a previously unheard conversation, sheds new light on an American success story and its tragic aftermath. Fans already suspect that Elvis's boneheaded decisions were enabled by newly acquired riches and reinforced by his circle of yes-men, the Memphis Mafia. Less known are poignant moments when the desperate singer reaches out for help or when others try to help him. Sadly, all is in vain, as connections constantly get missed. Not once, but several times, Elvis is implored by his mother Gladys, his early girlfriend Dixie Locke, and other level-headed intimates to stop the madness and get off the fast track, to return to Memphis and enjoy a quiet family life. After the whirlwind success of 1956, though, Elvis's response is always the same: "I can't. I'm in too far to get out" (1994, 479). Once he really is in too deep, he no longer has anyone looking out for his best interests.

After Gladys Presley's death in 1958, Elvis saw his last chance to find grounding. Guralnick narrates beautifully, if painfully, the entreaties Dixie Locke made to Elvis on the final night the couple spent alone together. Elvis tells Dixie that a backup singer he knew had recently gotten out of the entertainment rat race and given himself over to the Lord. "I wish I could do that," Elvis confesses. Dixie tells him it's still possible; he's already accomplished all he ever wanted. But Elvis says he's trapped. The following night, at a Graceland party, Dixie finds Elvis distant, lost among his hangers-on. She never saw him again (1994, 479).

Elvis Presley's story is a tragedy, but for Guralnick tragedy is not the occasion for moral judgment or cultural prophecy (1994, xiii; 1999, xi). Responding to filmmaker Bob Abel's question as to why he made those horrible Hollywood films and sang to a hound dog on the *Steve Allen Show*, Elvis offers a sad re-frain—"I had to, I had to"—but sheds no light on his motivation (1999, 468–69), suggesting that when postmodern American tragedy comes into view, it's as "malaise," and not merely as farce, Elvis embodying our collective enervation a good fifteen years before Jimmy Carter symbolized a nation running out of gas.[14] The biographer has an edge over the cultural critic when it comes to discussing malaise, for it takes a deliberate sorting through of mundane events to locate the moment someone admits defeat or simply stops caring. Poring over obscure interviews, old photos, and previously undiscovered contact sheets, Guralnick could see Elvis's life "all of a moment." Living with the biography every day, as one lives with a novel, he gained a new appreciation of human complexity, resisting commentary and building a narrative. "Over and over again," Guralnick told me, "you see the same manifestations of character in a subject—like shyness in Elvis or recklessness in Sam Cooke—but you can't use that detail or anecdote as a writer over and over. It becomes very important where you use it the one time in order to get maximum impact" (2010, 8/14 interview).

If quotidian facts read like revelations, it's because Guralnick, combining the doggedness of a reporter with the narrative chops of a novelist, places himself in situations where those facts resonate. For his profiles of blues and country musicians, he traveled to private homes as well as to clubs. For the Elvis biography, he spent years waiting patiently for Dixie Locke to share her memories of Elvis. When the two finally met, at an evangelical church where Locke worships, something about the place suggested the route Elvis might have taken if the clutches of "Colonel Tom" Parker and Hollywood weren't so strong. Secured in this setting, Guralnick found the interview with Locke "highly emotional on both sides," and the story she offered ("Elvis looked at me like I could save the world") "as eloquent as it gets" (2011, 12/15 interview).

Elvis chose not to settle down with Locke, or with another southern girl-friend, Biloxi beauty June Juanico. In his mind, he couldn't. Female fans covered his pink Cadillac with love letters and wrote their phone numbers in lipstick, but for Elvis intimacy was hard to come by, and maintain. When Elvis dated Natalie Wood, the press feasted on the details. Juanico, meanwhile, cried all the way through a photo session, giving her erstwhile mate a studio portrait in which she appeared awash in tears. Her portrait won second prize in a photo competition, but Juanico lost her boyfriend to the world of fame (1994, 349). Friends and fellow musicians felt the pinch, too. By the end of 1956, Elvis had struck it rich, but his original bandmates, Bill Black and Scotty Moore, were broke, living off a meager retainer and paying Hollywood prices, awaiting the beck and call of their famous boss. Embittered, they left Elvis's employment in 1957 (377, 432–33). Scotty Moore reappeared on the 1968 Christmas Special, then never saw Elvis again.

When Elvis played a "homecoming" concert in Memphis on July 4, 1956, he made a defiant announcement: "Those people in New York are not gonna change me none." But things had already changed. At his initial recording session for RCA in Nashville, engineers called out take numbers instead of shouting, "Hey, do it again" (237). It's a small but telling detail. Under Colonel Tom's management, Elvis became beholden to numbers and figures. In Guralnick's judgment, he became "the purest of American products, the commodity that had been missing from the shelves of an expanding marketplace of leisure and time and disposable cash" (241). Parker once told songwriter Jerry Leiber, "If you ever try to interfere with the business or artistic workings of the process known as Elvis Presley … you will never work for us again" (449). The business world's plastic language speaks for itself. The Colonel took a quarter of every dollar Elvis made. Qualitatively, he took much more than that.

On a personal level, Elvis tried to stay true to his roots, and to hometown innocence, but results were mixed. He lived in Memphis, but Graceland became a carnival. He posed on the mansion's lawn with a perky Hollywood actress, Yvonne Lime, on Easter weekend of 1957, and for a moment the balance seemed okay: the couple's celebrity flash cut through with malt shop innocence (382). Meanwhile, Elvis surrounded himself with local cronies, renting the Memphis Fairgrounds and cavorting from midnight to dawn in pursuit of extended adolescence. In time, his childlike behavior took on strange contours, similar to what fans saw decades later with Michael Jackson. There were donkeys in Graceland's swimming pool and peacocks in the yard. Elvis admitted into the Memphis Mafia one Scatter the Chimp, who at the promptings of the guys drank alcohol and had simulated sex with an ex-stripper. Like Wacko Jacko, Elvis bought a large ranch, the Circle G, as a playground for himself and his entourage. He delighted in fireworks displays and pillow fights. Looking at the moon and stars was a favorite hobby. He dabbled in New Age philosophy and adopted a Christ complex. He married a woman, had a child with her, but was thereafter rarely intimate with her. He liked his girlfriends to tuck him into bed as if he were a child. Most tragically, he put on his payroll a number of private doctors who kept him supplied with an array of pharmaceuticals up until his death (1999, 117, 147, 247, 254, 257, 313, 548, 633, 636). When the King of Pop followed the King of Rock and Roll down that road, one couldn't help but wonder whether fame in America has an identity all its own, drawing a diverse array of people into the same mistakes. In such instances, the divide between personal character and national character seems awfully thin.

Against all odds, Guralnick finds a moment of bliss near the bitter end. In Rapid City, in June 1977, just two months before his death, Elvis struggles heroically through a solo rendition of "Unchained Melody." Reportedly, the footage was deemed so raw that CBS executives declined to use it for their TV special. Guralnick recasts the event in his richest prose:

> It came at the end of the show when Elvis sat down at the piano and, with Charlie holding a hand mike, launched into "Unchained Melody," the Roy Hamilton number in which he so often seemed to invest every fiber of his being. Hunched over the piano, his face framed in a helmet of blue-black hair from which sweat sheets down over pale, swollen cheeks, Elvis looks like nothing so much as a creature out of a Hollywood monster film—and yet we are with him all the way as he struggles to achieve grace. It is a moment of what can only be described as grotesque transcendence, and when he signals to Charlie, "I got it," and goes on to complete the song with no help from Charlie or Sherrill Nielsen or any of the other background singers who frequently sustained his notes now in the more difficult passages, the expression on his face, the little-boy sense of relief that he has actually pulled it off, is both entrancing and heartbreaking. And then it is back to the standard finale, the giving out of kisses and scarves and the ritual departure that make up the carefully constructed façade he has built to wall himself off from everything but the approbation of the crowd. (1999, 638)

Sounding a lot like Marcus, Guralnick splits differences, balancing opposing trends without giving in to irony, trying to get to the heart of American contradiction. What Walt Whitman articulated, Elvis truly embodied, to our collective joy and eventual sadness. *Careless Love* didn't receive the same accolades as *Last Train to Memphis*, but it might be the greater achievement. The tale is too pathetic to render, but like Elvis in Rapid City, Guralnick pulls it off.

Despite Elvis's foibles, his defensiveness and insularity, Guralnick maintains that there is "no room for cool irony" when we see him make his great comeback (316), or at any other time. Whereas many rock journalists feed on irony, Guralnick reveals a fan's investment whenever Elvis squanders his talent or subdues his natural impulses. "One feels for him," Guralnick says, assessing the film *Blue Hawaii*, "one squirms with an embarrassment of one's own as he is asked to stand still for the trivialization of his music" (104). Many writers would trivialize the singer along with the trivial music, but Guralnick refrains, registering in human terms the commitments we make to art, and to commerce. The "democratic ideal of redemptive transformation" runs strong in the Presley saga, Guralnick explains. And for Elvis, comeback and redemption meant seeking out "a connection with a public that embraced him not for who he was but for what he sought to be" (661). Marcus could certainly abide such language. But as a biographer, Guralnick has a different emphasis. In assessing what Elvis "sought to be," and what America wanted him to be, he never loses sight of who Elvis really was.

In addition to the life stories being told, a crucial emphasis in Guralnick's books is race and integration in postwar America. Elvis Presley and Sam Cooke are compelling subjects because both were eager to "cross over," escaping racial categorization in pursuit of that most integrated American art form, the popular song. Actually, crossing over was Guralnick's own ambition while growing up in segregated Boston. Raised in upscale Brookline, he trooped over to Harvard Square at age fourteen to soak up the literary counterculture. After reading a Hemingway interview in *Paris Review*, he resolved to establish a daily writing routine. More influential, though, were the bohemians gravitating toward African American culture, especially its musical traditions. Music entered his life in a big way when a friend's brother came back from the Newport Folk Festival with a bunch of blues LPs. Guralnick was hooked, listening repeatedly to the discs and reading books on country blues by Sam Charters (*The Country Blues*), Paul Oliver (*Blues Fell this Morning*), and Frederic Ramsey (*Been Here and Gone*). In 1961, Guralnick saw Lightnin' Hopkins perform at Harvard and caught Big Joe Williams at Gerde's Folk City. He bought the Robert Johnson reissues, becoming a blues aficionado and in time, an equally ardent fan of soul music.[15]

Still a teenager, Guralnick traveled to Roxbury, Boston's largest black neighborhood, to visit Chitlin' Circuit nightclubs, which didn't ask minors for identification. He immersed himself in soul culture. During Freedom Summer, in 1964, he made friends with WILD deejays and worked as an usher for soul revues at the Donnelly Theater, facing a few predicaments with a rowdy clientele but getting access to the music he loved. Meantime, he maintained connections with Harvard Square friends, scoring his first interview with Skip James in Dick Waterman's Cambridge apartment in 1965 and placing his story in *Blues World*. Articles on Buddy Guy and Robert Pete Williams followed in *Crawdaddy!* By the time *Feel Like Going Home* appeared in 1971, Guralnick was the top translator of blues traditions for the rock crowd.

According to Guralnick, white hipsters picked up on blues so readily because black listeners had abandoned the form; it was uncontested ground (1999b, 251).[16] Soul music was another story. It largely escaped co-optation by white musicians and urban intellectuals. Perhaps for this reason, Guralnick gravitated to soul with great passion. Greil Marcus has associated 1964 and 1965 with the "pop explosion" led by the Beatles and Dylan, but at this time Guralnick identified more with James Brown (20). In Roxbury and elsewhere, he sought and found entrée in the soul world. This is not to say he didn't face roadblocks. "Tell me this, man, you won't take no offense," an unemployed black drummer asked Guralnick when he visited Big Duke's nightclub in Chicago, "but how does a member of the Caucasian race get to have soul?" (1999a, 226). Similar fish-out-of-water stories emerge in Guralnick's early books, as when he overhears label head Phil Chess using the language of the ghetto to curse back and forth with black artists. During their interview, Chess uses the same vernacular with Guralnick to describe the world of Chicago blues. Elated, Guralnick feels like he has stumbled upon a gold mine. But to protect his reputation, Chess breaks the audiotape of their conversation when the writer goes out for lunch (233, 239). The language of Chicago blues was gone; a vivid impression remained.

Important for Guralnick are the various assignations given blacks. He uses "Negro" in an early profile of Robert Pete Williams to register as conspicuously as possible the musician's limited opportunities in Rosedale, Louisiana (147–48). Elsewhere, he uses terms prevalent in the Black Power era, like "new breed" and "young blood," to identify a new generation assaying their musical progenitors. One young woman sporting an Afro seems bored and scornful of Howlin' Wolf (164), while other "young bloods" slap hands easily with Rufus Thomas (1989, 57). Likewise, in his biography of Sam Cooke, Guralnick freely adopts terms like "getting over" in his prose. Readers can judge for themselves whether stories of a rising gospel star "rhyming up" Bible stories, making congregations "overcome" or "upset," getting women to "fall out," and persuading collaborators to "have church" on stage benefit from the use of black vernacular.[17] But like Sam's brother L. C. Cooke, Guralnick is happy to "tell a story on Sam," adopting the lingo of key players to bring that story to light (2006, 7, 14, 20, 33, 482). The roots rock writer is "lucked in" and "caught out," attuned to the "steady talking" of an African American culture he has, in some sense, joined (413, 428).

Reading Guralnick is much like talking to him: you realize instantly that he's on the level and that his curiosity and lack of ego let him connect easily with all sorts of people. Short in stature and casually dressed, Guralnick looks odd next to the resplendent and larger-than-life Solomon Burke (1999b, 17), but the two were lifelong friends: soul brothers.[18] In Memphis, Guralnick was accepted as a member of the blues community. "It is just manifest good will," he explains; "people are glad to see you somehow and after a while you, too, begin to feel part of a community that has been created almost as a shelter against the storm outside" (1999a, 243). Unlike "noise boy" writers, renowned for their gonzo journalism, Guralnick focuses directly on musicians. His writing is atmospheric and simple. In the Val Wilmer photographs displayed in *Feel Like Going Home*, we see pride and perseverance in the face of hardship, along with the unalloyed joy and pain roots music communicates. That Guralnick's prose blends so well with an Englishwoman's photos of black musicians in the American South speaks highly of all the artists involved. Absent is the "shuck" that turned other contemporary writings on the blues into whitewashed promotional speeches.

In *Sweet Soul Music*, Guralnick provides a shadow history of the civil rights era, but keeps his perspective personal, his tone intimate. "It was a funny book for me to write," he admits, owing to the "odd process of self-revelation" (1999b, 397). Conducting numerous interviews, Guralnick shows how the "southern dream of freedom" was threatened by unpredictable forces of history and shaped by unbridled forces of personality. For that reason alone, *Sweet Soul Music* stands as a valuable cultural document. But for me its message would have meant far less had Guralnick not also supplied personal anecdotes about attending soul shows in Roxbury, listening to black radio, and encountering the unpretentious generosity of working musicians. If his profiles of Solomon

Burke and Booker T. Jones are especially vivid, it's because he reveals his own impulses and affections in advance. Booker T.'s awestruck recollection of working with Otis Redding hits home because of the empathy Guralnick displays. So does the story of Stax's awkward collapse. Writing from the standpoint of a fan, enjoying the access of a peer, Guralnick gets invested in outcomes history has already determined.

Reflecting upon the tenuous position of white soul men like Dan Penn and Steve Cropper in a tumultuous era of race relations, Guralnick realizes that he was "seeking to transcend my origins through art, just like them" (390). But mostly he lets the musicians speak. It's more useful to hear Duck Dunn or Johnny Jenkins discuss Otis Redding's rise to mainstream success than it is to hear Robert Christgau, in his *Esquire* review of the Monterey Pop Festival, dub the black singer "Superspade" or to hear Jon Landau proclaim Redding the "future of rock and roll" years before he used that phrase to herald Bruce Springsteen's rise. Listening to people in Memphis and Macon showed Guralnick a side of Redding few glimpsed in concert arenas or read about in the rock press. Truth is, once fame arrived, the singer put on airs; he consorted with prostitutes. "He wasn't no damned idol. He was a human being," Jenkins tells Guralnick. "That's a man's life. You *must* tell the truth" (328).[19]

Sweet Soul Music honors Jenkins's request. Guralnick stresses that "this romantic story did not always take place in the most splendiferous or romantic of settings, and when you think of Otis Redding, you should think of the sheer nasty funk as well as the dignity of the man; we should always remember that soul music could stink as bad as the nastiest blues, could offer redemption, like the church, only after acknowledging the basest of human deeds" (264). "People sometimes ask: don't the flaws bother you?" Guralnick writes in his Cooke biography. "But I had no interest in whitewashing either Sam Cooke or his surroundings." Like Lithofayne Pridgon, a girlfriend and confidant of Cooke (and Jimi Hendrix), Guralnick is wised-up to the pragmatic choices people take when trying to "get over," when they abandon their search for a "wonderful white picket fence." He wants "to be true to a world that celebrated life in all its variegated glory, to a community that never failed to acknowledge that without sin there is no salvation, that if we deny human nature we deny the only truth to which we have access" (2006, xvi).

If the best roots rock writing mirrors the soulfulness of music, its feel and power, its vibrations of shareable experience, then Guralnick stands as its exemplar. There are a few moments, however, when enthusiasm pushes him into dangerous territory. "I've tried to express the pulse of the music, not just its formal definition," he writes in *Sweet Soul Music*, "the idea that here was a truly democratic arena open to anyone as much on the basis of desire as technique, as much on the basis of gut instinct as careful calculation" (15). This sounds innocuous, but trouble ensues whenever Guralnick overcompensates, replacing analytical methodology with personal attempts to straddle the color line. After talking to Burke and other soul musicians about time spent on the Chitlin' and Fraternity Circuits, Guralnick finds himself attracted to their ribald adventures. The picaresque travels in the segregated South are harrowing, he admits, yet the resigned humor of soul musicians leads him to declare, "It all sounds like a lot of fun" (92).

Coming upon this passage while reading about segregation's ugly legacy left me a bit shocked. The tone just seems strange. Guralnick approaches the excesses of the "White Negro," a bohemian archetype introduced by Norman Mailer in a 1957 *Village Voice* essay and thereafter adopted by various writers and musicians. Forecasting the desires of an emerging counterculture by claiming that black artists are America's true existentialist heroes, Mailer reasoned that the "organic growth of Hip depends on whether the Negro emerges as a dominating force in American life" (1992, 604). The same year Mailer's essay appeared, Jack Kerouac published *On the Road*, postwar America's ultimate "kicks" novel, which included an extended reverie, narrated by main character Sal Paradise, reminiscent of Mailer's existential musings: "At lilac evening I walked with every muscle aching among the lights of 27th and Welton in the Denver colored section, wishing I were a Negro, feeling that the best the white world had offered was not enough ecstasy for me, not enough life, joy, kicks, darkness, music, not enough night" (1986, 180).

When Guralnick recalls attending a soul revue in Roxbury in June 1964, he uses similar language to recognize personally what black audiences recognized when they looked up toward the stage of the Donnelly Theatre:

> I wished with every fiber of my being that the recognition would include me, or at least my good intentions, that I, who was so visibly not part of the community, could somehow be absorbed within it. Everyone has their stories of being the lone white face in the crowd, and I don't think mine or anyone else's are particularly significant, but there was clearly

a sense—both then and now—of entering into an alien environment, of stepping out of my world into a land uncharted and inviolable. Perhaps this added to the romance of the occasion, perhaps it added to the suspense, knowing that at any moment all this oneness could turn on you—but I don't think so. I think I was merely envious and scared; my exclusion was only one more impetus to make me wish I was black and free of all the encumbrances of a bourgeois world, the same duality that Donnie Fritts must have come face to face with in Florence, Alabama, or Mick Jagger in Dartford, England. (1999b, 248)

When you read Guralnick's complete body of work, however, you realize how far he is from Mailer's or Kerouac's White Negro excesses. Personal context means a great deal to Guralnick, whether he is conversing with the ebullient and playful Solomon Burke or finding provisional acceptance at the Donnelly Theater as a teenager attending a soul revue. It isn't just his own enjoyment that is reflected on the page, it's also the enjoyment of those he joins in such musical settings. At the same time, Guralnick underscores the historical circumstances of the American music he chronicles: "Soul music ... was the product of a particular time and place that one would not *want* to see repeated, the bitter fruit of segregation, transformed (as so much else has been by the encompassing generosity of Afro-American culture) into a statement of warmth and affirmation" (3).

Guralnick's understanding of soul and blues derives from some serious hang time. Spending hours with Burke, Bland, and other musicians awakened him to the complexity of their lives. Just as white southerners like Dan Penn, Chips Moman, Charlie Freeman, and Duck Dunn became accomplished soul men by hanging out with black musicians, and just as the black songwriting team of Isaac Hayes and David Porter benefited from hanging out all day at Stax studios, Guralnick honed his craft by immersing himself in soul, country, and blues social circles.[20] Doing so allowed him to "operate by feel" (2010, 8/14 interview). It was the *feel* of black culture Mailer and Kerouac were seeking in their Negro reveries (both writers use that word). But Guralnick brings a greater self-assessment and respect for the communities he studies. "That I was not of that community, that I could not even presume to seek inclusion, was not of real consequence," he says of southern soul singers. "It was heartening simply that this unified feeling could exist at a time when I saw society fragmenting all around me, not least on the issue of race. I could introduce quotes from my writing at this point which would mortify me for their assumption of liberal guilt … But my firmest memories are of the music" (1999b, 252).

Circumventing the hipster's pose of existential darkness, Guralnick recognizes that laughter served a real purpose in Solomon Burke's difficult life. Guralnick knows he joins the black man's "fun" at his own peril, obeying the vagaries of internal response rather than the protocols of political correctness or the laws of cool. Maybe that's his point. He simply manifests his acceptance of (and in) soul's brotherly culture. Among brothers, trust is paramount, and with Burke, Guralnick felt that: "There is no story that Solomon has told me that does not appear to have a basis in fact" (87). Greil Marcus, writing about Bob Dylan, takes the opposite tack, arguing that "to promote an individual as the source of meaning in an individual's work is to promote pure solipsism" (2010, 127). But that's a cultural critic speaking. In Guralnick's view, trust offered new perspectives on American culture.

Guralnick's negotiations of the color line are thrown into greater relief when he writes about White Negroes like Phil Walden, the young manager of Otis Redding, or Dewey Phillips (1994, 6), Elvis's earliest champion on Memphis radio. Prevented by Jim Crow laws from attending performances of black musicians (even the R&B group he managed), Walden absorbed black culture from the airwaves (1999b, 137), joining a "secret but growing legion of young white admirers who picked up on rhythm and blues on the radio and took it as the key to a mystery they were pledged never to reveal" (2). Walden's education came courtesy of Hamp "King Bee" Swain and the legendary John R., who worked the 1–3 a.m. shift on Nashville's WLAC. When Walden's displeased parents cut off funds, Redding collected money from fellow musicians so Walden could continue attending college (142). A decade prior, in Memphis, "transracial" Dewey Phillips made a name for himself on integrated airwaves. An eccentric, boundary-breaking networker, a shape-shifter of sorts, he suggested for white teens new ways of being in the world. Rufus Thomas called Phillips "a man who just happened to be white" (quoted in Guralnick 1994, 97). Dewey may have been a shock jock, but he offered opportunity to youngsters who knew civil rights primarily through R&B. In his own weird way, Dewey Phillips kept his eyes on the prize.[21]

And then there was the cadre of Dan Penn, Spooner Oldham, and Donnie Fritts, white songwriters and session men from the rural South who brazenly called themselves "a bunch of niggers" (Guralnick 1999b, 197). During the 1960s, in the studios of Memphis and Muscle Shoals, Alabama, these White Negroes laid down probing lyrics and luscious soul grooves, evading fame's spotlight, their anonymity consistent with the level of respect they had for the black singers fronting their singles. According to Penn, an almost impossibly hip Alabamian whose words and music casual listeners mistakenly attribute to Aretha Franklin and Percy Sledge, "We didn't know nothing until black people put us on the right road. I would have learned nothing if I'd have stayed listening to white people all my life." Penn found the atmosphere he was looking for in the studio: "It was the black people singing; we did the picking and grinning" (quoted in Guralnick 1999b, 199, 403). Whatever backlash Penn suffered in his family and hometown dissipated once he found a like-minded group of integrationists. Describing Penn and Moman, Guralnick says, "Each was a lonely voice in an isolated outpost evangelizing for freedom and R&B" (1999b, 216). When Penn and Moman first met in 1966, they didn't need language to communicate. Both realized that the general listening audience was not ready for a white guy who sounded black (any more than Elvis Presley or the Righteous Brothers already did), so they wrote songs, made demos (Penn's are legendary), and produced the artists they loved. Humor saved them from becoming precious or overly presumptuous. "There was an irreducible element of put-on even in what they most fiercely believed," Guralnick says (294).

Not that there weren't dangers awaiting White Negroes in the American South. Hanging out in black clubs was "very hip—*until* someone started shooting," Phil Walden recalled (quoted in Guralnick 1999b, 141). As in any archetypal American tale, contradictions abound. As Guralnick says, the half-dozen backwoods kids who changed the face of soul music were "too hip for their environment but too comfortable with it ever to want to break out" (181, 197, 214). White Negroes like Jerry Lieber and Jerry Wexler (in the 1950s and 1960s) and Tom Waits (in the 1970s) could play the "White Spade" angle from safe removes in New York and Los Angeles.[22] By contrast, Penn, Moman, and Oldham wrote and played black music—with black performers and for a black audience—in the Deep South of the 1960s. They were cultural pioneers, yet they remained good old boys who rarely strayed from home. They kept it real. Hailing a kindred spirit, Guralnick calls Penn the "secret hero" of *Sweet Soul Music*, mimicking the language Sal Paradise employed to praise Dean Moriarty in Kerouac's *On the Road*. "Somehow through radio and empathy,

[Penn] picked up the message from the air" (188). Granted, it's hard to line up these evaluations with critical race theory. Yet the messy process whereby diverse characters relate honestly to each other in real time, as in good fiction, was a truth Guralnick accepted and printed as legend. In Memphis and Muscle Shoals, story and personality trumped theory.

Guralnick shows how ordinary people who exchanged racist hatred for communal joy changed the rules of southern culture. He re-creates the atmosphere of southern clubs on "white nights," when mixed-race audiences discovered ecstasy, despite long odds. Whites were admitted to black clubs and made to stand on one side of a rope. Late at night, the rope came down, and everyone could dance together in joyous defiance of laws and social mores (1989, 123–24). "Black music *took* liberties long before black people were *granted* them," music historian Ted Gioia says (2009, 51), and in Guralnick's writings we see southern whites taking notice, gambling away liberties granted them in segregated society to follow liberties on the other side of the rope. Ernest Tubb, Mickey Gilley, Hank Williams Jr., Charlie Rich: few associate these country performers with black music. But Guralnick shows them working alongside blacks in the fields, praying with them in church, and listening to them on the radio. By the same token, we find black southerners tuning in to the Grand Ole Opry to hear whites pioneer new directions in country music (Guralnick 1989, 278). Abetting this trend were deejays like Bill Randle in Cleveland, who bucked convention to a "schizophrenic" degree, giving Elvis a chance to be heard up North as well as in Memphis (Guralnick 1994, 177). Even before Elvis, crossover dreams were in the air. "Race" was finished as an official musical genre in 1949, when Jerry Wexler, working for *Billboard*, coined the term "rhythm and blues" as something "more appropriate to more enlightened times" (Guralick 2006, 84). Some racial barriers collapsed. Under-the-counter sales of black artists' records to white teenagers made Lloyd Price's "Lawdy Miss Clawdy" a breakout hit in 1952. Immediately, record stores in southern cities were obliged to stock and display R&B selections (87–88).[23]

Without discounting the idealism of would-be communicants, Guralnick complicates the R&B worldview, highlighting the inevitable pitfalls, the charged moments when segregation's rope foiled crossover dreams or when the marketplace ran counter to the musicians' purer visions. R&B was "just a rubric," Wexler later admitted, looking back in cynicism, if not in anger, and the "name of the game was whatever the traffic would bear" (quoted in Guralnick 1999b, 4, 357). Guralnick himself says that "the story of soul music represents both the triumph and the tragedy of the free enterprise system; the cross-fertilization by which soul music came to exist and influence in its turn the entire spectrum of American music was no more an accident than the invention of the Model T" (1999b, 6).

The example of Sam Phillips looms large here. His Memphis Recording Service recorded Rufus Thomas, Howlin' Wolf, Ike Turner, Little Junior Parker, and B. B. King, leasing some of their sides to Chess and Modern before using Thomas's "Bear Cat" to launch the Sun Records label in 1952. Promoting southern aura, Phillips told a Memphis reporter that he was looking for "Negroes with field mud on their boots and patches in their overalls ... battered instruments and unfettered techniques" (quoted in Guralnick 1994, 5–6). All the same, he eyed crossover success, reportedly telling his secretary, Marion Keisker, "If I could find a white man who had the Negro sound and the Negro feel, I could make a billion dollars" (quoted in Guralnick 1989, 172). Phillips found Presley, a young man whose insecurity, he observed, "was so *markedly* like that of a black person" that he resembled Sun's roster of blues singers, "simultaneously proud and needy" (quoted in Guralnick 1994, 43, 93). By giving Elvis his chance, Phillips changed the face of American roots music. "I don't sound like nobody," Elvis told Keisker during his early visits to Sun. His statement was as much confession as boast. Elvis was terrified at how he'd be perceived. The night Dewey Phillips played his record on the radio, Elvis went to the movies to hide. "I thought people would laugh at me," he said in 1965. "Some did, and some are still laughing, I guess" (quoted in Guralnick 1994, 61, 100).

For Sam Phillips, Presley's unique voice represented a business opportunity. In 1956, when he sold contractual rights to Elvis to RCA, Phillips did not receive anywhere near a billion dollars (that goal remained for Colonel Tom).[24] Neither could Phillips go back and cash a dividend of goodwill with Sun's black performers, whom he had jettisoned in pursuit of Elvis, Johnny Cash, and Carl Perkins. "Just like he catered to black, he cut it off and went to white," Rufus Thomas lamented (quoted in Guralnick 1989, 63). Phillips has argued in his own defense that by 1954 labels like Atlantic, Chess, Specialty, and Checker were on hand to record black artists, as they were not back in 1950, and that these labels could do black artists more justice than he could at Sun. Maybe so. But the hurt Thomas registered was undeniable. Phillips boasted that with Elvis, he "knocked the shit out of the color line" (quoted in Guralnick 1994, 134), but he evidently failed to calculate what that meant for black artists.[25]

Rufus Thomas faced disappointment once more with Stax Records, another Memphis label he helped put on the map. The Stax headquarters on McLemore Avenue was dubbed "Soulsville, USA," but owner Jim Stewart was unwilling to let Thomas, his daughter Carla, or any black performer, for that matter, enter his private home.[26] The upshot was that an Atlantic distribution deal, brokered for Carla's hit single "Gee Whiz," was completed in Wexler's Memphis hotel room. Adding insult to injury, Rufus was obliged to enter said establishment through the back door, near the garbage cans. Nationally, soul music was breaking down social barriers. Behind the scenes, Rufus Thomas wearily noted, it was "the same old shit" (quoted in Guralnick 1999b, 106).

Segregationist bias cut both ways, though in decidedly different ways and to markedly different degrees, affecting white performers more subtly and far less painfully. Nonetheless, it's sobering to learn that Charlie Rich's long-standing plan to record a country blues album with a black sharecropper friend was ignored by industry insiders once Rich found success as a "countrypolitan" crooner. Asked by Nashville suits to tamp down his blues roots, Rich walked around with a briefcase full of unrecorded music he'd written and stashed, much as Guralnick saw *Sweet Soul Music* go years without a publisher. The implicit message given both men was that the mainstream (white) public wouldn't care. Neither, perhaps, would a black populace that daily suffered such slights.

The question of what material succeeds in crossing over, and at what time, is fundamental in determining the identity of soul music. What is soul? Who decides? Do we know it when we hear it? Guralnick praises "When a Man Loves a Woman," Percy Sledge's 1965 hit, calling it not just "the first expression of southern soul to go mainstream" but also an "integrating factor" on the level with Elvis's "That's All Right," Little Richard's "Tutti Frutti," and Martin Luther King's March on Birmingham. But how soulful does Sledge's hit sound two decades later, after it has been given the Michael Bolton treatment and used to flesh out scenes in *The Big Chill*, a movie in which white thirty-somethings blab on guiltily about abandoning their 1960s idealism while engaging in some of the least soulful singing and dancing ever put on screen? Consider also the fate of Aretha Franklin, whose hits have been so overplayed that my first association is suburban cocktail party or Starbucks coffeehouse, not Detroit or Muscle Shoals. In some radically altered context, did the "Soul Provider" (Bolton) and "Lady Soul" (Franklin) come to occupy the same airspace? Guralnick doesn't comment on these particular whitewashing trends, perhaps because when *Sweet Soul Music* was written, they were just on the verge of occurring.

Or maybe Guralnick knew they were a denouement. Far more powerful are the tales told in "The Death of the Dream," *Sweet Soul Music*'s tragic climax. In this lengthy and emotionally gripping chapter, Guralnick implies that the unraveling of Stax Records signified something larger than the individual experiences of musicians and producers. He is talking, rather, about the dissolution of a black-white partnership and also, importantly, the breakup of a family. Sadly, the safe haven for interracial musical collaboration that Estelle Axton and Jim Stewart created could not survive the King assassination, which took place down the road, at the Lorraine Motel, in April 1968. In June, *Time* ran a cover story on Aretha Franklin and the rise of soul music, but the soul coalition was already crumbling. In a well-placed anecdote, Guralnick recalls that on the day King was shot he was attending a college class, and on the subway ride home the "bitter unreality" of what happened in Memphis sank in, preventing him (and thousands of other fans) from attending the James Brown show at the Boston Garden the following night. The show went on as scheduled. Few attended, but many watched its simulcast on WGBH-TV. Brown was brilliant, heroic, and as responsible as anyone for keeping things peaceful on Boston streets.[27] Guralnick watched the show on TV and dutifully wrote his piece for the *Boston Phoenix*, lauding Brown as "king" but lamenting the new era that had dawned. "That was virtually the end of my direct involvement with soul music," Guralnick recalls in *Sweet Soul Music* (354), a bizarre statement given his publishing history.

Yet Guralnick is correct to suggest that for the musicians and writers on the soul scene, things would never be the same after April 1968. "That was the turning point for relations between races in the South," Booker T. Jones said ruefully, "and it happened in Memphis" (quoted in Guralnick 1999b, 355). The day after the assassination, his bandmate Duck Dunn went to Stax to get his bass. When Isaac Hayes came over to talk to him, the Memphis cops came out with their guns drawn, assuming the black man was assaulting the white man. The place Dunn lived and worked was suddenly off-limits. Racial strife and backstabbing infiltrated his safe haven. When Jim Stewart ran the studio, he became a common target for musicians wishing to register their resentment. At first, Guralnick explains, Stewart knew enough to "surround himself with people not simply of talent but of character," like the Boston Celtics in basketball (1999b, 131). But divisions emerged, and grumbling ensued. The atmosphere took a turn for the worse when Stewart brought in black executive Al Bell, who stoked internal rivalries between blacks and whites, including the incredibly tight house band, the MGs. Bell subsequently tapped Don Davis, who replaced Steve Cropper as de facto A&R head and took the label in a slick Detroit-style direction, to the chagrin of white instrumentalist Jim Dickinson, who preferred (as he called it) the old guard's "nigger music." Also arriving on the scene were a hustling producer, Johnny Baylor, and his thuggish bodyguard, Boom Boom, who interrupted recording sessions with one-armed push-ups and threatening grunts. "Morale started being chipped away at," Carla Thomas remembers (quoted in Guralnick 1999b, 362–63, 367). Some, like songwriter Homer Banks, viewed the arrival of these men in a positive light, praising the self-awareness of black musicians and executives determined to take their rightful share of profits and offering as proof hits from Isaac Hayes, the Staple Singers, and Luther Ingram. According to Banks, Stax gained more respect with Bell, a black man who came through the civil rights movement battle-tested and proud (Guralnick 1999b, 368). Stax forged ahead with this new aesthetic, climaxing with Wattstax, a festival of black pride held at the Los Angeles Coliseum in 1972.

Arguably, things had begun to change for Stax in 1967 with the sale of Atlantic Records, their distributor, to Warner Brothers, and with the death of Otis Redding late in the year in a plane crash (under mysterious circumstances, given Redding's impending decision to break away from Stax and Phil Walden, some have said).[28] At Stax, the double whammy hit hard. Black society in general was in a period of turmoil. Love Generation rhetoric didn't apply. Muhammad Ali was stripped of his heavyweight crown for resisting the draft. The civil rights movement gave way to militancy as H. Rap Brown became chairman of the Student Nonviolent Coordinating Committee and the Black Panthers gained strength. Detroit and Newark burned during a "long, hot summer." *Ebony* called it "the summer of 'Retha, Rap, and Revolt" (Guralnick 1999b, 345). It was all that.

A loud warning shot had been fired during a transcendent but ultimately disastrous recording session that took place at Fame Studios in Muscle Shoals in January 1967. Aretha Franklin arrived with her husband Ted White and Atlantic executive Jerry Wexler for a summit with Spooner Oldham, Chips Moman, and other white session men assembled by Fame head Rick Hall. Dan Penn came too, bringing "Do Right Woman," a new song he'd co-authored with Chips. The first track they laid down, "I Never Loved a Man (The Way I Love You)," was a pinnacle of black-white communion. Besides Penn, few had heard of Aretha before her arrival in Alabama. But when she sat down at the piano and hit the first chord, Oldham, hired to play keyboards, immediately ceded the bench, moving over to electric piano and organ. Moman played a resplendent guitar, and a patched-together horn section did their part. "It was beautiful," Penn recalls, "better than any session I've ever seen, and I seen a bunch of 'em" (quoted in Guralnick 1999b, 340). But it fell apart just as quickly. Musicians and producers took a break. Drinking ensued. Off-color comments were exchanged between the good old boys and Franklin's husband. Aretha couldn't get into the flow of "Do Right Woman," and eventually Penn went out to do the vocals on a demo.[29] When the day's music was finished, the trumpet player reportedly pinched Aretha's ass, setting off a welter of accusations, including racist barbs Wexler couldn't smooth over. Rick Hall squared off with Wexler and White, digging deep into his redneck lexicon to insult the black man. The next morning, Aretha Franklin left Alabama for New York, where she cut Penn's song and completed her album with some of the same musicians (Hall, tricked by Wexler, thought he was sending Oldham, Penn, and guitarist Jimmy Johnson to New York for a King Curtis session). Aretha's stint at Fame Studios was cut short after one sublime song. Within a span of twenty-four hours, soul music's "southern dream of freedom" was realized then dashed, never fully to recover.

Guralnick says we can either blame the ruptures of 1967 and 1968 on the "classic failures of liberalism" and simply shrug our shoulders, or instead seek a "single bullet theory" of the soul coalition's collapse (1999b, 381). Aretha Franklin's aborted session at Fame represents one bullet. Wexler's interloping manipulation of southern studios, label heads, and session men represents another.[30] No bullets flew at the Soul Together concert held at Madison Square Garden for the Martin Luther King Jr. Memorial Fund in June 1968; it was merely a last-ditch effort to get whites and blacks on the same stage. And yet a lethal bullet was fired at the soul coalition during the National Association of Television and Radio Announcers (NATRA) convention in Miami that August.

The official theme: "The New Breed's New Image Creates Self-Determination and Pride." There were appearances by Coretta Scott King, Julian Bond, and Jesse Jackson, articulate spokespeople for the cause. But on the convention floor, things turned ugly. Wexler, a symbol of white, Jewish, northern, major label power, was hanged in effigy. Marshall Sehorn, a white New Orleans R&B entrepreneur, was pistol-whipped. Phil Walden, attending the conference with legendary deejay Hamp Swain, received death threats and was blamed for orchestrating Otis Redding's plane crash. Fistfights broke out and rumors flew around the convention, the atmosphere of which was sanctioned by something called the Fair Play Committee. Fair or not, Soul Power now meant Black Power (382–84).[31]

Sweet Soul Music tells this story so effectively because Guralnick emphasizes the detailed recollections of musicians and producers rather than the broad arguments of cultural theorists. Admittedly, the book is thin on trends in soul music after 1968, offering brief consideration of the Wattstax festival and the Hi Records story. Preston Lauterbach's The Chitlin' Circuit fills in some gaps, going back in time to describe juke joints and inner-city corridors ("strolls") where black-white relationships weren't an issue because they weren't possible, then leaping ahead to Hi Records' production of smooth soul hits in the early 1970s.[32] Readers should also track down Robert Gordon on the Stax Records story (Respect Yourself), Greil Marcus on Sly Stone (2015, 60–89), Nelson George on the death of R&B, or Jeff Chang on the history of hip-hop. When Guralnick decided to write again about black self-determination in music, he did not compete with these accounts. He explored the origins of soul in a biography of Sam Cooke.

After the success of the Elvis biography, Guralnick was approached by major publishers to write biographies of Michael Jackson and Bob Dylan (2010, 8/14 interview). No dice. He had his heart set on Cooke, and his decision made sense. "Sweet Soul Music," the 1967 hit by Arthur Conley that gave Guralnick a book title, derives from Cooke's "Yeah Man," a rare but vibrant track from 1964. In Dream Boogie: The Triumph of Sam Cooke, Guralnick enriches the chronicle he began in Sweet Soul Music while tapping the biographical skills he honed in Last Train to Memphis and Careless Love.

In a 2005 interview with James Marcus, Guralnick says that Dream Boogie evolved much the way his Elvis biography had:

I tried to go into the [Cooke] book, just as I did with Elvis, without pre-conceptions, and in that sense everything was a discovery—everything was a revelation. What I wanted to do was to write the story without foreshadowing, allowing events to unfold (as they do in real life) without any more knowledge of the outcome than Sam or J.W. [Alexander] or anyone else had at the time. What I was looking for was a deepening of perspective, and in that sense Sam became more and more real to me (and I hope to the reader) through the revelations and perspectives of those who knew him best: his family, his wife, friends like Lou Rawls and fellow Soul Stirrer LeRoy Crume, J.W., and Bobby Womack … As people, they were very different. Elvis was far more instinctive, nowhere near as self-confident as Sam. Sam was a deeply analytic person who saw every new situation as a challenge to broaden his knowledge and perspective. Both were highly intelligent, complex, and ambitious but Sam's brilliance, his intellectual discipline and almost visionary reach seem to me as unique as Sam Phillips's or Walt Whitman's or James Baldwin's both in the territory he sought to encompass and in his boundless confidence in his ability to get there. (Guralnick 2005)

The biographical continuum served Guralnick well. Presley and Cooke were perfectionists in the studio, doing multiple takes in an effort to get inside a song. For a time, they were on the same record label, RCA. Both were persistent and proud, returning triumphantly to the sites of early failure in order to prove naysayers wrong. As budding supper club entertainers, Elvis bombed in Vegas and Cooke at the Copa in New York, but they took these venues by storm a few years later.[33] Perhaps most important, Presley and Cooke were intent on bridging racial divides in popular music, albeit in decidedly different ways and under markedly different circumstances.

Presley appropriated rhythm and blues motifs, mixed them with country traditions, and fashioned a style of rock and roll that sent young white listeners into a tizzy. He had little traction among black audiences, except in Memphis. "We had a lot of fun with him," Nat D. Williams of WDIA Memphis said of Elvis during his initial run. "Always he had that certain humanness about him that Negroes like to put in their songs" (quoted in Guralnick 1994, 206). But if Elvis's appeal derived from his borrowing of black styles, he rarely engaged black listeners, especially after off-color comments ascribed to him began to surface.[34] Musically, he was a riddle. "Sings hillbilly in R&B time," a Louisiana radio executive said early on. "Can you figure that out?" (182). Well, millions of white teenagers figured it out, even if Elvis confounded them by putting out gospel albums between pop releases. Despite the sidetracks he made into Hollywood and Vegas schlock, Elvis hung on to his roots as best he could, and that included music picked up in the poor neighborhoods of Tupelo and Memphis: not just blues, but gospel, both black and white. Hearing Elvis singing hymns backstage, Ira Louvin walked up to him and said, "Why, you white nigger, if that's your favorite music, why don't you do that out yonder? Why do you do that nigger trash out there?" To which Elvis responded, "When I'm out there, I do what they want to hear—when I'm back here, I can do what I want to do" (253). Even as the press expressed revulsion at his animalism, Elvis would sing hymns or spirituals backstage or in the studio to get the feeling necessary to perform (285, 335–36).

Sam Cooke enjoyed a deeper immersion in gospel, performing with the Singing Children in his father's congregation and later with Chicago's Highway QCs, fully hitting his stride as lead singer of the Soul Stirrers, replacing gospel star R. H. Harris in 1950. Cooke was famous among black listeners but virtually unheard of among whites until he turned to secular music. He found crossover success with "You Send Me," a #1 hit in 1957, shortly after Elvis struck gold. Cooke's move to the mainstream was controversial, but as Reverend Charles Cooke told his son, there's no prohibition in the Bible against worldly success (Guralnick 2006, 64, 156).

Cooke's ambition made him a quick study. "What was most extraordinary about Sam Cooke was his capacity for learning, his capacity for imagination and intellectual growth," Guralnick explains (2006, xvi). Whereas Elvis usually kept his curiosity hidden and came out publicly against intellectuals (1999, 135–36), Cooke actively courted intellectual advancement, reading books at every opportunity and trying to get his cohorts to do the same.[35] Not that most whites noticed. "His body flows with tiger grace," the press reported, denying Cooke the intellectual recognition he deserved. "He's as happy as a boy pushing upward on a swing" (quoted in Guralnick 2006, 589–90). Guralnick's biography stands as a welcome corrective. We see Cooke as a thinker as well as a "symbol of an era that glowed with racial pride, ambition, and promise" (651).

Like his friend Muhammad Ali, Cooke made racial solidarity a priority for black entertainers. Cooke refused to play segregated concert halls, emboldened by Louis Armstrong, who urged the U.S. government to "go to hell" in the wake of the Little Rock crisis (202), and by Clyde McPhatter, who warned Cooke against the predatory practices of white label owners, including Jerry Wexler at Atlantic (307). Others, like Nat King Cole and Fats Domino, initially resisted black boycotts and obeyed Jim Crow (371, 490–91), but in time they came around and joined Cooke's resistance. One night in 1963 in South Carolina, police dogs roamed the aisles, making sure black concertgoers on one side of segregation's rope wouldn't do more than stay seated and politely applaud. Cooke decided he'd had enough. "We the gladiators out here," he told Bobby Womack. "I can't do this no more" (quoted in Guralnick 2006, 481). Cooke took a stand, and before long the social consciousness of soul music was emanating from microphones and radios. Just as Mahalia Jackson urged Martin Luther King from the podium to share his dream in the March on Washington speech, Cooke's "A Change Is Gonna Come," the black man's answer to Bob Dylan's "Blowin' in the Wind," challenged listeners to envision a more equitable America.

Cooke protected his own interests as well. His intellectual autonomy allowed him to resist strong-armed management more effectively than Elvis did, and ultimately it helped him carve a place for blacks in the business side of music. Joe McEwen refers to Cooke as the "man who invented soul." But Guralnick refers to Cooke (along with Solomon Burke and Ray Charles) as one who paved the way for a new black capitalism, years before James Brown became famous for doing so. Cooke set up his own publishing company (KAGS) and record label (SAR) to nurture black talent and keep proceeds in the black community. Told by manager Allen Klein that RCA was treating him "like a nigger," Cooke agreed. "You're right. I want you to go after them" (quoted in Guralnick 2006, 474). Cooke knew Elvis wasn't getting treated as poorly by RCA as he was, and when working with Klein, he demanded from the label the same respect. If respect wasn't forthcoming, Cooke could turn deceitful, as when he assigned songwriting credit for "You Send Me" to his brother L. C. so that royalties would stay in his pocket and not go to Specialty Records owner Art Rupe, who still held the contract on Sam's songwriting.

More through blind ambition than deceit, Cooke compromised his civil rights principles from time to time, so strong was his pursuit of mainstream success. "I want to be black. I'm not going to desert my people," he told Bobby Womack in 1964. "But to cross over, you must appeal to that market." Cooke was talking of the Copa, the renowned New York City nightclub, where he had bombed in 1958 but still hoped to connect with an upscale white audience, even if that meant eliminating soulful material like "Bring It On Home to Me," "Ain't That Good News," and his traditional encore, "Having a Party." Cooke told Womack: "White people are not gonna come to the black side of town … You have to be all around, you have to be universal" (quoted in Guralnick 2006, 569). Alas, his second run at the Copa was a success, and it looked as though "supper club soul" had arrived. A month later, however, Cooke was back on the Chitlin' Circuit, playing the Club Harlem in Atlantic City, getting funky and preaching uplift. This was Freedom Summer. Riots occurred in Harlem. President Johnson signed the Civil Rights Act. The Impressions' "Keep on Pushin'" was one theme song. Cooke's "A Change Is Gonna Come" was another. Four years before *Time* leapt on board, the *Philadelphia Tribune* proclaimed soul "the word of the hour, a spiritual return to sources" (Guralnick 2006, 407). Wherever he appeared, Cooke stood tall, telling a reporter from the *Atlantic City Press*, "I have no doubts about myself" (quoted in Guralnick 2006, 588–90). Confidence helped him accommodate diverse audiences, but it created a fractured public perception. Cooke at the Copa is better known than Cooke at Miami's Harlem Square Club. But listen to both recordings, then tell me where the soul is.

American to the core, Cooke was contradictory and hard to figure. The man who sang gospel was hit with three separate paternity suits at age twenty-one. Gospel bobby-soxers and Sister Flute characters proved hard to resist. In subsequent years, he was served a bastardy warrant and arrested backstage for failing to pay child support (47, 93, 105, 217, 222, 381).[36] Cooke was reckless. He met white girls for trysts in the woods outside southern towns, knowing full well what would happen to him if caught. Instructed by a Memphis policeman to push his out-of-gas car out of the road, Cooke responded, "You wouldn't ask [Frank Sinatra] to move no car." Nor was he finished. "You push the car," he told the cop. "You may not know who I am, but your wife does. Go home and ask your wife about me" (quoted in Guralnick 2006, 369).

In *Dream Boogie*, Cooke emerges a picaresque character, a rambler on par with Kerouac's fictional heroes. "Sam took to the road as if he were born to it, which in a way he was," Guralnick muses, thinking back to Sam's early travels with Reverend Cooke and the Singing Children. At the same time, Guralnick shows Cooke suffering unfair roadblocks as a black man in a racist society. Cooke aspired to be the "perfect American boy" (220), but the road to success took its toll. Some in the gospel community called his move to secular music a deal with the devil. They understood Cooke's serial tragedies—his first wife's fatal car crash in California, his cohort Jesse Belvin's crash in Arkansas, his own crash on Highway 61, and the death by drowning of his infant son—as signs from God (265, 282, 327). By the time Cooke was gunned down by a motel manager in December 1964, the possibilities and limits of his American life had taken a fatal turn. Americans who sought racial justice suffered for the tragedy.

In 2015, Guralnick published a biography of Sam Phillips. Once again we find him "telling a story on Sam." The key question this time is whether a personal relationship with the subject affects the biographer's writing. Guralnick met Phillips in 1979 after having been put off a full decade in his interview requests. The meeting occurred in one of Phillips's radio stations, which had suffered severe flooding. Guralnick abandoned the interview and helped clean up. After eight hours of toil, Phillips turned to Guralnick and said, "I'm not sure everybody has the love for what I feel and what I have felt, so therefore I'm very cautious about talking to a quote unquote writer" (quoted in Guralnick 2015a, 533). If Guralnick's physical labor that day earned him some good will, his long-standing friendship with Knox Phillips, Sam's older son, also brokered the deal and led to unrestricted access to the Sun Records founder over twenty-five years.

Guralnick's challenge was to flesh out in a massive biography what he hadn't already said in earlier profiles on Phillips (1999a, 170–75; 1989, 325–39), in his huge biography of Elvis (Phillips's most famous discovery), or in the essays he'd written about other musicians Phillips recorded at Sun Studios (Rufus Thomas, Howlin' Wolf, Charlie Rich, Scotty Moore, Jack Clement, Jerry Lee Lewis). In this regard, Guralnick is moderately successful. The famous moment when Elvis walks into Sun Studios to record a song for his mother gets its due, although it's revealed that Marion Keisker and Sam Phillips had a disagreement about who recorded Elvis first (2015a, 552–54). It's further revealed that Phillips and Keisker were involved at the time in an extramarital affair (which broke off suddenly in 1956, when Sam turned his sights to a young Memphis Recording Service employee, nineteen-year-old Mississippian Sally Wilbourn).[37] Guralnick gives special attention to the early days of the Memphis Recording Service (as Sun Studios was initially known), and particularly to Sam's belief that anybody should be able to record what they want to say or sing. Like Harry Smith in the same era, Phillips was fascinated by the variety of American sound, a belief solidified when a man dressed in overalls unexpectedly entered Sun Studios in 1956 and sang "Old MacDonald Had a Farm," complete with dead-on imitations of the animals' voices, then promptly left, never to be heard from again (310). Among the lore that defines Americana, this moment represents for lovers of roots music the mystery of democracy.

Phillips's mission was "the cause of human communication" (54), a loaded issue in the South. He was dedicated to serving "people of little education and even less social standing, both black and white, who had so much to say but were prohibited from saying it" (60). Phillips was influenced early on by Silas Payne, the black sharecropper his family more or less adopted in the 1930s. Guralnick says that Payne became "the epicenter of everything Sam Phillips ever believed both about himself and the 'common man,' in that most uncommon narrative that became the lodestar for his life" (12). Drawn as well by the rough democracy and "absolute freedom" of Beale Street, Phillips headed to Memphis to act upon his progressive impulses (15). In the early years at Sun Records, when Ike Turner, Little Junior Parker, and Rufus Thomas were granted opportunities to record, Phillips established, in Keisker's words, "a facility where black people could come and play their own music, a place where they would feel free and relaxed [enough] to do it" (quoted in Guralnick 2015a, 64). "I knew what I opened the studio for," Phillips told Guralnick. "I was looking for a higher ground, for what I knew existed in the soul of mankind. And especially at that time that black man's spirit" (73). Howlin' Wolf stood as an exemplar. Phillips couldn't tell whether Wolf's voice was the worst he'd ever heard or the most beautiful, but he was sure that he sang "with his damn soul" (119), and that made all the difference. Also crucial was the young southerner who rushed out to hear the new music, defined by *Billboard*'s Paul Ackerman as "the kid with the 89 cents [who] feels it is time for a change" (quoted in Guralnick 2015a, 285).

Working outward from there, Guralnick equates Phillips's daily labors in the 18′ by 30′ studio with the main tenets of American democracy, especially equal opportunity. Guralnick points out that as a boy growing up in Florence, Alabama, Sam was enamored with Clarence Darrow's legal fights against various injustices taking place in the nation. But the biographer also maintains that whorehouses and pool halls were just as influential as Darrow's courtrooms in shaping Sam's "study of humanity" (28). Sam's lifelong study was based on spontaneity and intuition, his "feel" for any given situation. Sun's famous recordings owed everything to the feel Phillips had as a producer and engineer, and to the feel he encouraged in the musicians' performances. Accordingly, "Mystery Train" is defined as a "feel song"; no one could have predicted either Little Junior Parker's or Elvis's version in advance. Remember, it was the "Negro feel" as much as the Negro sound that Sam was looking for when he discovered Elvis. "It's a feel at the touch end of your fingers. It's the feel that you see mentally … It has nothing to do with religion—but we're all spirit," Phillips tells Guralnick when asked to explain his studio magic. "How could I help but agree," Guralnick says in response (194, 207, 586). The esteemed biographer turns to melted butter here, as Marion Keisker predicted he would: "What [Sam] wants is an amanuensis," she warned (quoted in Guralnick 2015a, 556). But Guralnick, too, always made "feel" the basis for his investigations, so how to determine the line of influence?

Somewhat conspicuously, Guralnick mimics Phillips's phrasing and lingo. "Hell, it was a complete *original*" (334). That's Guralnick talking about Jerry Lee Lewis's cover of Ray Price's "Crazy Arms." Compare that with Phillips talking to Elvis after his cover of "Blue Moon of Kentucky" at Sun in 1955: "Hell, that's *different*. That's a pop song, nearly about" (quoted in Guralnick 1994, 103).[38] Other stylistic flourishes take hold as well. Twice, Guralnick uses qualifying modifiers ("seemed to forget"; "almost painful") only to tell readers to ignore his cautiousness ("forget about 'seemed'"; "forget 'almost'") (614, 653). He even takes to swearing a bit, dropping the F-bomb on several occasions. Emphasizing "American individualism" (537), Guralnick tries "to write a book that conforms to Sam's definition of what a recording session ought to be, as epic as, well, take your pick of epics, but as intimate as sexual relations. That tells a story that, like most stories, can be both heroic and tragic at the same time, in its own mortal way" (xvii).

Sam Phillips is in many ways collaborative: it's the autobiography Sam never got around to writing. Guralnick's interviews with Phillips take place for many hours, over many days, over many years, the eccentric subject spinning his tale at his own pace. The tone is indeed intimate. The Phillips family refers to Guralnick as "Peter." Unlike Presley and Cooke, Phillips lived a long life, the final half out of the public eye. Granted unprecedented access, Guralnick had to negotiate the living man's version of himself, without downplaying his painful circumstances: electroshock therapy, a tempestuous partnership with his brother Jud, and marital infidelity. Guralnick admits to believing certain stories more than others, and he owns up to his limitations when dealing with tricky subjects, such as Sam's evangelical faith in Elvis, whom he once compared to Jesus (522–23), or his ongoing love affairs ("Knowing Sam, and Becky, and Sally, and Marion as I do, I have no easy answers") (580). At the end, the seasoned biographer admits to being a little disoriented when dealing with Sam Phillips, as though he was under the sway of a force more powerful than himself: "With all the intricacy of narrative and detail, I felt sometimes as if I had been caught up in a torrent of eloquence and insight, balanced by an earthiness that retained the capacity to shock, to a degree that I had never before encountered in my life" (585). Indeed, Guralnick's personal investment seems stronger here than it does in *Sweet Soul Music*, which is saying something.

Peter Guralnick writes life stories that matter. In his books, American roots music and the people who perform that music bear out fundamental truths readers can consider in a new light. Always, the emphasis is on the musicians themselves. Clinton Heylin once criticized Guralnick for hewing to straight reportage in his Elvis Presley biography, and specifically for not asking an important question: "Did it have to be this way?" (Heylin 2003, xv). But empathy doesn't allow for such questions. A responsible biographer is too busy feeling what others have felt. In writing, as in music, the goal is not to let judgment spoil what's otherwise possible.

Perhaps the best thing about Guralnick's biographies is the way he ends them: not with words, but with a photograph. In *Careless Love*, after hundreds of pages detailing Presley's sad decline, we turn the page and find a casual portrait of Elvis, Vernon, and Gladys taken just after the singer's rise to fame. Everything, for that moment, seems fine. Likewise, after reading about Cooke's violent death at age thirty-three, we find a photo of Cooke laughing, taking a record off a shelf, with nary a care in the world. The biography of Phillips concludes with a posed family photo taken at the Memphis Fairgrounds in 1955, when Sam's influence was at its peak and domestic bliss reigned. I once asked Guralnick whether he regarded these photographs as redemptive. He said that he did. Of the happy figures that appear, alive as you or me, at the end of each book, Guralnick said, "That's why you tell the story in the first place. I didn't choose to write about Sam Cooke because the man was killed at the Hacienda Motel" (2011, 12/5 interview).

Recording life's little ups and downs, Guralnick writes as honestly as his subjects sing. John Milward described Guralnick well in *No Depression*, the alternative country magazine, calling him "an American author with a foreigner's curiosity" (2006). American roots music offers cries of joy and pain, to be listened to attentively and empathetically. Many fields depend on biographers of Guralnick's stature, yet never do his books smack of self-importance. In the acknowledgments section of *Dream Boogie*, Guralnick tells his team of supporters, "I hope we can all do it again!" And in *Sam Phillips* he praises colleagues who gave him "the courage (and enthusiasm) to go on!" Fifty years on the job, his spirit remains infectious. Here's hoping Peter Guralnick will go on for many years to come.

★ **3** ★

"Searching for a Truer Sound": *No Depression* **Magazine**

Soliciting southern radio markets in 1955, Sun Records founder Sam Phillips attempted to promote his latest musical discovery, Elvis Presley. To his chagrin, he faced a round of rejections from R&B deejays who played Sun's early singles but wouldn't play Elvis. Fats Washington explained his rejection of Presley in decidedly down-home terms: "This man should not be played after the sun comes up in the morning, it's so country" (quoted in Guralnick 1994, 112). Once Elvis found success, much was made about how his unique style, "hillbilly in R&B time," altered American popular music. But as Washington's comment suggests, there remained resistance to the hillbilly side of Elvis's repertoire. To hip tastemakers in an emerging rock and roll market, country music was an embarrassment, best shunted off to predawn hours, when rockers were just going to bed and nobody but a damn farmer would be alert enough to absorb cornpone lyrics set to twang and lilt (or care to). The recording industry may have regarded R&B as lowbrow, but country music occupied an even lower rung on the cultural ladder.

It wouldn't always be that way. At the tail end of the 1960s, after psychedelic rock had run its course, Bob Dylan, the Byrds, the Band, the Grateful Dead, Michael Nesmith, New Riders of the Purple Sage, and Neil Young led a countercultural return to roots music. Sadly, the genre known as "country rock" turned flaccid by the 1970s, when the Eagles and their ilk laid on too much

L.A. gloss. Punk rockers in particular chastised country rock for its laziness, its smugness, and its blandness. But the tides continued to turn. Heralded by the rockabilly sounds of the Blasters' *American Music* (1980) and the Nashville strains of Elvis Costello's *Almost Blue* (1981), country styles were embraced once more by young music fans, including those who traced their roots to punk scenes. Texas roots musician Joe Ely was touring with the Clash (*No Depression* [hereafter cited as *ND*] #16 1998). In Los Angeles, the punk musicians in X consorted with Bakersfield's new country hope, Dwight Yoakam. Energized by emerging bands like Green on Red and the Meat Puppets, this new alliance took hold among indie rockers. By the 1990s, the new movement had become known as "alternative country," or "alt-country."

Making this movement recognizable to itself, and giving it a forum, was *No Depression*, a bimonthly (originally quarterly) magazine that derived from an AOL discussion folder, as well as from the Postcard and Postcard 2 e-mail lists (Pecknold 2008, 31). *No Depression* magazine was launched in 1995 and ceased its print run in 2008, by which time alt-country music had risen in stature. Today, *No Depression* continues as a website and online newsletter, providing updates on concerts and record releases, reviews, and blogs, all of it composed by its 20,000 members. As was true twenty years ago, *No Depression* still regards itself as a community. This chapter salutes its unique brand of roots rock discovery.

From the beginning, *No Depression* tried to escape the pitfalls of rock journalism (slickness, self-importance), striking an unpretentious tone even as it featured professional writers (Bill Friskics-Warren, Ed Ward, David Cantwell, Allison Stewart) and courted advertising revenue necessary for a national publication. With no intent to make a killing (to paraphrase Son Volt's "Loose String"), co-editors Grant Alden and Peter Blackstock sought a unique strain of roots rock discourse, merging the brash attitude of the indie scene with the traditional values of country, the liberal with the conservative, the hip lingo of urban America with the plain speech of the outlying areas, the professional polish of mainstream rock periodicals like *Rolling Stone* and *Spin* with the exuberant subjectivity of cheaply produced fanzines. For more than a dozen years, their experiment worked. In a nice twist, alt-country musicians joined readers in embracing *No Depression*'s communal spirit. After Jayhawks guitarist Gary Louris wondered aloud about the fate of one of his favorite lost bands, Souled American, in issue #6, two readers dug up the information and sent

Louris a reply in the next issue's "Box Full of Letters." Named after a Wilco song, "Box" was the magazine's most important column. In it, writers, musicians, and fans became equal partners, adhering to Generation X ideals and tapping countercultural trends without the self-absorption they saw plaguing Baby Boomers. If these correspondents sometimes failed, succumbing to familiar traps of pretense, taste policing, and dilettantism, they were nonetheless committed to finding common ground for a contemporary revival of folk culture, often referred to as "Americana."

"Americana" is a term I used in chapter 1 to analyze Greil Marcus's music writings. It's a term Peter Guralnick adopted in his books on roots music. And yet it's a term Bob Dylan, assaying its increased circulation after the publication of Marcus's *Invisible Republic* and the reissue of Harry Smith's *Anthology of American Folk Music* in 1997, said he didn't understand. Those in the alt-country movement tended to be more sanguine than Dylan. *No Depression* writer Bob Townsend pointed out that back in 1986, when Peter Case's first solo album was deemed "barbed Americana" by *Trouser Press*, the term triggered "a sociological rather than a musical meaning" (*ND* #14 1998). A decade after Case became so classified, Americana got launched as a radio format, around which a community of young adherents began to coalesce. "I like the term Americana," bluegrass musician Johnny Staats reported from Jackson County, West Virginia. "It encompasses a lot of things—bluegrass, country, folk. Hopefully, we're starting something that more people will follow" (*ND* #27 2000).

"Americana" summons mysteries, cloaked in symbol and myth, which can be applied liberally to any core American experience. Perhaps it is merely "the idea of the idea of America," a tagline the Firesign Theatre used to parody mortgage bankers selling bunk (Marcus 2015a, 379). But Americana need not be considered so cynically. In *Mystery Train*, Greil Marcus saw in bluesman Robert Johnson an Americana icon, someone who articulated "the ultimate American image of flight from homelessness," someone who "lived for the moment and died for the past" (2015, 22). Marcus found that spirit embodied as well in the Band, a group "committed to the very idea of America: complicated, dangerous, and alive" (35); a group whose songs "were made to bring to life the fragments of experience, legend, and artifact every American has inherited as the legacy of a mythical past" (50). Eventually, such old-fashioned values became a rallying point for members of Generation X, or as former *No*

Depression writer Kurt B. Reighley tagged it, "Generation DIY." As Reighley notes in *United States of Americana*, music was just one component of the new iteration:

> In music, the umbrella term *Americana* encompasses a variety of contemporary artists who use time-tested sounds, such as delta blues or classic country, as a jumping-off point to something new. That impulse isn't limited to songwriters and bands. Its sphere expands every day, throughout fashion, grooming, food, and entertainment. Plenty of people would rather bolster their sense of identity, and become better acquainted with neighbors and friends, by exploring essential favorites from every corner of America's past. They are going back to their roots, in pursuit of goods that will endure and the know-how to maintain them, to the sustenance of tastes and sounds that delighted their grandparents and great-grandparents" (4).

For Reighley, Americana signifies whatever's time-tested, genuine, authentic, and still, in some way, cool. It celebrates fashionably unfashionable art made by spirited folks content to live "off the grid" (12), as hippies enamored with the *Whole Earth Catalog* and the Band once did, albeit with more of an edgy, punk rock vibe. Generation X's attraction to Americana "isn't about going Back to the Land," Reighley says; "it's [about] importing the best of the land into daily activity" (13).

Americana's low-key character made it attractive to indie rockers. By the mid-1980s, thanks to trailblazing post-punk groups like the Mekons, who unplugged on *Fear and Whiskey*, or the Knitters (comprised of L.A. musicians from X and the Blasters), who did the same on *Poor Little Critter on the Road*, it was regarded as a punk rock move to abandon stage lights and head for the front porch, metaphorically at least, playing country music with old-fashioned acoustic instruments (151). Bands like Lone Justice, the Long Ryders, and the Blood Oranges—whose lead singer, Cheri Knight, joked that she came to alt-country six years too early (*ND* #4 1996)—were part of what producer Eric "Roscoe" Ambel deemed "the great roots-rock scare of '84" (*ND* #33 2001). Although some were more punk in attitude than others, it's clear that alt-country standard-bearers of the early 1990s—Uncle Tupelo, the Jayhawks, the Bottle Rockets, Whiskeytown—owed much to their 1980s predecessors.

Defining the alternative country amalgam, Bloodshot Records co-founder Rob Miller says he "connected some of the lack of artifice we found coming out of the punk scene with some of the three-chords-and-the-truth aspect of country music, and how it's really stripped down" (quoted in Reighley 2010, 14). Those three-chord truths could hurt, but many Gen Xers were into that kind of thing. The sordid aspects of country and folk certainly appealed to Throwing Muses front woman Kristin Hersh, who covered traditional songs on her solo albums: "I remembered these beautiful songs. I was struck by the reality of the yuckiness. It was punk to talk about liquor and murders and Jesus and Hell. It was titillating. The chick always dies. She's stabbed and poisoned and drowned" (*ND* #20 1999). The same bug hit Rennie Sparks, part of a "countronica" outfit, the Handsome Family: "My psychiatrist recently said, 'I've noticed you're talking a lot about amputations and root cellars. Do those things have any special meaning for you?'" (*ND* #15 1998).

The connection between punk and country remained strong well into the 1990s, as Bloodshot introduced "insurgent country" to the market and other small labels devoted to alt-country began sprouting up.[1] Alternative rock had fast become, in Greil Marcus's estimation, "no alternative" at all (2000b, 105), and thus country music served as a welcome antidote. Alt-country aficionados sought an authentic sound, a soundtrack for a subtle revolution. "You start hearing things like Johnny Cash and Hank Williams," Rob Miller said, "and you think, 'Wait a minute. There is this other music that was completely devoid of artifice … even if it was created fifty years ago'" (quoted in Reighley 2010, 14). For Miller, "Americana" was a buffer term helping urban hipsters overcome cultural and regional prejudices. More precisely, Americana was "geared toward breaking through that stench that hangs over the C-word. Country music has (stunk) for so long to rock-going audiences that it takes an umbrella term like Americana for people to put away their prejudices" (quoted in Pecknold 2008, 39). *Gavin Report* editor Rob Bleetstein rejected the term "alternative country" because he believed "both words at the time just had been used and abused." "Americana," on the other hand, granted him the leeway he desired. "I thought about what it meant musically, which was really nothing, so it was our chance to define it as something" (quoted in Pecknold 2008, 39). Resolutely DIY in spirit, the Americana movement has proved predictably pragmatic. "You scrutinize the past to solve a problem in the present," Reighley says in *United States of Americana*. "That's not indulging in nostalgia. That's common sense" (16).

Regardless of whether the alt-country movement is susceptible to nostalgia, I remain nostalgic for its heyday. I was an overeducated, underemployed "slacker" in 1991 when Richard Linklater's art house film put that word into wider play. That same year, a bookstore colleague handed me a homemade cassette containing the first two Uncle Tupelo albums, *No Depression* (1990) and *Still Feel Gone* (1991). The music possessed Janus-faced qualities, dipping into an American past but pointing toward new possibilities in Gen X art. Today when I hear Uncle Tupelo songs, I am struck by what had come out of the gate: a genre of music melding the in-your-face attitude of post-punk with the down-home performances country musicians had long dished out, which could mean the ferocious rockabilly antics of Jerry Lee Lewis (Jason and the Scorchers' role model) or the reflective, folk-based styling of Neil Young (Whiskeytown's territory, more or less).[2] Alternative country satisfied something Gen X kids otherwise lacked. Some revisionists, like Jon Smith, have suggested that members of Generation X gravitated to country musicians because they loathed 1960s hippies and 1980s yuppies as much as 1970s punks did (2008, 54), but that's obviously not true in all cases. For alt-country poster boy Ryan Adams, punk spirit was wherever you found it, even among hippies. "I don't care what anybody says," he brayed from an Austin stage after a cover of "Wharf Rat." "The Grateful Dead are punk as fuck" (*ND* #52 2004). Maybe it's because, as Steve Earle said, "Bluegrass is the original alternative country music" (*ND* #20 1999). The influences cut several ways. The Avett Brothers, a young bluegrass act with rock ambitions, insisted that they adopted their Everly Brothers–style harmony from Seattle grunge heroes Jerry Cantrell and Layne Staley of Alice in Chains (*ND* #52 2004). Who knew? Meantime, country legend Merle Haggard's albums could be found on Epitaph, a renowned punk label (*ND* #30 2000). Under Americana's big tent, the confluences were often astounding.[3]

More than any other band, Uncle Tupelo epitomized the alt-country genre. On albums and in concert, the garage band roar of "Left in the Dark" (their inspired cover of midwestern rockers the Vertebrats) and "Blues Die Hard" co-existed with stripped-down fare like "No Depression" (an equally game-changing cover of the Carter Family) and "Life Worth Livin.'" The Tupes could sound like Dinosaur Jr. one minute and Waylon Jennings the next. They could take an Iggy Pop punk anthem ("I Wanna Be Your Dog"), play it rapid-fire on acoustic instruments, and make it sound like it emanated from some

Carolina holler. In their hands, the roots of rock and roll spread in unforeseen directions. I experienced this as a listener. Though they hailed from southern Illinois, a place I've never been, Uncle Tupelo took me back home. I'd traveled from the hinterlands of western New York to live in Boston. Before hearing the Tupes, I knew the indie scene fairly well, or was beginning to, but I had largely forgotten, or otherwise put behind me, the rustic sources alt-country was tapping. *No Depression* and *Still Feel Gone* helped me make peace with my rural upbringing. Grant Alden once called Generation X "a rootless people rooted to music" (*ND* #61 2006). I guess I am among their number.

Imagining myself a part of two cultural geographies has helped me understand success and failure on several levels, and failure's role in alt-country music cannot be underestimated. Dava, the art student who made me the Uncle Tupelo tape, had seen her share of it, wafting in and out of school and suffering through a series of menial jobs. Conscious like many Gen Xers of her uncertain career trajectory, she asked me to pay particular attention to Uncle Tupelo's "Watch Me Fall," its downcast message cut through with bemusement. In herky-jerky rhythms, the Tupes conveyed the same message X relayed a decade prior in "We're Desperate," another of Dava's favorite anthems. "I always thought that the point of punk was coping with bullshit," X vocalist John Doe told Geoffrey Himes in a *No Depression* feature (*ND* #28 2000), "and humor is an important part of that." Add to Doe's assessment country music's laconic attitude toward daily crap, and you have an interesting mix indeed. "The lyrics were so truthful," Doe said of George Jones and other country artists, "and the singers had such good haircuts." The blend of country and punk songs Dava included on her mix tapes manifested the slacker aesthetic of embracing loss and limitation, or knowing what to make of a diminished thing, namely the dwindling opportunities for young people in America. Members of Generation X bonded over their thwarted ambitions, emboldened by their decision to say "screw it" and live off the grid, as Boomers once bonded over plans to change the world. Like the Vertebrats, the obscure Illinois band whose songs Uncle Tupelo and the Replacements covered, Xers were "left in the dark," enamored with certain aspects of 1960s culture but left in its penumbra, facing a foreclosed future.

At times, it seemed best not to care. "Whatever," we sighed. In indie rock circles, the Replacements "Shiftless When Idle," an ode to wasting time, spoke to those feelings, as did the Gear Daddies' wistful acoustic lament, "Statue of

Jesus," and X's aforementioned "We're Desperate." In alt-country songs, punk rock's acknowledgment of failure grew a bit scarier owing to the terrors of rural isolation, yet failure also emerged as a vibrant, creative force. As country singer Lee Ann Womack put it, "Singing about pain, whether it's something you went through specifically yourself or you can empathize with whoever did write that lyric, you know what pain is. So I think it helps to have lived a little, been knocked around a little, maybe" (*ND* #27 2000). Anomie, fostered by an intellectual appreciation of pain, was common across the Gen X soundscape. It's no mistake that a Replacements fan was the one to hip Peter Blackstock to Uncle Tupelo's first album.[4] Bassist Jeff Tweedy sang about sitting around and watching stuff go by ("That Year"), partly to admit to laziness, partly to brag, and partly to send out an SOS, as Paul Westerberg had done on countless Replacements songs, giving punk rock desperation a whiff of small-town restlessness.

Behind alternative country's emphasis on "Losering" (a Whiskeytown song) there existed a serious meditation on how failure facilitates creative success (a Gen X obsession I explore in depth in chapter 4). Gen X artists were assisted in this endeavor by beautiful losers from the Boomer generation: derelict-by-choice geniuses like Gram Parsons, dreamy creator of "Cosmic American Music"; Townes Van Zandt, inveterate yarn-spinner about loveable screwups; Tom Waits, scruffy purveyor of dissonant "junkyard Americana"; a variety of down-on-their-luck Memphis musicians, especially Alex Chilton; and even John Lennon, who upon moving to America threw away success whenever he felt like it.[5] Uncle Tupelo's "Watch Me Fall" wasn't mere whining; traps were put there by design. Here as elsewhere, the sad-sack consequences alt-country slackers sang about were more real than their detractors let on. Lest anyone think "That Year" or "Train" (another Tweedy composition) revealed a lazy ne'er-do-well's penchant for trainspotting, we should recognize that following his father into railroad work was Tweedy's fate if the music thing hadn't worked out so well.[6] In this regard, Tweedy differed from Parsons, heir to a Florida citrus fortune, or from Van Zandt, who came from Texas oil wealth. This much seems congruent: Tweedy, Parsons, and Van Zandt all failed by the standards of traditional country, just as Waits failed by the standards of L.A. singer-songwriters. In so doing, they recalled the bold decision-making of musical pioneers like Miles Davis, whose "failure in the eyes of jazz critics and advocates of classical trumpet playing was a sign that [he] was operating under a different set of standards" (Mather 2008, 163). A key question in this chapter is whether the journalists in *No Depression* hewed to similar principles, disregarding expectations, embracing failures, and thereby matching their favorite musicians' genre-busting prowess.

In 1995, five years after Uncle Tupelo's debut album got released and one year after the band dissolved, its principal songwriters, Jay Farrar and Jeff Tweedy, started new bands and issued competing LPs (Son Volt's *Trace*; Wilco's *A.M*). That same year, *No Depression* magazine emerged as the chronicle of the alternative country movement, as *Rolling Stone* had for rock back in 1967 and *Vibe* for hip-hop in 1993. It was an auspicious time to start such a publication. Gillian Welch and Whiskeytown put out acclaimed debut albums and fueled heated discussions about alt-rock authenticity.[7] The Bottle Rockets signed with Atlantic and saw the re-release of their best album, *The Brooklyn Side*. A year later, Wilco's sophomore effort, *Being There*, upped the ante in the Farrar-Tweedy battle, alt-country's equivalent of the Lennon-McCartney rivalry.[8] Americana was now a radio format with its own chart in *Radio and Records*, the trade journal of the Americana Music Association. Roots music had been influencing alternative rock for some time, but there was a new spirit in the air, solidified and given a home base by *No Depression*. Grunge and alternative rock had become homogenized and bland, prompting musicians and listeners to seek new adventures in sound and writers to debate the sounds they heard.

I didn't pick up a copy of *No Depression* until 2005, a full decade into its print run, discovering it on a newsstand. Instantly, my sense of alt-country coalesced. The knowledge I gathered went beyond music toward an atmospheric conception of nationhood. One of the first issues I bought (*ND* #60 2005) focused on New Orleans in the aftermath of Hurricane Katrina. The haunting cover image signified a communal commitment to beauty, care, and truth in the Crescent City, awash at that time in natural destruction and governmental neglect. On the cover, an angelic statuette lies supine, as though sleeping, on a pile of dirt and debris. "Lost in the Flood," the caption reads. "The cultural cradle of New Orleans lies scattered amid muck and mud. Can this sleeping beauty rise again?" Inside, *No Depression* staff writers, along with musicians such as Mary Gauthier and Peter Holsapple, mused on the fateful hand the city had been dealt. In time, I'd glean more details about Katrina from Douglas Brinkley's book *The Great Deluge* and Spike Lee's documentary film *When the Levees Broke*. But in the autumn of 2005, inspired by Americana music,

I marveled at the feedback loop *No Depression* offered. A shared passion for southern roots music led writers to express love for the troubled, beautiful land whence it came. "I was making my own depression," Bob Dylan announced with swagger in the early 1960s ("My Life in a Stolen Moment"). Well, here were my contemporaries doing the same, wearing boundary-breaking allegiances on their sleeves and rolling up those sleeves to create art. I felt welcomed back to a community I hadn't realized I'd abandoned.

The welcome *No Depression* offered readers was evident in its format, which changed remarkably little over its thirteen-year print run. "Miked" provided live reviews; "Town and Country" supplied brief regional profiles; "The Long Way Around" contained extended features on artists; "Waxed" and "Not Fade Away" contained reviews of new and reissued albums, respectively. Think pieces like "Sittin' and Thinkin'" and "A Place to Be" also appeared occasionally. The corrections notice was called "All the Fixin's."⁹ In the "Front Porch" section, the opening letter from the editor was titled "Hello Stranger," after the old Carter Family song. In the "Back Porch" section, the valedictory column was titled "Screen Door," after an Uncle Tupelo track. Together with the magazine's title, these bookend columns suggested that the circle between 1930s roots music and the new breed of alt-county was indeed unbroken.¹⁰

Thus encouraged, I circled back to my bohemian days. Before entering academia, I wasn't forced to specialize in a literary period or genre, categorize what I knew, or hold forth as "an authority" on particular topics. I absorbed knowledge as it got shared. Sure, my postgraduate friends and I were a bit cocooned, hanging out on a ramshackle screened-in porch on Berkshire Street in Rochester, New York. Maybe we anticipated there'd come along a song describing scattered scenes like ours. It arrived with "Screen Door," an Uncle Tupelo track. In Jeff Tweedy's song, as in our lives, a screen door allowed for permeable exchange. Notoriously crummy Rochester weather came through the Berkshire Street door, but so did friends who stopped in to catch up and enjoy some music. Were we naïve? No doubt. But so are those who disparage the situations out of which alt-country songs arise.

Take, as a prime example, *Old Roots, New Routes: The Cultural Politics of Alt.Country Music* (2008), a collection of essays edited by Pamela Fox and Barbara Ching. Although I have a better opinion of it now, this book's relentless attack on exuberance and fandom struck me at first as one-sided and smug. Its contributors strive for academic rigor, abandoning enjoyment. They seem out of touch with the scenes they consider. Not that they mind. "What I find so delightful about so many of the essays in this collection," one contributor wrote, "is their refusal to valorize the narcissistic ontological lacks of youth culture that fandom, hipness, and subcultural capital seek so vainly to fill" (J. Smith 2008, 76). When Fox and Ching consider Uncle Tupelo's *No Depression* album and see a "genre of cover shot [that] could have been taken by fans," they seem unduly suspicious, even a bit disgusted (15). *Old Roots, New Routes* is right to analyze the underpinnings of alt-country, but as Sleater-Kinney might say, this book is "no rock and roll fun."

Fox and Ching critique the alt-country movement with regard to race, gender, age, and "the cultural politics of commercialism." That's fine. Those perspectives shape my own thinking, as you will see shortly. I find equally relevant, however, the situations Fox and Ching regularly dismiss, such as the one Beth Orton shared with *No Depression* readers upon release of her 2002 album, *Daybreaker*:

> One time, I was coming back from a friend's house, and we had been up all night drinking and laughing and talking and listening to records. He gave me a copy of *Dusty in Memphis* to go home with. I put *Dusty in Memphis* on and listened to it and watched the sun come up. Lovely. It was beautiful. That is a daybreaker, to me. You know, when you are a bit off your nut, the sun is coming out, and you are listening to the most incredible music. That is pure joy to me. We used to think music could change the world. But I think it is wonderful to put on a song and have it change your day, have it make everything seem a bit better. That is when music matters. Maybe that's all we can expect of music. (*ND* #40 2002)

Geoffrey Himes supplied a similar anecdote in *No Depression*'s 2003 feature on Lyle Lovett, praising the "sense of community [that] is the key element in the whole Texas singer-songwriter ethos,"

> that habit of sitting around someone's house or a nightclub after it's closed and sharing new songs produces a different kind of songwriting. In those situations, away from paying audiences and check-writing executives, when empty bottles cover every flat surface and an acoustic guitar rests on every right thigh, the motivation for singing a new song is not to win applause or a contract but to impress your peers. Craftsmanship

becomes the highest goal, and you try to come back each month or each week with a new song that might finally win that elusive nod of approval from Guy Clark or Townes Van Zandt or whoever the unspoken arbiter of the gathering happens to be. (*ND* #47 2003)[11]

Alternative country isn't only about history or sociology. It's about enjoying the moment, making original music with acoustic instruments, working on craft, and cultivating friendships.

Jealousy can erupt anywhere, and music scenes inevitably run their course. It's not unusual for key players in a tight-knit community to take off for the bright lights of industry towns. Lyle Lovett recalls that Guy Clark, Steve Earle, and Rodney Crowell left Texas for Nashville and "made it work for themselves" (*ND* #47 2003), but not everybody left unscathed. Nanci Griffith, who departed Austin for Nashville in 1985, endured backlash from musicians and journalists, including *Austin American-Statesman* writer Michael Corcoran, who dismissed Griffith's band as "Nashville hacks" and gratuitously labeled Griffith "the type to get married in a vintage white Victorian dress." Decades later, in *No Depression*, Griffith reflected: "There are so many great artists in Austin who have never gotten out of Austin, and that is always difficult. You can be totally famous in Austin, but if you drive to Dallas, no one's heard of you" (*ND* #56 2005). Eventually, artists must decide whether small is beautiful, but Griffith's case suggests that some divisions are also exacerbated by gender bias. Here, Fox and Ching's book proves useful. No scene is so cocooned as to be free of politics and prejudice, especially when one participant's breakout success is thought to eclipse the talents of others.

It was only a matter of time before commercialism affected alt-country. Halfway through its print run, *No Depression* paused to consider Americana's ongoing negotiation with big-budget simulacra. *O Brother, Where Art Thou?* had just come to theaters, and with its T Bone Burnett–produced soundtrack it gathered an armload of Oscars and Grammys. The album sold eight million copies, occasioning a "Down from the Mountain" tour with Alison Krauss and Ralph Stanley, even as Farrar and Tweedy saw their experimental albums (*Sebastopol* and *Yankee Hotel Foxtrot*) rejected by major labels. A year after the movie's release, Grant Alden noted that *O Brother* had "so pervasively entered the world around me that the newness of hearing bluegrass at Target has finally worn off" (*ND* #34 2001). Chris Thile, of the bluegrass group Nickel

Creek, was similarly bemused by the film's impact: "I think *O Brother* made the people realize that there was music like that … I do cringe when I think that Americans might be thinking, 'O, how quaint. Our roots, how sweet'" (*ND* #59 2005).

Americana was trending. Ryan Adams appeared alongside Willie Nelson, mugging his way through a Gap television ad. In 2006, *Vanity Fair* photographers commissioned alt-country musicians for a fashion spread, "The Country and Western Music Portfolio," assuring elites that this new breed was "cerebral, devoid of anything hick" (2006, 291). Even the craft movement reached a tipping point, filmmaker and crafts maven Faythe Levine remembers, since a slew of slick magazines closed in on what had been an activist outlet for punk girls who simply wanted to knit together (Reighley 2010, 211). Facing such developments, how might grassroots music communities retain their integrity?

If the Americana explosion ushered in by *O Brother* helped *No Depression* gain readership, it also prompted its editors to think twice about what they had wrought. Just as Tweedy and Farrar claimed to be flabbergasted by the sustained attention accorded Uncle Tupelo, Peter Blackstock and Grant Alden used disarming language to explain their publication's lasting impact on Americana music. "Our magazine's name came to tag a scene," Alden lamented in a 2010 post to *No Depression*'s online newsletter, "even though we tried actively … not to be limited to anything which might be described as a scene. The operating hunch I shared with Peter at various times was that we covered artists who were too loud, too weird, or too old for country radio, but even that expanded. We covered the music we liked, plain as that" ("Field Notes"). Blackstock had used similar language at the outset of their venture:

> A curious breed are these animals we endeavor to define as "movements" or "trends" or "scenes." They're rarely, if ever, the result of any conscious directional effort on the part of the artists that encompass them; yet these artists clearly share certain aesthetics, values and visions that inevitably invites [*sic*] association among listeners who also identify with these qualities. In essence, the artists and their fans constitute a community—not in the literal sense, but on ideological grounds that are as binding as common geography. (*ND* #4 1996)

The geographic hook was crucial. Sleater-Kinney's Carrie Brownstein recalls that in the 1990s, to be a fan of music also meant to be a fan of cities, or places. Regionalism—and the creative scenes therein—played an important role in the identification and contextualization of a sound or aesthetic. Music felt married to place, and the notion of "somewhere" predated the Internet's seeming invention of "everywhere" (which often ends up feeling like "nowhere"). (2015, 79–80)

Scenes are eventually constrained by media hype, and *No Depression*'s co-editors—who met in Seattle, writing for *The Rocket* during the heyday of the grunge movement—knew enough not to get caught in that trap. They were well aware that once a scene gets defined, people start showing up for the wrong reasons. Looking back at the grunge explosion in a profile of Mark Lanegan, Alden spoke wincingly about "the time friends began to speak of the teenagers they were meeting who had moved to Seattle to become heroin addicts. Some of them hung out in the coffee shop up the street from my old neighborhood, nodding out over lattes." Alden admits that Seattle rock had become hard to write about. "Those were not the chords the music had played in my heart, but one never knows how words and sounds will be heard by others. Nor how they're meant, in the end. So I started this damn country magazine" (*ND* #16 1998).[12]

Luckily, *No Depression* found success on its own terms. A full decade into his venture, listening to music in his car, mulling over midlife realities (settling down, raising children, not getting out to clubs much anymore), Alden takes comfort in what alt-country still provides him:

For many, music becomes simply a set of markers to be manipulated by canny advertisers. The rest of us gather in peculiar communities such as this, for our lives still demand expression, and the habits of our quest will be put to sleep no more easily than a hungry child. And so we are drawn to explore the simpler yet complex power and, yes, the sheer transcendence of great songwriting, though we now listen in the stolen privacy of midnight headphones or solitary drives, and the songs that touch us now may not so easily be shared. (*ND* #55 2005)

With *No Depression*, Blackstock and Alden offered a creative space where maverick strains of American music could be enjoyed and shared, without unnecessary categorization.

If *No Depression*'s title pointed backward to the Carter Family and forward to Uncle Tupelo, it likewise honored the grassroots community that used the name in an early 1990s message board. "Our magazine's title extends that tip of the hat to the *ND* online regulars who got the ball rolling," Alden and Blackstock announced in their inaugural "Hello Stranger" column. The editors invoked Uncle Tupelo's hometown in southern Illinois for another measure of homespun authenticity: "Now it's up to us to take it and run. Today, Belleville; tomorrow, the world" (*ND* #1). The editors repeatedly insisted that the "alt-country" tagline, affixed to the magazine's subtitle in early issues, was just a joke, a way of poking fun at alternative rock. Notably, "Americana" never made it onto the magazine's banner. "Peter and I actively sought to distance ourselves from that word," Alden said in 2010, "simply because we thought what was played on the Americana chart [in the *Gavin Report*] was generally … too wimpy" ("Field Notes").

Alden's antinomian spirit sparked *No Depression*'s earliest issues. Asked to account for the inclusion of so many Hank Williams photos in the first few numbers, he said:

> Bottom line? We wanted to, which is pretty much the same reason this magazine started four issues back, and which will remain our guiding principle, and never mind that the thing's grown like Topsy. For whatever reason, people get caught up in labeling music, and proclaiming the arrival of musical movements. And so the question becomes, should this particular movement be called twangcore, insurgent country, alternative country … doesn't matter. The music predates (and will survive) whatever labeling and movement the movement ascribes to it. We just want to write about it. ("Hello Stranger," *ND* #4 1996)

For the first time since the inaugural issue, Blackstock joined his co-editor in *ND* #4's "Hello Stranger" column to account for their magazine's change of subtitle. "Folks occasionally ask Dad what the kids are up to," Blackstock humbly explained. "When he tells them about *No Depression*, he usually receives puzzled looks in return, so his stock answer has become 'It's a magazine about alternative country music—whatever that is.'" Hence the new subtitle: "The Alternative Country (Whatever That Is) Quarterly." In *ND* #59 (2005), that subtitle evolved to "The Past, Present, and Future of American Music," but for nearly a decade the equivocal phrase Blackstock borrowed from his father reflected Generation X's "whatever" aesthetic; it was wide and useful as a "lasso," one reader enthused ("Box Full of Letters," *ND* #7 1997).

Inevitably, that lasso collected some acts at the expense of others, leading to some friction. Dismayed by a negative review of the band High Noon, one reader wrote, "If you think the vague, lackluster and uninspired ramblings of Wilco, Sunvolt [*sic*], the Jayhawks, et al. are the next phase in the evolution of modern country, then I can understand why you subtitle your magazine 'The Alternative Country (Whatever That Is) Bimonthly.'" As was their wont, Blackstock and Alden sent the High Noon fan a cleverly titled rejoinder: "We Must Be High" ("Box Full of Letters," *ND* #8 1997). In the next issue, the editors went one better, temporarily changing the subtitle to "The 'How Would You Define Alt-Country?' Bimonthly" (*ND* #9 1997). Their insouciant attitude colored future issues as well. *ND* #21 (1999) featured on its cover a hard-to-perceive horizontal shot of the Old 97's, and thus the subtitle was changed to "Turning Alt-Country Upside Down (Bimonthly)." When Johnny Cash died, the editors obscured their title with an inset photograph of Cash, for as Blackstock explained, "No single artist meant more to alternative country than Johnny Cash. Whoever he was" ("Hello Stranger," *ND* #48 2003). When Cash won a posthumous Grammy for *American Recordings IV—The Man Comes Around*, the magazine honored him in their first annual critics poll, titled "The 40 Best Alt-Country (Yeah, Whatever) Albums of 2003." Alden, who hadn't included the poll's eventual winner (The Jayhawks' *Rainy Day Music*) anywhere on his list, duly shrugged: "That, of course, is the duality (or plurality; whatever) which has always made this a fun magazine to create, and, we hope, an interesting magazine to read, and to argue about" (*ND* #49 2004).[13]

For better or worse, alt-country's "whatever" aesthetic brought diverse groups of people together. The fusion of punk rebellion and country traditionalism made for some scene-stealing moments, as a member of the Red Dirt Rangers attests: "One night while playing at this private party I saw a kid slam dancing in one corner and an older couple swing dancing in the other—to the same song! I guess that's the best description of what we do" (*ND* #3 1996). The same dynamic held sway at Henry's, a North Austin bar where University of Texas students mingled with traditional country fans. "I played for both kinds of 'blue hairs' at Henry's," Don Walser recalled (quoted in Fox 2008, 96). Ryan Adams of Whiskeytown lent his oft-quoted description of alt-country to the title track of *Faithless Street*, explaining that he started a country band because punk rock was too difficult to sing. Suddenly, country music became a refuge for those, like Jeff Tweedy, who felt "maimed" or "tamed" by rock and roll (Wilco 1996).

Slackers half in love with easeful failure had found their métier, although they endured some puzzled looks. "I used to hate country music, mostly out of ignorance," Danny Heifetz of the San Francisco–based band Dieselhed told *No Depression* in *ND* #14 (1998). "Today I was looking through 'zines, trying to find places to send our CD, and one said 'No country.' I felt I couldn't send it there, because we are a little bit country." Seems the prejudice of hipsters against anything "country" was hard to shake. The savviest alt-country types learned to shift colliding allegiances to their advantage, but real divisions remained. "Country music, so the cliché went, was about an acceptance of life's limitations, but rock 'n' roll was about rejecting those limitations altogether," David Cantwell wrote in "Elvis Presley—Fanfare for the Common Man," his brilliant essay on the King. "Where country represented resignation, rock 'n' roll reached for freedom" (*ND* #11). Arriving several decades after Elvis debuted, alt-country showed what happened when rock's eternal promise of freedom didn't work out, when the decision to play country music, as Neko Case maintained, became a punk rock choice (*ND* #12).

Searching for that truer sound, in writing as well as in music, *No Depression* adopted a transparent DIY vibe. In early "Hello Stranger" columns, the editors revealed what it was like getting their magazine to press, Blackstock reenacting "mad-scramble-to-the-finish-line production weekends" and explaining that the "Hello Stranger" column was the last thing he wrote after everything else was finally set (ND #8 1997). Blackstock's sprints to deadline were inspired, he claimed in *ND* #13 (1998), by musicians like Butch Hancock and Mark Olson, both of whom had retreated to small desert towns (Terlingua, Texas; Joshua Tree, California), leaving renowned bands (Flatlanders; Jayhawks), big cities (Austin; Minneapolis), and midsized record labels (Sugar Hill; American) in one fell swoop, releasing music independently and informally, sometimes through mail order.[14] In indie production, you learned fast that all sorts of problems cropped up, but at least they were *your* problems.

Anecdotes about Sunday's rush to deadline remained an endearing component of *No Depression*. As Alden put it, "Four years on, this magazine still feels like a small miracle each time it goes to press. And a curse at least once the night before. Not so long ago Peter and I stood in the midnight gloom of an office kindly loaned by Seattle designer Art Chantry and pieced together a first issue from Kinko's laserprints, breaking briefly to drive down the road to the Tractor Tavern to see the Bottle Rockets. Happily, both we and the Rockets are still around, though that old truck expired long ago" (*ND* #23 1999). As years passed, the upstart editors extended their base to thousands of subscribers, but they kept the tone intimate, befriending far-flung readers long before Facebook came around. In one column, Blackstock informed readers of his wedding and suggested that even if he and Grant didn't get out to see bands quite as often, the magazine was the place where their love for music could be shared with people who mattered to them (*ND* #51 2004). Through the very last issue, home addresses and phone numbers of the editors were posted on the masthead.

In alt-country circles, strangers didn't stay that way for long. Various "Screen Door" columns spoke of the fortuitous meetings *No Depression* made possible. In an essay titled "Someday, the train will return to these parts," Blackstock remembered visiting a group house at 406 West 30th Street in Austin, a way station for bands, writers, friends, and hangers-on. Someone there provided him the name of a Wild Seeds fan in Mobile (who'd sent a fan letter to the Austin address). The name Jack Pendarvis proved handy when Blackstock's car broke down in Mobile en route to New York. In ensuing years, Blackstock came across Pendarvis's name in album liner notes, in kids' TV shows featuring members of the Mekons, and elsewhere, proving that the alt-country world was a small world after all (*ND* #12 1997). Perhaps that's why when AOL discussion board member Kim Webber introduced herself to Blackstock at a concert, she merely raised her name badge. When Webber contracted multiple sclerosis, Blackstock used a "Screen Door" column to spearhead grassroots fundraising efforts (*ND* #28 2000).

Blackstock's memorial essay for Dan Bentele, another discussion board original, underscored the magazine's emphasis on friendship. Bentele had been the organizer of St. Louis's Twangfest, which tried mightily to avoid the corporate trappings of Austin's behemoth South by Southwest Festival (SXSW). "You have known someone like Dan," Blackstock wrote,

> one of those someones through whom you discovered and shared this music, with whom you tossed back a beer and bobbed your head to good grooves, from whom you received a mix tape or CD, and about whom

you perhaps didn't know enough. You felt the kinship all the same. The culture of alternative country (if you'll permit the phrase; you know what it means because you've lived it too) turns around such feelings, such individuals. Bands that survive by word of mouth need mouths like Dan's: smart, unpretentious, enthusiastic, friendly. They need spaces like Schubas, the Continental Club, the Station Inn, the Duck Room: big enough for stretching out, but small enough for recognizing familiar faces, for bonding without losing individual connections and private excitements—the kind that initially inspire every kid with a guitar, every fan with a 45 or an mp3." (*ND* #57 2005)

Long before Blackstock wrote these words, he and Alden recognized a "culture of alternative country," which is what prompted *No Depression* to become more than just a music magazine.

Sincere and poignant the magazine could certainly be, but witty repartee remained its calling card. The "weird-like-us" bonding that Ann Powers championed in indie rock circles (see chapter 4) regularly manifested itself in *No Depression*'s "Box Full of Letters" column. One time, a question arose as to which professional wrestler invented the "heart punch." A stream of educated guesses (Stan Stasiak, Blackjack Mulligan, Big John Studd) got published over several issues. But a Kansas City correspondent signing off as "Down for the Count" maintained that none of the readers was correct: "It was my ex-girlfriend Michelle who perfected the devastating heart punch" (*ND* #12 1997). Case closed. The forum was relaxed enough that Blackstock and Alden good-naturedly chided readers whose judgments they found faulty, and they adopted a bemused tone ("Thanks, thanks a lot") whenever they received profuse praise. One reader from Minnesota announced, "I will not be renewing my subscription to *Rolling Stone*, as *No Depression* gives me all the music news I need. So, thanks, and keep up the good work!" The editors seized the moment with a typically quirky heading, "Unlike a Rolling Stone," thanking the reader while comically laying waste to Boomer-style ambitions, journalistic and otherwise.

As happened in the vintage clothing explosion, alt-country revered past traditions but used humor to loosen up all definitions. If alt-country musicians were not completely ironic, neither were they fully earnest. "These folks are mining the classics with real love and a feel for the stuff," Phil Fuson said of BR5-49, a band whose name was inspired by Junior Samples's used car salesman shtick on

Hee Haw, "but not to the point that the compositions feel like museum pieces" (*ND #3* 1996). The irony inherent in other band names like Southern Culture on the Skids, Drive-By Truckers, Future Farmers of America, and Backyard Tire Fire provided alt-country aficionados sufficient distance from conservative aspects of the Deep South. Writers at *No Depression* enamored with BR5-49's "party fog of irony" (*ND #16* 1998) were prepared to share the chuckle.

At the same time, *No Depression* had a real mission, providing underappreciated country artists their due. This was especially true in the "Not Fade Away" column, which reviewed reissues. It was here that Billy Joe Shaver's 1973 release, *Old Five and Dimers Like Me*, got recognized as a classic. Shaver was also credited as the writer behind Waylon Jennings's greatest hits. "Not Fade Away" positioned vintage roots music in insightful historical contexts. Consider the column from *ND #67* (2007). Of Tony Joe White's *Swamp Music: The Complete Monument Recordings*, Edd Hurt wrote, "It survives not only as first-rate music, but as a portrait of a time [1968–1970] when white soul meant taking risks with a style and feeling that quickly became unfashionable, even as the message of hope became even more relevant." To me, that's a fairly concise take on shifting race relations among young southerners forty years ago—a comment Peter Guralnick might make—even if it's buried in the middle of a record review. Ed Ward was equally perceptive when reviewing *Friends of Old Time Music: The Folk Arrival, 1961–1965*, a Smithsonian Folkways box set featuring southern musicians brought northward to perform for urban elites. For Ward, "these were amateur musicians coming from a very different milieu from the one its audience was living in: pre-mass media, rural, and rooted in ways that spoke to previously unarticulated needs of urban intellectuals." Despite its "whatever" attitude, *No Depression* fostered serious musicological discussion.

In time, alt-country's respect for traditional country music matched the title of a George Seitz album: *The Good Old Days Are Here*. Reviewing that album, Kevin Roe linked its musical message with *No Depression's* larger mission: "It's just one more reminder that this magazine—and the bands it profiles—are just the latest in a long line of colorful musical ancestors without whom the term 'alternative country' would just sound like some archaic Yankee word for the Great White North." Peter Blackstock sounded an equally humble note in his review of *First Ladies of Country*. "Many folks today who are coming at country music from a bass-backwards perspective—won over by such alt-country heroes as Uncle Tupelo and the Jayhawks and then seeking out the music's history (yours truly is largely included in this camp)—can be well served by an occasional primer on the basics" (*ND* #4 1996).

Others, especially academics, were less sanguine about alt-country's relationship with traditional American music. In his influential 2002 article "Why Isn't Country Music Youth Culture?" Trent Hill argued that contemporary alt-country musicians "are not, unlike the urban, college-graduate hillbillies of the folk revival interested in recovering an authentic past so much as articulating a set of connections and alliances within a marginalized present" (quoted in J. Smith 2008, 59). Presumably, young hipsters "making their own depression" had co-opted the difficulties others truly suffered. For Hill, that kind of cultural borrowing worked fine for Dylan and folk revivalists of the 1960s but not, apparently, for Gen Xers. Perhaps their love of irony was to blame. While New Traditionalists of a certain vintage—Emmylou Harris or Dwight Yoakam—largely escaped the criticism Hill leveled, the quandary affected younger and more playful alt-country musicians. Saddled with laughable names, the hybrid genres they fashioned—like "Newgrass," "Gangstagrass," or "Rappalachia"—were viewed as amusing but potentially harmful, as was a bluegrass tribute to Van Halen, *Strummin' with the Devil.*

Meantime, young musicians who sought an unadulterated return to the past, such as self-proclaimed "analog snob" Grey DeLisle (*ND* #50 2004), country blues enthusiast Lucinda Williams, or acclaimed folkie Gillian Welch, were shot down by various commentators for their pretenses, and specifically for their "class transvestism" (P. Fox 2008, 142). Greil Marcus regularly skewered Williams for her "shtick mournfulness" and her florid "Hard Road" clichés. "Her father was a college professor, but she spent her childhood out by the barn eating dirt, which is why her own songs ring so true today," Marcus sneered in *Real Life Rock* (2015a, 193, 367, 373).[15] Some complaints emanated from within the *No Depression* community. Calling himself a "sixth generation 100% authentic hillbilly," a reader named Jeff Kerr wrote "Box Full of Letters" to blast DeLisle, a Hollywood actress, suggesting she should "team up with that other Caliphoney singer Gillian Welch and do some hard hittin' songs about the hills … Beverly Hills, that is. I am absolutely sick and tired of having my culture carpetbagged. Hey, I like burritos and tacos. Maybe I should record a record of Norteno music" (*ND* #51 2004). An avalanche of responses defending Welch and DeLisle appeared in the following issue under the title "Jeff Kerr: You've Got Mail!" "Come on Jeff, celebrate the world, and don't try to own it," wrote Sean Hogan, a "100% authentic internationalist" from Cork, Ireland. "Even hillbillies came from somewhere else, once." Welch's musical partner, David Rawlings, also wrote in, wryly telling Kerr, "You should be grateful that magazines like *No Depression* exist to provide you with artists' background information. Otherwise you would have to judge them by their music." Fittingly, Rawlings's dateline read: "geographical location withheld" ("Box Full of Letters," *ND* #52 2004).

Taking the measure of Kerr's complaints while simultaneously underscoring their appreciation of past treasures, the editors put older musicians such as Porter Wagoner, Ralph Stanley, and Loretta Lynn on the magazine's cover, wrote long features on their life and work, and ran other articles on veteran songwriters like Mickey Newbury who were overlooked by mainstream media. Some current Nashville stars such as Patty Loveless got the cover treatment, but so did Hank Williams, proving that the magazine was nothing if not eclectic. "I think Hank Williams records have a lot more to do with the Sex Pistols than they have to do with Brooks & Dunn," Steve Earle mused aloud in *ND* #3. After repeated shout-outs to "old Hank" in early issues, readers were already inclined to agree.[16] But the "Box Full of Letters" contretemps put the relationship between old and new in a different perspective and pushed the editors toward a broader definition of alt-country.

For the most part, the magazine's preference for younger, rock-related country scenes led it to disparage traditional country outlets, especially Nashville, with its Music Row, its Hat Acts, its Countrypolitan and New Country cronies, and its "NashVegas" glitz. Alden, who moved to Nashville in 1997, lamented that the clubs were half empty during the workweek. "I don't think most of Music City views music as art, but as product," he surmised, searching for a reason.

That's the culture of session players and punched-in vocals and cloistered songwriters on top of which is placed a lead singer in a cowboy hat, all served up to the handful of radio programmers who—far as I can tell—really run this place. If you work on an assembly line, the last thing you want to do with your nights is turn a wrench … My sense is that too many people who work behind the scenes in Nashville have lost the joy of the music, have turned a rare opportunity to make a living doing something they love into … into a job. And jobs stop at five o'clock. (*ND* #10 1997)

Alden's complaint was later echoed by Dave Hickey, who championed Waylon Jennings, Willie Nelson, Tompall Glaser, and other so-called "Outlaws" as "the only folks in Nashville who will walk into a room where there's a guitar and a *Wall Street Journal*, and pick up the guitar" ("Farther Along: Waylon Jennings," *ND* #39 2002).

But like the people who reside within them, cities have multifaceted personalities and complex histories. *No Depression* dutifully revealed that in the 1980s many intelligent songs got composed in Nashville courtesy of Guy Clark, Rodney Crowell, Townes Van Zandt, and others. "It's often forgotten what a special time the '80s were for country music," Geoffrey Himes explained in his feature on Clark. "It was an era when intelligent lyrics could get on the radio, when country-pop was not a dirty word. For the community fostered by Clark and Van Zandt was not traditionalist; they were injecting irony and minor sixths into the music as never before. The high standards and the work ethic these writers learned in the Clarks' living room kept their work from getting stale even when success came along." Neither was this group of musicians unique in its commitment to craft. "We didn't invent this stuff," Clark told Himes. "Writers like Kris Kristofferson, Roger Miller, Mickey Newbury, Billy Joe Shaver and the whole outlaw crowd were writing really good songs before we came along. We wanted to live up to their example. They proved that you don't have to sell the audience short; the public is a lot hipper than the music biz gives them credit for" (*ND* #41 2002).

It was in the 1990s that things turned worse, with Garth Brooks and Shania Twain ("the highest paid lap dancer in Nashville," Steve Earle snickered) ruling the airwaves. "Until Shania's people stop buying pickups, Shania will be a country artist, Iris DeMent (the most country singer imaginable) will be an alt-country artist, and Merle Haggard will be a has-been," Peter Cooper coolly observed (*ND* #23 1999). Articulating alt-country's reaction against Nashville's Hot Country format, punk-roots chanteuse Neko Case shifted blame from high-profile musicians like Brooks to the industry titans who marketed them:

> I generally blame the programmers and the marketers for the travesty that is the new country promotional train. Have you seen those commercials where they have some young yuppie-lookin' guy going, 'This isn't my grandfather's country, it's not like some guy's dog's dyin' on my radio, this is real music'? It makes me so fuckin' mad ... Or those ads that

just say 'all country, no bumpkin'? Who the fuck do those people think they are? It makes the artists on the station look bad too; you'd never hear Garth Brooks on TV going, 'Oh, Hank Williams was a redneck hick'; you'd never hear that. None of those artists would ever downplay old country to make themselves look good; why the hell would anyone say anything so ignorant? Obviously, those people don't care about the music; they just think of their audience as a demographic, which is also insulting to the people that listen to country music. (*ND* #12 1997)

Throughout the 1990s, alt-country musicians railed against Nashville glitz. Webb Wilder's nutritionally correct group, the NashVegans, was one. Comedic songster Todd Snider took a bemused view, releasing *East Nashville Skyline*, an ironic play on what was already a revisionist Nashville offering, Bob Dylan's 1969 album *Nashville Skyline*. Some thought this criticism too facile. Jason Ringenberg, leader of Jason and the Scorchers, lamented how alt-country types repeatedly took potshots at the city, when in fact so many great musicians lived and worked there (*ND* #6 1996). But most in the *No Depression* crowd agreed with "insurgent country" musician Robbie Fulks, who expressed his discontent succinctly in his anti-Nashville screed, "Fuck This Town." Fulks's song made waves, but within a year he too had sold out, L.A. style, signing with Geffen and churning out overproduced alt-rock on his one-and-done major label effort.

Given the vituperative outbursts of musicians and readers, it was surprising to hear Grant Alden praise Nashville as his new domicile in *ND* #29, heralding the five-year anniversary of the magazine with a grown-up tone he hadn't expected of himself or his peers. "Mind you, I'd imagined nothing of the kind five years ago. I expected—anticipated, hoped for, desperately needed—a broad, punk-led country renaissance. Didn't happen, not really. Might still, might not" (*ND* #29 2000). Alden settled comfortably into Music City, serving as president of the Americana Music Association. When Alden revealed in "Hello Stranger" that he was moving to Morehead, Kentucky (*ND* #50 2004), he said it was done to be closer to his in-laws, not because he was irritated with Nashville. As proof, he placed Nashville favorite Miranda Lambert, an "emerging platinum country singer," on *No Depression*'s cover. He even admitted that on a trip to Nashville he'd flirted with the idea of starting a mainstream country magazine, explaining that "the battle with Music Row that was there at the inception of *No Depression* is now largely over" (*ND* #69 2007). Yet most fans of *No Depression* remained suspicious of the industry town, one reader in "Box Full of Letters" lambasting Bill Friskics-Warren for his pick of Brooks and Dunn, pure "Music Row crap," in an annual critic's poll (*ND* #50 2004). Glossiness in general came under siege. *No Depression*'s decision to give "teen-pop singer" Mandy Moore a six-page spread and to place chart-toppers The Shins on their cover met with anxious outcries from readers and self-conscious backpedaling from the editors, Blackstock going so far as to tally the number of older (over-sixty) artists who had previously graced the cover (*ND* #68 2007; *ND* #70 2007).

But alternative rock remained a part of the magazine's mix. While Alden was making his separate peace with Nashville, Blackstock regularly hailed Raleigh-Durham, North Carolina, renowned for its indie scene. Very early in the magazine's print run, Blackstock called Raleigh-Durham "the most vibrant alternative-country community in America" (*ND* #4, 1996). So frequent and laudatory were *No Depression*'s reviews of North Carolina bands (Whiskeytown, the Backsliders, 6 String Drag) that some readers suspected a local conspiracy, especially after the magazine's advertising director quit to manage one of those bands. Poignant in retrospect is Blackstock's feature on Whiskeytown prior to the band's major label debut, *Strangers Almanac* (*ND* #10 1997). By this point, the band and magazine were primed for megawatt recognition, which never really came. Maybe that was for the best, at least for *No Depression*. From the beginning, the editors apologized for each milestone. Filing incorporation papers, Blackstock told readers, "If we've grown faster and bigger than we expected when we started this thing two years ago, we ain't exactly movin' on up to the East Side. And maybe that's not the goal." As Americana adherents, Blackstone and Alden sought homespun pleasures. "Sitting here in our production office (a.k.a. Grant's living room) on a Sunday night as we prepare to go to press, I pause for just a moment, proud of what we've created, secure in the knowledge that we're still having loads of fun. And that we're going to see Glen Campbell tomorrow night" (*ND* #11 1997).

Still, the commercial appeal of Americana was growing fast. Alt-country was ready for its close-up, and folks repositioned themselves, hoping for their big break. Raised in Austin, Blackstock moved from Seattle to North Carolina in 2000 ("Hello Stranger," *ND* #26) to enjoy his favorite alt-country scene first-hand, then abruptly moved back to the Seattle area in 2004 ("Hello Stranger,"

ND #54), only to bounce back to Raleigh in 2007 (*ND* #71). At the dawn of the millennium, Raleigh kingpin Ryan Adams hightailed it to Nashville, joining Todd Snider and other rebels trying to nurture an alt-country scene in the shadows of Music Row. But before long, Adams moved to L.A. to chase rock star dreams. Panning Adams's major label debut, *Gold*, for its Hollywood slickness, Blackstock decried the ornery musician's abandonment of a genre, and a place, he had done so much to promote ("Hello Stranger," *ND* #35 2001). The Texas alt-country community was dealt the same blow when Rhett Miller of the Old 97's took a Hollywood star turn. "We may still be foundering for a definition of No Depression," a perturbed reader wrote after seeing Miller's transformation, "but I'm pretty sure it's not an L.A.-living, model-wife-having, *Elle* magazine photo-shoot-taking, ruffled-purple-shirt-wearing pretty boy. If I'm wrong then I'll expect a glorious appreciation of the Eagles in the next issue of this magazine" ("Box Full of Letters," *ND* #42 2002).

Alt-country's mainstream flirtations took on a diabolic cast when roots duo Kelly Willis and Bruce Robison starred in a television advertisement for Claritin allergy medicine. As fans debated their heresy, the musicians explained their choice, using humor as a foil. "We're not really a duo. We just play one on TV," Willis chortled in concerts. Jeff Tweedy, Joe Henry, and Chuck Prophet likewise suffered abuse from *No Depression* readers for having strayed from the alt-country fold, trading back porch vibes for a big studio sound and pop music dollars ("Box Full of Letters," *ND* #28 2000).[17] In Raleigh, Blackstock celebrated those who kept alt-country real, folks like Van Alston, who gathered musicians for Alejandro Escovedo benefits (Escovedo suffered from hepatitis C) (*ND* #49 2004). But the spotlight on Americana had caused some ruptures.

Amid commercial growth, media attention, and artistic experimentalism, salt-of-the-earth authenticity remained an alt-country ideal. *No Depression* noted that popular acts like Michelle Shocked (on *The Texas Campfire Tapes*) and Lori McKenna (on *The Kitchen Tapes*) were willing to take a step back and pursue lo-fi projects, abandoning studios to record music in intimate settings with acoustic instruments, as Bob Dylan had done on *The Basement Tapes*, or Bruce Springsteen on *Nebraska*.[18] Even then, there lurked the possibility for widespread success and overexposure. A *No Depression* reader named David Wilds, enamored with the "small is beautiful ethos," suggested a gold status sales cap (500,000 copies), worrying that what happened to the Beatles and Garth Brooks would happen to Lucinda Williams after the success of *Car Wheels on a Gravel Road*. Besides warding off "insanity," not to mention "lobster eaters and lawyers," Wilds predicted that a sales cap would kill corporate involvement in alternative music and let hundreds of small labels bloom: "Rather than five or six empires, we would have hundreds of Oh Boys or E-Squareds or Dead Reckonings or whatever. Small sales would give us small groups of committed people" ("Box Full of Letters," *ND* #27 2000).

Perhaps the most endearing (and enduring) moment in alt-country's quest for authenticity can be found in "Windfall," the opening track of *Trace* (1995), Son Volt's superlative debut. In the era of Clear Channel Communications, the AM station Jay Farrar located on his car radio sounded like 1963, and thus sounded like heaven. The sound of roots music wafting through the American night evoked an eclecticism that was not quite gone, and not yet forgotten. Like Farrar, alt-country fans in the 1990s twirled radio dials "searching for a truer sound," even on the FM band. WFUV in New York City and KEXP in Seattle did their part (despite some slickness), as did WDVX, a tiny nonprofit station transmitting from a trailer near Knoxville, Tennessee. Nick Spitzer's New Orleans–based show "American Routes," syndicated on public radio, provided a learned perspective on roots music and those who made it.[19] But there was something magical about the all-night AM station Farrar discovered serendipitously in the southern night. I am reminded of Kerouac's *On the Road*. Its mad transcontinental dashes were made palpable when different radio stations came into range, playing music particular to regions the characters were traversing. And I recall that those great country pop hits of the 1960s and 1970s ("Wichita Lineman," "Suspicious Minds," "Behind Closed Doors") sounded better on AM radio, where I first heard them, than they do in digitally enhanced versions. In their 1985 song "Left of the Dial," the Replacements scored the ultimate salute to college radio. The song engaged indie fans because it carved out a space of belonging. A decade later, Son Volt did the same for Americana music, saluting the small radio outlets resisting corporate makeovers. Today, during Son Volt concerts, it's the line about the Louisiana radio station that encourages the greatest number of fans to sing along, even if most in the audience get their music via satellite or the Web.[20]

Through the static on Farrar's radio, there arrived an understanding of what American tradition was and could be once more, if the alt-country experiment reached its full potential. Folk and country were reclaimed as young people's music, plain and simple. Sarah Lee Guthrie, an erstwhile punk, was brought back to her grandfather Woody's music by a rocker husband moving in the folk direction: "That's what folk music is anyway—singin' your grandpa's song, no matter who your grandpa is" ("Town and Country," *ND* #35 2001). The Del Fuegos had already said as much: "It's folk music, you know, music for folks" (*ND* #13 1998). Brad Tyler defined country by virtue of the West Texas borderlands he and his favorite musicians (Jimmie Dale Gilmore, Joe Ely, Butch Hancock, Jerry Jeff Walker) called home: "Maybe country music, most broadly defined, is music that springs from a country landscape, music with a regional base and a regional basis. Maybe country music, to the extent that it's distinct from other categories, is music that's planted, and grows, in a particular patch of earth" (*ND* #7 1997). If there exist here personal connections missing from Marcus's abstract discourse on folk music ("a version of the song the song itself wanted to hear") (2015a, 442), *No Depression* certainly set out to nurture them.

The contours of community matter. In the old days, AM stations playing roots music were able to "reach across broad swaths of rural America" (A. Fox 2008, 99); regionalism was shareable. Polluting this river of influence was the poison well of suburbia, the affluent but disconnected demographic Nashville has targeted since the rise of "Countrypolitan." Alden explains:

> Suburbs push out to the freeway at the edge of larger cities, vast tracts of uniformly manufactured townhouses abutting the rootless, restless, rushing American imperative that makes such subdivisions good business. Generica, a friend calls it. For the moment the transition seems complete. In less than a century we have moved from rural to urban, from urban to suburban. And, from the comfort of their suburban gas fireplaces, only the most wealthy can now aspire to return to the country. And no matter where you go, nor what road you take, country radio sounds the way those new homes look. (*ND* #15 1998)

Alden repeated his warning a couple years later in his feature on Lee Ann Womack:

> In the suburbs, where most of the people who tune in country radio on their way to work live, the blues are all but forbidden. Banished in a flurry of church groups, prescription pills, self-help infomercials, soccer games, and the forced hilarity of drive-time chatter … in the end there is only exhaustion, and a mortgage to pay. No wonder so much modern

country music resembles a commercial jingle and fits unobtrusively into the wallpaper of unexamined lives. (*ND* #27 2000)[21]

To counter suburban blandness and solidify the power of place, *No Depression* included in its "Town and Country" section "brief regional features" of bands, complete with datelines. Even more precisely situated was "A Place to Be: About a Place," a column that ran in early issues then sadly disappeared. The "down here, where we're at" focus epitomized by Uncle Tupelo's "Screen Door" was linked to local sites, even as Americana got marketed to a broader cultural arena and the Internet began to erase geographical boundaries.

The magazine's emphasis was on the quirky, and that led writers to explore topics beyond music. Early columns featured stories about Paradise Gardens, a reservoir of folk art created by Howard Finster in Georgia and compared by Alden to the Watts Towers (*ND* #10 1997). Additional Americana art spots such as the Highlander Research and Education Center in New Market, Tennessee (ND #28 2000), and the Southern Folklife Collection at UNC-Chapel Hill (*ND* #34, 2001) received attention. In Tampa, lovers of the grotesque were given a tour of a Gram Parsons theme park, described by its owner as a "Field of Dreams type thing" (*ND* #39 2002). Spring training baseball received a shout-out in "A Place to Be" (*ND* #20 1999), as did New York City's Cowgirl BBQ restaurant, proud home of Frito Pie, Chicken-Fried Chicken, and Rootin' Tootin' Western Cocktails (*ND* #12 1997). David Cantwell kicked the food discussion up a notch when he proclaimed Arthur Bryant's Barbecue at Eighteenth and Brooklyn in Kansas City, Missouri, "the single best restaurant in the world," refuting John Morthland, who had declared central Texas barbeque "king of 'em all" (*ND* #48 2003). Cantwell used the same space to contest Greil Marcus's gratuitous depiction of Memphis as ugly (*ND* #46 2003), bolstering *ND*'s love of the regional underdog.

Readers in search of lonely American spots let "A Place to Be" spirit them away to an abandoned Greyhound station in Eau Claire, Wisconsin, where they met the longtime but newly unemployed station manager, true heir to the Wichita Lineman (*ND* #30 2000). They were also transported to Terlingua, a dusty desert town near the Rio Grande that had become a refuge for Texas troubadour Butch Hancock and small groups of fans coming to hear him (*ND* #32 2001). In my favorite "A Place to Be" essay, "The Big Lake They Call Gitchee Gumee," Peter Blackstock recounted his low-budget automobile tour of the western Great Lakes. Meeting former Replacements manager Peter Jesperson in a cabin outside Sault Ste. Marie, Michigan, then traveling west along the Lake Superior shoreline, Blackstock listened to low-wattage pirate radio from Duluth and heard firsthand accounts of the wreck of the *Edmund Fitzgerald* (*ND* #24 1999).

No Depression gave writers the chance to display their literary chops. Of the co-editors, Blackstock was the more lyrical composer. His 1998 "Screen Door" offering, "The Northwesternmost Cut of All," was a geographically specific essay on par with Gary Snyder's bioregional writings. Blackstock describes his trip to Port Angeles and Neah Bay, in Washington State, to catch sight of the World War II survivor USS *Missouri* on its way back to Pearl Harbor. Missing the *Missouri* in Port Angeles, Blackstock travels deep into the wilderness. Hugging the coastline, hiking its cliffs, he does not merely want to catch sight of the ship; he aims to find the precise northwestern corner of the lower forty-eight states. Just as Henry David Thoreau once stood at Provincetown, Massachusetts, and marveled at his ability to put all of America behind him, Blackstock transports *No Depression* readers to his own transformative lookout:

> The trail zigs and zags through old-growth forest so dense and moist you could almost swim through it. Felled trees expose root-bases bigger than cars. The sound of water crashing ashore against giant rocks beckons in the distance, drawing you forth toward the magnificent sights to come ... It was more than worth it in terms of majestic visual wonder. On either side, waves slam into towering cliffs of rock, carving out sizable caverns in several places. To the south, the Washington coastline tapers down and gently eastward, clearly delineating this spot as the northernmost on the U.S. part of the continent. (*ND* #17 1998)

Who expected such writing in a music magazine?

Literature had a home at *No Depression*. The issue containing Blackstock's bioregional meditation included a feature on Emmylou Harris penned by Cecelia Tichi, professor of English at Vanderbilt.[22] In a later issue, southern fiction writer Larry Brown celebrated the songwriting of Robert Earl Keen, even as songwriter Steve Earle was dismissed as a Larry Brown wannabe in a separate review of Earle's debut fiction collection *Doghouse Roses* (*ND* #34 2001).[23] An early feature on Chip Taylor was titled "As a Man Grows Older" after an Italo Svevo novel (*ND* #10 1997). Michael Perry's profile of songwriter

Greg Brown was written with Old Testament phrasing, and in an accompanying interview, Brown shared his literary proclivities: "I like reading Thomas Hardy in the fall" (*ND #66* 2006). Scott Manzler thought it pertinent to link a Texas community's hands-on competition to win a Nissan truck with Willa Cather's *Death Comes for the Archbishop* (*ND* #21 1999), while Edd Hurt boldly declared that songwriter Bobby Braddock's memoir "stands alongside the work of Flannery O'Connor and Robert Penn Warren as an account of a south in its first throes of self-consciousness and urbanism" (*ND* #68 2007). As the above examples suggest, the literary crosscurrents could be dizzying. As Bill Friskics-Warren intimated in a 1999 review of Freakwater, what we had here was a group of alt-country types who believed they could "woodshed with a clutch of Buck Owens LPs and a Southern Lit reading list and come out making records" (quoted in P. Fox 2008, 147).

The striving for literariness got to be a bit much for some readers. In "Box Full of Letters," Geoffrey Himes was lampooned for his writer's workshop prose (*ND* #29 2000). Bill Friskics-Warren, lecturer at Vanderbilt, was criticized for his "Greil Marcus impersonations and the namedropping that dilutes the review to the point that I can't tell if he liked the record or not" (*ND* #43 2003). Mike Logan, already infamous for his highly ironic double review of Molly Hatchet and Commander Cody reissues in "Not Fade Away" (*ND* #46 2003), wrote a review of a Richard Thompson concert that said nearly nothing about the guitarist or his music (*ND* #53 2004). But it was another reviewer named Claire O, renowned for her over-the-top style, who suffered the most abuse. In "Box Full of Letters," one reader complained that Claire O's review of the new Dirt Ball record "reads like it was written in a college creative writing class." Another reader critiqued Claire O more bluntly: "Who is this Claire O. henry miller (not) lite weight gain no pain in the ass wordsmith with the I.Q. of a fencepost? Get rid of her ass. She not only sounds like a cutesy sophomore who thinks she's a poetess, she is a hindrance to the career of anyone she chooses to 'critique.' Her writing 'style' is more about her own ego than the work of the people she supposedly writes about" (*ND* #29 2000). Although Blackstock and Alden had fun with the heading ("No fair piling on [but she probably likes it]"), they defended Claire O, picking her 1998 review of Jerry Jeff Walker's *Cowboy Boots and Bathin' Suits* as one of the magazine's highlights. "As one is the loneliest number who not whom harbors like a loaded boat deep respect for Walker, Texas Arranger," Claire O wrote, Jabberwocky-style, on that occasion,

"I am like Paula Jones unsettled that like sand in my dandies, this album leaves me uncomfy in the end. It's pleasey like the breeze, but passes like the wind" (*ND* #16 1998). Might not the same be said Claire's efforts?

The perceived gap between alt-country's truer sound and pretentious literary effusions was given new articulation by Laurel Snyder, a veteran of the Iowa Writers' Workshop, who in a *No Depression* essay recalls defending country music in literary settings:

> I know that even as I write this, somebody is finishing their thesis on the curious emergence of alt-country music in the new millennium, and that's fine. But for those of us seeking comfort from the clever or indirect sarcasm of graduate school and indie-rock, country music is more than an idea. Dogs die and lovers leave and trucks break down. Other things happen in this world too, but an awful lot of people get left and an awful lot of people cry and an awful lot of people drink too much. Clichés happen for a reason ... And yes, there are bad offensive stupid country songs. Of course there are. But at least when they're bad, they're usually honest. ("Screen Door," *ND* #38 2002)

Actually, the gap between literary studies at the university and alt-country music in the clubs wasn't all that wide. Whiskeytown's Caitlyn Cary studied creative writing at North Carolina State with fiction writer Lee Smith (*ND* #38 2002) and invited Smith to deliver the spoken word outro to her biggest solo hit, "Cello Girl" (*ND* #45 2003). Smith in turn wrote acclaimed novels about Appalachian folk music. Singer-songwriter Tift Merritt studied literature and writing at University of North Carolina (*ND* #39 2002). Pieta Brown, daughter of songwriter Greg, earned a linguistics degree from University of Iowa (*ND* #40 2002). Exene and John Doe of X started their career as Venice Beach poets. Their cohort Dave Alvin was close behind; transfixed by Bukowski, he gave literary readings on the coast when he wasn't playing music (*ND* #52 2004). Following the example of Steve Earle, esteemed Texas troubadour Joe Ely wrote a novel, *Reverb*, published by the aptly named American Roots Publishing (*ND* #46 2003). Peter Case, Chuck Prophet, and Jay Farrar published memoirs and on-the-road ephemera. And in 2009, Melville House published a collection called *Amplified: Fiction from Leading Alt-Country, Indie Rock, Blues and Folk Musicians*, featuring "narrative songwriters who had never published or had barely published fiction before but were willing to take a chance." In any event, these were writers who, the editors believed, "*should* be writing fiction" (Schaper and Horwitz 2009, 10).

Political discourse likewise shaped the community *No Depression* created and nurtured. On albums and in performance, alt-country musicians Todd Snider (on *Peace Queer*) and Steve Earle (on *Jerusalem*) shared their political sentiments, taking the liberal side of Bush-era debates. *No Depression* subscribers had divergent opinions on this development. Facing the ugly attitudes that passed for patriotism in post 9/11 America (detailed by Grant Alden in a previous "Hello Stranger" column), a Sikh reader found solace in the liberal politics *No Depression* had begun to broadcast: "I sometimes have wondered whether, and where in America I fit. So thanks to everyone who shares the big-hearted spirit of America and Americana, because I realize where I fit, and it is exactly the place Woody Guthrie laid out" ("Box Full of Letters," *ND* #39 2002). Newly emboldened, Alden took a decidedly leftist stance in ensuing issues, sometimes beginning his columns with "We liberals" (*ND* #49 2003), despite complaints from readers who honored country music's conservative politics (and canceled subscriptions in frustration). Things came to a head in *ND* #53, when Alden used the "Hello Stranger" column to endorse the Kerry-Edwards presidential ticket (after a lengthy harangue). Ed Ward followed with a "Sittin' and Thinkin'" dispatch from Berlin, railing against Ugly American behavior. Profiles of Sally Timms and Camper Van Beethoven made 2004 look like 1968, as renegade alt-country performers freely shared leftist political views.

No Depression readers sounded off in the following issue's "Box Full of Letters," most lamenting the stance Alden had taken, one reader asking, "What does the staff of an alternative music magazine know about alternative politics?" That question was answered implicitly by another correspondent: "I bought your magazine for the Buddy Miller article. And prior to that for the Patty Griffin article. And prior to that for Sam Phillips/Loretta Lynn ... Notice—politics wasn't the reason." Some countered Alden's political stance with their own. As one letter put it, "Left-leaning *ND*ers should be singing praises that U.S. intervention in Iraq and Afghanistan rang the chimes of freedom for millions of women, children, and men in what were previously two of the most repressive countries in the world. Your *ND* readers in those countries were probably a bit dismayed with your comments. They just want to rock out to the new Silos and Tandy albums like us Americanos, without getting their hands chopped off in the process" (*ND* #54 2004).

Like many a politician, Alden may have underestimated or misperceived the mindset of his constituency. Although he had a long-standing policy of not responding to letters to the editor, he felt compelled now to do so:

> I am particularly struck by the blind fury with which some readers responded to our endorsement of a mainstream candidate for president. If we are really a country so bitterly divided, we are headed for a rough and rocky road, no matter who is elected.
>
> You may or may not wish it to take place in these pages, but we have to be able to talk about our differences, and preaching to the converted only weighs down the collection plate. They may rarely be so explicit, but politics have always been—and will always be—among the textures of these pages. Great songs (and good writing) come from hard thinking, and surely we wish our best artists to grapple with the most difficult and important subjects they encounter ... The lengthening tradition of rock criticism is inextricably interwoven with politics. So is the music in the pop marketplace. I've spent my entire adult life studying both music and politics with equal interest and passion. There are of course, at least an equal number of readers who, over the years, have pronounced me wholly equally unfit to write about music. (*ND* #54 2004)

Blackstock rushed to his co-editor's defense in *ND* #54's "Hello Stranger" column, but that didn't stop the sour letters from coming. Alden offered another explanation of his political turn in the 2004 critics poll, envisioning an Americana movement that bridged a divided citizenry:

> Let me refill the glass and start again: We never knew who we were. But we thought we did, and we've lost that, I think; and, worse, we've lost the habit of thinking about it. In these moments we find it difficult to live out personal and national dreams, for in the rush of technology and CNN and a lousy job market and the looming sense that something big is about to go wrong, we have largely stopped looking to see who we might be, who we might become. But the records I most liked and listened to this year were beginning to poke carefully at that question again. It is dangerous to place too much faith in musicians, but great songwriters often get to where we're going long before we realize there's a journey to take. (*ND* #55 2005)

Maybe Alden was envious that musicians had the opportunity to express their views before thousands, in concerts or on records, even if some got "Dixie Chicked" in the process. In fact, conflicts between performers and audiences were more combustible. On March 21, 2003, the day after the Iraq War began, minutes before she was to hit the stage, with 600 people in their seats, Iris DeMent canceled a show in Wisconsin, telling her audience, "It would be trivializing the fact that my tax dollars are causing great suffering, and sending a message that might makes right" (*ND* #54 2004). Right wing radio had a field day with this news, and DeMent subsequently received death threats. A public station that played DeMent's music had its state funding revoked when a conservative activist mounted a challenge. Jill Sobule faced similar criticism, telling *No Depression* that while opening for Don Henley in Florida she was booed for expressing her politics (and for sporting a tee shirt that read "My Bush Would Make a Better President"). Yet Sobule held steady to her Blue State mantra. "You don't want someone in *Cats* to get up and talk about their political views, but if you're a songwriter, an artist, of course you have every right to. And people have every right to clap or get pissed off too" (*ND* #54 2004).

Political correctness in *No Depression* had its limits owing to its demographics. In a 2003 survey, the magazine learned that an astonishing 86 percent of its (replying) audience was male. Seventy-five percent were college graduates and 55 percent were married. The mean age: 41.6 years old (*ND* #50 2004). Those masses of middle-aged men had a lot of gender-biased coverage to page through. In a cover feature, Silas House concentrates so much on Kelly Willis's looks it's downright uncomfortable (*ND* #40 2002). Similarly, in his feature on the all-female bluegrass group the Be Good Tanyas, Geoffrey Himes lingered over the members' dress, height, and hair color rather than their musicianship (*ND* #44 2003). John T. Davis frothed at the mouth in his appraisal of Patty Griffin: "A pink sweater over black trousers, glittering dark eyes juxtaposed against an alabaster complexion, and her justly celebrated coif of red hair tied back into a neat ponytail made Griffin a one-woman riposte to the drab morning" (*ND* #50 2004). Finally, a reader in the following issue's "Box Full of Letters" expressed dismay: "Shocking to me are the pictures of Patty Griffin … that include credits for makeup, styling and hair. I think it is safe to say that you have achieved a "new" level.… " But in answering this complaint, the editors didn't cede much ground. "Don't expect a swimsuit issue," they said (*ND* #51 2004). When Don McLeese profiled Rilo Kiley, he didn't repeat the mistake of *Village Voice* critic Robert Christgau, who called the group's lead singer, Jenny Lewis, a "wet dream for indie boys"; McLeese merely quoted him (*ND* #71 2007).

Although Alden never revealed survey results, race was another hot-button issue. "The alternative-country movement, it's safe to say, is largely music by and for white people," Jenni Sperandeo wrote in her review of Jim Goad's *The Redneck Manifesto* (*ND* #17 1998). Going a step further, musician and provocateur Will Oldham wrote in to say, "*No Depression* seems like a culturalist, racist magazine to me, about a certain kind of white music" ("Hello Stranger," *ND* #20 1999). Support for *ND* arrived in the next issue's "Box Full of Letters" from several black readers, including a teacher of African American studies, and from staff writer Ed Ward. But the race controversy did not disappear. In a "Sittin' and Thinkin'" column titled "The Unbearable Whiteness of Being Country," Crispin Sartwell tried to lighten the discussion with humor, albeit awkwardly: "Listening to country music—or playing it—is not standing in the schoolhouse door with George Wallace. It's just enjoying a certain culturally situated art, an art whose artists and audience are principally white. White folks got rhythm, baby. We're naturally musically gifted, just as we're naturally gifted in polo and bobsledding" (*ND* #41 2002).

Faced with this evidence, I decided to do a little survey of my own. I looked at *No Depression*'s seventy-five printed covers and discovered that blacks were featured on five of them: Isaac Freeman (*ND* #38 2002), Little Miss Cornshucks (*ND* #45 2003), Lizz Wright (*ND* #58 2005), Allen Toussaint (with Elvis Costello) (*ND* #64 2006), and Solomon Burke (*ND* #66 2006). I did not count the Grand Ole Opry's blackface star, Honey Wilds, who appeared alongside Hank Williams on *ND* #4 (1996). Inside the cover, *No Depression* occasionally saluted black performers like Opry stalwart DeFord Bailey, heir to the lost black string band tradition (*ND* #37 and #38 2002), deeming him worthy of the Country Music Hall of Fame. The magazine also described how T Bone Burnett and the Lomax family tracked down an ex-con named James Carter, the singer of "Po' Lazarus" (recorded by Alan Lomax at Mississippi State Penitentiary in 1959), to deliver a royalty check in the wake of *O Brother*'s multiplatinum sales (*ND* #39 2002). The Carolina Chocolate Drops received a brief feature in the last print issue (*ND* #75 2008). Record reviews, especially those in the reissue section, covered influential black artists. But overall, sustained interest in black traditional music seemed paltry. Prefacing Barry Mazor's cover article on Little Miss Cornshucks, Alden said that her music wasn't the magazine's usual fare but that it was interesting in a musicological sense. A year later, Alden trumpeted the magazine's recent incorporation of blues artists, discounting the notion that *No Depression* hadn't done enough due to the racism inherent in all things country ("Hello Stranger," *ND* #52 2004).

Through the years, *No Depression*'s self-consciousness about racial matters seemed to linger, attributable in part to the paucity of black writers. Where diversity and inclusion were concerned, the tone was sometimes forced. Coincidental or not, separate features in *ND* #58 (2005) revealed that jazz musicians James "Blood" Ulmer and Lizz Wright were prompted to incorporate blues into their repertoires because, as blacks, they were already "living the blues." Worse yet was Michael Goodwin's article on James Brown's death, in which he applauds himself for taking the A train all the way up to Harlem for the Apollo Theater wake and for being called "brother" by African-Americans standing in line to view Brown's body (*ND* #68 2007). As noted in chapter 2, Peter Guralnick proved a far wiser commentator, telling Bill Friskics-Warren in a *No Depression* interview that the best contemporary soul musicians "don't replicate the feeling, they achieve the feeling" (*ND* #27 2000). Many racial crosscurrents emerged. One African American reader from South Central L.A. wrote in to applaud the diversity of country music to which she'd been exposed in *No Depression*, divulging her growing interest in bluegrass and revising her previous assumption that country was all CMT and Toby Keith ("Box Full of Letters," *ND* #57 2005). Most everybody's heart was in the right place, but it would have been great to see *No Depression* devote more space to black performers.

Despite its shortcomings, *No Depression* stands as one of the most influential music magazines in the rock era. Over the course of a decade and a half, Grant Alden and Peter Blackstock launched an online discussion board on alt-country music, presided over seventy-five print issues of their magazine, organized an online archive of back issues available on their website, and passed the baton to Kim Reuhl and Kyla Fairchild, who managed the online operation. To Reuhl's delight, the site's "crowd-sourced content" garnered nominations for 2012's *Best Music Writing* anthology. The newsletter was informative, keeping members up to date about albums and tours, but bloggers simply could not match what professional writers did during *No Depression*'s long print run. But the world of journalism, like the music business, keeps changing. In 2014, Fairchild left, and Reuhl, funded by the FreshGrass roots music foundation, was able to publish a few print collections and hire former *ND* staff writers.

Poring over back issues of *No Depression*, I have decided that Americana, like the country for which it's named, is mostly what you believe it to be. I will hold on to my print copies of *No Depression* because the magazine created a community in which such beliefs could be shared, debated, and enjoyed. Country music will continue to go in and out of style with critics and trend-setters. But *No Depression* leaves as its legacy a far-flung community immune to their consultation. Like the music it chronicled, this magazine, a "hobby run amok" (Alden and Blackstock 2005, ix) was deeply rooted and eminently soulful. Its writers pursued the truer sound they heard, on car radios and in their minds, to our lasting benefit.

★ 4 ★

"Learning to Live on Your Own": Growing Up in DIY America

In 1986, having just graduated from college, I lived in a furnished room in a rickety apartment house one block down from the independent bookstore where I earned the minimum wage. I was in a new city, broke, staring college loans in the face, but actually pretty happy. Many nights, I dined alone on spinach salad, Progresso soup, and Genesee Cream Ale. But it wasn't then that I learned to live on my own. Rather, it was when I left the garret for a semi-communal situation, a "group house," actually another apartment, several blocks away. It had not dawned on me that striving for intellectual independence could be a group activity, but clearly it could. In the end, I learned as much about literature in this freewheeling environment as in any classroom. When friends moved from Boston to San Francisco on New Year's Day in 1990, they sent back a mix tape illustrated with photographs from their cross-country automobile journey. The tape included the Mekons song "Learning to Live on Your Own." I listened again and again. The song dealt with the band's adventures in the recording industry, but it also spoke to my situation of freedom and responsibility. Flush with the optimism of youth, I had found my soundtrack.

During this time, roughly 1986–1992, America witnessed the media-saturated crest of alternative rock, a reductive manifestation of an indie scene that included punk, post-punk, hardcore, and college rock. As Greil Marcus pointed out in 1994 after viewing a Taco Bell television ad featuring well-scrubbed "grunge" kids bodysurfing to Cracker's "Low," "alternative" was no alternative at all: it was indie stripped of its independence by record companies and corporate marketing machines. Hip-hop has always concerned itself with "keeping it real," but indie rock had its own attitude about grassroots purity, particularly in the early 1990s, when it faced the national spotlight, and even before that, in the mid-1980s, when Hüsker Dü, the Replacements, and REM jumped to major labels. As a mid-career academic, I find something poignant about a community measuring its ideals as it confronts professional challenges. Looking back, I realize that gifted writers have helped me gain perspective on what I was hearing at the time, and what I myself have been sorting through on an intellectual level.

Important to my ongoing appreciation of indie rock are the environments giving rise to it, especially in Generation X bohemia, described by critic Ann Powers as "more a path than a place" (2001, 27). In *Weird Like Us*, her engaging 2001 book, Powers combines sociology and memoir, reflecting her "concern of being a whole person, all the time" (154). Hers is an emotionally complex coming-of-age tale, one that is less interested in celebrating particular musicians than it is in mapping enclaves where young people foster a communitarian spirit. "Become what you are," Juliana Hatfield once urged listeners. Citing Hatfield, Powers underscores the personal liberty she and other Gen Xers enjoyed in San Francisco and New York. Like Dylan decades prior, Powers was in the 1980s and 1990s "busy being born." *Weird Like Us* tells her tale; to a certain extent, it tells mine.

But what happened to teenagers with less desirable zip codes? Gen X subcultures existed beyond San Francisco and New York, Austin (home of the "slackers" Richard Linklater filmed) and Seattle (home of grunge), or even Portland (mocked by indie rocker Carrie Brownstein in *Portlandia*, an IFC comedy series) and Boston (hotbed of college radio). Generational rebellion was not articulated solely in the music predominant on college campuses. Accordingly, *Teenage Wasteland*, Donna Gaines's portrait of suicidal heavy metal kids in Bergenfield, New Jersey, stands as a useful counterweight to Powers's chronicle of overeducated slackers. "People like us are often accused of running away—from responsibility, from society," Powers says in *Weird Like Us*. "We were running, it's true. This book is about the luminous corners where we stayed" (37). But Powers is relatively well-off, and her slacker status is something Brownstein links with societal privilege and smug entitlement.

"It's an inverted dynamic," Brownstein says, "one that sets performers up to fail, but also gives them a false sense of having already arrived" (2015, 192). Gaines, a native of Queens (home of the Shangri-Las, singers of "I Can Never Go Home Anymore"), knows that running away is not so easy for the financially strapped, undereducated youth residing in "turnpike suburbia." Beset by low self-esteem and beat down by authority figures who pay little heed to their aspirations and lifestyle choices, these teenagers occupy corners far darker than those Powers describes. Like the arty kids of Seattle and San Francisco, the Jersey teens were labeled "losers" by mainstream society, but they weren't nearly as apt as Gen X scene-makers to claim that tag. The word was simply hurtful. Deflective irony and reassuring safety nets were in short supply where they lived (and died).

Reading Powers and Gaines in conjunction with watching *The Breakfast Club*, a film by John Hughes, and comparing their models of self-discovery to Baby Boomer Patti Smith's memoir *Just Kids*, I have traced the bifurcated nature of Generation X alienation, "once all the flurry of Woodstock nation had died down" (Gaines 1998, 11). Clearly, certain factors determined whether you inhabited the heart of a scene or an anonymous nowhere, whether you listened to trendy alternative rock or unfashionable heavy metal, whether others considered you a free spirit charting your own path to success or an irredeemable failure dragging others down. Ultimately, I found the gray zones that exist between such binaries to be the most fascinating, and this led me to consider biographies of two indie icons, Kurt Cobain and Alex Chilton, written by Charles R. Cross and Holly George-Warren, respectively. One became a poster boy for Gen X alienation. The other was a 1960s teen star whose career derailment made him a cult figure. What Cobain and Chilton shared was an ability to straddle the line between success and failure, to articulate that process in unflinchingly honest songs, and to have listeners identify with their sadness and anger.

Kurt Cobain's journey from a high school underachiever (weathering abuse in an impoverished out-of-the-way town) to a worldwide megastar (hounded by the press, ravaged by drug addiction, and destined for early death) is a well-rehearsed American story. Rebellion strikes a chord with masses of young people, only to be quickly identified and co-opted by marketing monsters with dollar signs for eyes. The rebel artist suffers the consequences of misunderstanding and exploitation. Behind the psychological aspects of this artist's rise and fall lies a sociological case study, one that Charles Cross, more than any other Cobain biographer, rigorously pursues. In fact, up until the time he formed Nirvana and found success, Cobain's story resembles that of the Bergenfield teens. And although he seemed reluctant to revisit his painful adolescence in interviews with the rock press, in several of his songs Cobain did just that, sharing a profound inner hurt, a feeling of worthlessness that never really went away.

Alex Chilton's teenage years were markedly different, and his long decline offers an interesting contrast to Cobain's meteoric rise and fall. Chilton's parents encouraged aesthetic repartee in their Memphis home, a bohemian enclave that functioned as an art gallery and an informal salon, through which many a jazz musician passed. When Kurt Cobain was sixteen, he was failing school. He was also homeless and spending hours alone underneath a bridge. When Chilton was sixteen, he too was flunking out. Yet he had a #1 single with the Box Tops. He basked in adulation while performing on tour, hanging out with the Beach Boys. Alas, fortune's wheel turned, and a decade later in the trajectory of each man's life, the roles had reversed. In his mid-twenties, Kurt Cobain was arguably the most popular musician in America (having dislodged Michael Jackson from the top of the Billboard album chart). Chilton in his mid-twenties was reeling from the commercial failure of his band, which bore the ironic moniker Big Star, sinking deeper into addiction and depression. Chilton's bitter-grapes withdrawal from rock star ambition was hauntingly rendered in one of the great "lost albums" of the 1970s, *3rd*, also known as *Sister Lovers*. Cobain's bitterness found its fullest expression on his group's final studio album, *In Utero*, which reached #1 but intentionally alienated the bandwagon listeners Cobain so despised.

In the biographies by Cross and George-Warren, the spiraling lives of Cobain and Chilton are chronicled empathetically, without sensationalism. Yet as I read this work, I kept wondering how a novelist might render such fraught musical journeys. Several fiction writers born in the 1960s (Zachary Lazar, Michael Chabon, Jonathan Lethem, and Jennifer Egan) have done just that, inhabiting the lives of musicians, producers, or listeners, as the spirit moved them. For me, the best fiction about rock weaves the music into cultural contexts, as happens in Dana Spiotta's *Eat the Document* (2006) and Eleanor Henderson's *Ten Thousand Saints* (2011). The wise teenage characters in these novels show that whether we are making music or simply listening to it, rock and roll facilitates the alternative fictions Americans have always craved. Through music, we see ourselves as key players in fantastical narratives, especially when we are young. Whether it is the dreamiest 1960s pop or the brashest 1980s hardcore, rock welcomes isolated teens into dynamic force fields.

The books and films I highlight in this chapter comprise a diverse lot, but each honors lives shaped by rock music and does so with style, verve, and originality. Memoir, sociology, biography, and fiction: each of these genres accommodates the maverick nature of rock artists and explains our attraction to them. Aided by Patti Smith, Ann Powers, Donna Gaines, Charles Cross, Holly George-Warren, Dana Spiotta, and Eleanor Henderson, I have rekindled in my own memory the fruitful intersections of independence and communal bonding, intellectual growth and sensory euphoria that I experienced in the heyday of Generation X.

The personal pronouns in the title of Ann Powers's *Weird Like Us: My Bohemian America* imply that the book will be both memoir and social history. Populated with folks Powers befriended on her journey toward adulthood, *Weird Like Us* shows that an artist's sense of self is reliant on the people she encounters and nurtures. We are fortunate with Powers and Patti Smith (in *Just Kids*) to have a written record of how such interchanges occur. Many years earlier, another Catholic girl, Mary McCarthy, titled one of her memoirs *How I Grew*, and this is an apt description of what Smith and Powers convey in their revealing books.

An openhearted personal chronicle, *Just Kids* won a National Book Award in 2010. Published a decade after *Weird Like Us*, it describes the experiences of an earlier generation, groundbreaking moments that made Powers's book possible. Happily, she doesn't crow about it. Smith is a Baby Boomer, born in 1946, but as a punk pioneer she is less interested in reflecting 1960s idealism than she is in pursuing edgier expressions of personal freedom. If her tale of leaving a dead-end situation in South Jersey to pursue the artist's life in the big city seems overly familiar, it is also, by virtue of her imagination and warmth, never boring, never trite.

Like many teenagers who have yet to find like-minded compatriots, Smith possessed an independent perspective that assuaged her social isolation. Looking back, she never engages in self-pity, probably because she found the right balance. Smith was fiercely determined to "enter the fraternity of the artist: the hunger, their manner of dress, their process and prayers" (12). But she rarely denigrated those who chose different paths, except to fight back against narrow-minded people unwilling to grant her the same leeway. Consider her early prose poem "Piss Factory," an extended rant against petty worldviews. We learn that Smith's artistic stance did not sit well with her fellow factory workers, illiterate women who teased her for reading Rimbaud at lunch break and who once pushed her head inside a toilet bowl (23). She got out, and in the 1970s her memory was written down and set to music. Suffice it to say, Smith's defiant stance met with greater approval at the Mercer Arts Center in Lower Manhattan, where she performed "Piss Factory" on a bill with the New York Dolls (218).

Ever proud, Smith was willing to endure homelessness in New York City rather than suffer in her hometown. Her first morning in the city, she awoke alone on a brownstone stoop. It was Independence Day 1967, and radio stations broadcast her tale. The Beatles' "She's Leaving Home" was popular. So was Bobbie Gentry's "Ode to Billie Joe," a song about a daughter whose family remained clueless about the trouble she shared with the departed title character. "Tears of Rage," yet another song about a wayward daughter, was composed around this time by Bob Dylan and secretly recorded with the Band in Woodstock. In a sugary pop song that made the Top Ten, Scott McKenzie promised young runaways that if they put flowers in their hair and traveled to San Francisco, they were sure to meet some gentle people. Smith's situation in New York City was not as neatly encapsulated, but in *Just Kids* she does a marvelous job recounting what it meant, at that time, to live on your own:

> I can't say I fit in, but I felt safe. No one noticed me. I could move freely. There was a roving community of young people, sleeping in the parks, in makeshift tents, the new immigrants invading the East Village. I wasn't kin to these people, but because of the free-floating atmosphere, I could roam within it. I had faith. I sensed no danger in the city, and I never encountered any. I had nothing to offer a thief and didn't fear men on the prowl. I wasn't of interest to anyone, and that worked in my favor for the first few weeks of July when I bummed around, free to explore by day, sleeping where I could at night, I sought door wells, subway cars, even a graveyard. Startled awake beneath the city sky or being shaken by a strange hand. Time to move along. (30–31)

After meeting Robert Mapplethorpe, Smith shared her journey to artistry. "I don't think, I feel," Mapplethorpe told Smith (71), evoking faith in personal intuition. Mapplethorpe may have feigned jealousy when Smith captured popular success, but the companions always supported each other while ensconced in the secure nest bohemia provided. "Nobody sees as we do," Mapplethorpe reminded Smith (80, 104). In actuality, the artists around them (Bobby Neuwirth, Sam Shepard, Harry Smith, Allen Ginsberg, and Jim Carroll) subscribed to the same mantra. Smith wasn't in a piss factory anymore

Like Smith, Ann Powers left her blue-collar Catholic family to pursue an artist's life in a major metropolitan area while never fully abandoning her parents or their values. Was she a bad kid trying to be good or a good kid trying to be bad? For Powers, as for Smith or Mapplethorpe, it was a matter of semantics. Following aesthetic passions to their conclusion was key. "I drew no line between life and art," Smith confesses in her memoir, and we can see in her songwriting, and in the creative work she admires, that hers was no mere pose (2010, 9, 186, 188). Powers saw her poetry go nowhere, and yet she remained dedicated to the arts and to the art of self-expression. In *Weird Like Us*, she talks of "turning everyday life into an art project" (2001, 122), and for her, rock journalism was part of the mix. Powers wrote for *The Rocket*, various Bay Area weeklies, *The New York Times*, and *The Village Voice* before penning her memoir.

Crucial to Powers's recollections of bohemia is the ideal of "sustainable youth" (4), which she admits borrowing from Robert Christgau, her editor at the *Voice*. For Gen Xers, Powers says, youthful impulse was complicated by the uncertain legacy Boomers bequeathed. Powers and I were born in 1964, the year the Baby Boom officially ended. When it came to models of rebellion, we knew we could not live without the older Boomers, and yet living by their codes could seem confusing.[1] Watching Boomers exchange countercultural idealism for narcissism during the Me Generation galvanized punk and indie communities seeking an alternative culture all their own. The ideal of sustainable youth was thus modified. "The perception of adulthood as a phase when questioning gives way to cool contentment doesn't make sense in an era when no basics, not your dress code nor your family structure nor the shape of your career, are solidly in place," Powers writes. "Slackers refuse to act like grown-ups because they believe that to do so would be to lie" (206).

That youthful spirit shaped the indie underground from 1981 to 1991, a decade Michael Azerrad chronicles in *Our Band Could Be Your Life*. Betrayed by the incomplete revolution put into motion by the Boomers, Gen Xers sought new roads to freedom. The decision was more practical than conceptual. For Dean Wareham, leader of the seminal indie bands Galaxie 500 and Luna, "there was no such thing as being proud to be indie. There was simply no other option at the time" (2009, 109). Perhaps Wareham believes that nobody but a damn fool ever performed music, or wrote about it, for anything other than money. Fugazi's indie-cred model doesn't work for everybody, he says (147). Powers herself does not believe rock is at any level divorced from commerce, but she honors the spirit of independent artistry anyway. "Rock and roll showed me how to be something else," Powers declares in *Weird Like Us* (30).

Growing disaffected with "academia's knotty lingo" after entering UC Berkeley's graduate program in English, Powers recalls that she ditched her assigned readings and "spent more time with the rock criticism of Greil Marcus, Robert Christgau, Lester Bangs, Simon Frith, and Ellen Willis, which taught me that writing about music was really just a way of writing about the world—a bastard way, it's true, but there were possibilities in that very border identity." Academia couldn't hold a candle to the vision burning in her mind: "I realized that selling out its elitist rules meant joining a much larger social dialogue" (254).[2] In my own weird way, I appreciate her choice. In 1992, when Powers left UC Berkeley to work for the *New York Times*, I was heading west to pursue graduate study at another UC campus. Our crossed paths mark a convergence, a pivot point where a love of music and intellectual inquiry find happy balance, a prime motivation for *It's Just the Normal Noises*.

It helps to have specific spots on which to pivot. The clubs hosting indie rock shows were important. But so were group houses where outsiders gathered to create a scene. Just as post-punk fans were busy "getting awesome" during concerts, the folks who broke bread in group houses and toiled in alternative working environments found strength in numbers, forging new ways of belonging, tweaking 1960s communal ideals to fit new realities.[3] We made do. Albums stacked against the wall were regarded as furniture, as evident in the film adaptation of Nick Hornby's *High Fidelity*. Discs were flipped and paperbacks tented as friends turned each other on to something new. "I always figured that was the best thing that could happen to you, to be caught up with a group of people with heroic enthusiasm for what they're doing," Memphis musician Randall Lyon told Robert Gordon when recalling Dylan's 1966 swing through his city (2001, 133). A similar sentiment infused the domiciles of Gen X bohemia. I need only think back to my own salad days.

"It's just the normal noises in here!" A background shout at the beginning of Tom Petty and the Heartbreakers' "Even the Losers"—a shout initially uttered on a home audiotape by guitarist Mike Campbell's wife, Marcie, who was monitoring a broken washing machine (Zanes 2016, 154)—became for inhabitants of our Rochester apartment a collective cry of joy. We could relate somehow to this mysterious exclamation emanating from the vinyl grooves. Taped to our wall was a page from a graphic novel identifying a character as a "goddamn intellectual." My housemate Chris, who posted the image and played the Petty, was exactly that. Like the persona in Petty's song, Chris showed us the stars, informally presiding over a group he tagged "the whole sick crew," borrowing from Thomas Pynchon's *V.* Music was a huge part of our lives. The hum of conversation and blare of LPs became virtually indistinguishable. In the summer of 1987 we created our own Summer of Love, twenty years after the official version. Petty was a mainstream choice, of course, and so was Zeppelin, however ironic we claimed to be when taking discs from album sleeves (or naming our houseplant "Robert"). Other selections—Captain Beefheart, the Flying Burrito Brothers, Jonathan Richman, Scruffy the Cat, and Opal—were not as mainstream. Neither were Hüsker Dü or the Replacements, despite their recent signings to major labels, nor Bobby "Blue" Bland and Taj Mahal. As the music played, poetry by Robert Creeley, W. S. Merwin, and Carolyn Forché got passed around, as did Bard paperbacks by Latin American novelists. If you are what you eat, I was toasted pita smeared with honey and washed down with black coffee. Smokes and drugs were available, but I held to my athlete's code. We were all fortified by a diet of music, literature, and conversation. That's what we called normal.

It's easy to grow nostalgic for a time when having nothing meant having everything. It's a bit harder to admit, as Kim Gordon does, that "all that [youthful] idealism is someone else's now." Living on grits, noodles, onions, potatoes, pizza, and hot dogs, walking fifty blocks home from part-time jobs because subway tokens cost too much: that's not a life to which Gordon, now in her sixties, can return, although it's still "alive in [her] head" (2015, 11). Something of those days just stays with you. In *Just Kids*, Smith recalls the humble situations she shared with Mapplethorpe, beginning with an apartment at 160 Hall Street in Brooklyn (43–45) before recounting the atmosphere of the Chelsea Hotel, where eccentric residents and visiting artists lent color. At its worst, the bohemian hotel on Twenty-Third Street represented an art hustle, "an open market, everyone with something of himself to sell" (107). Nevertheless, the Chelsea became for Smith and Mapplethorpe a "new university" (138), a place where knowledge was easily accessed, where they felt more fully themselves. Through it all, Smith and Mapplethorpe remained locked in; others took a backseat to their special relationship. "You're my family," he told her (17). "At its best," Smith says, "our relationship was a refuge from everything, where [Robert] could hide or coil like an exhausted baby snake" (236).[4]

In *American Hardcore*, Steven Blush reveals a different set of circumstances when talking about group houses in 1980s punk communities. In the Dischord House in Washington, D.C. (where Minor Threat front man Ian MacKaye held court), the Church and the Black Hole in Southern California (the former featured in the documentary film *The Decline of Western Civilization*), and the infamous Vats squat in San Francisco, hardcore kids eked out a meager existence with fellow transients (Blush 2001, 75, 88, 143, 145). These houses doubled as rehearsal spaces and as default hotels whenever touring bands arrived by the vanload. Electricity and heat were often unavailable. "We're Desperate" by X was one theme song, since any given week, hardcore kids needed a new address.

The houses Powers inhabited in San Francisco seem sunny and bright by comparison. As rotating casts of young people followed their dreams, Powers identified "one of the first tasks any would-be bohemian faces: to create a sense of home that lasts while your life changes, to cultivate a family spirit beyond the boundaries of the white picket fence" (2001, 40–41). Despite the taken-for-granted aspects that infuse all partnerships, she found "a family that was a reverie, conjured up within a whimsical Eden where we all named ourselves" (48). Her group house bliss had several iterations: in the Mission District, in the Western Addition, and on Steiner Street. "Home was no board game here," Powers says of the Steiner Street house, "not when you had people who'd stake their lives to determine home's definition. The dominant personalities on Steiner Street made pledges that intense" (56). Sacrifice and hard work were necessary. The experiment paid off when the definition of family expanded beyond what was previously known. "These new clans are not simply accidental formations," Powers enthuses; "they represent self-conscious choices to remake society from within its most personal sphere" (71). Or as Rob Sheffield said, reviewing Kristin Hersh's memoir, "The kids took care of each other because they knew nobody else would" (2010).

Group houses accommodated a hodgepodge of influences. In a chapter entitled "Soul Trash," Powers describes the vintage clothing and recycled furniture lending the shabby abodes their deep culture, and their inhabitants a necessary sense of security. Amid the bohemian's scramble for freedom lies a desire for something meaningful and lasting, something that has weathered the storm and has a survivor's tale to tell. "Homemaking as a popular art form" requires of Powers and her housemates curatorial practices reminiscent of Frankfurt School theorist Walter Benjamin, who was enamored with authenticity and aura. As Powers muses:

> If the modern condition is slippery loneliness, with people roaming from connection to connection wondering why all this contact doesn't satisfy, treasured objects form the record of our desire to rest. Not the things we acquire to keep moving—the new car, the status-proving gizmos, the keep-up-with-the-Joneses home furnishings—but those that weigh us down and make us more ourselves. A pile of rocks gathered from every beach I've ever walked, a shelf full of books on medieval saints, my father's high-school pin, every record Brian Eno has ever made, the plastic animals from atop the ice cream cake at my sixteenth birthday party: these are my rabbit's feet, guarding me against the great danger in this crowded world: that I'll lose myself. They are also messages, the first words in all my stories, my biography in junk. Gifts we share in the showing, rather than through physical exchange, they allow us to know each other in ways that our running, quotidian selves can't share. Come visit me and stay awhile, and I'll take you through my collection. And you, among your things, could do the same for me. (194)

I quote the paragraph in full because to leave out any of the collected items would give short shrift to the life they help narrate. With such menageries, Powers and her friends could adopt an experimental identity, a fluid center, knowing they were safely anchored by past impressions. "Every passion borders on the chaotic," wrote Benjamin, "but the collector's passion borders on the chaos of memories" (quoted in Powers, 214).[5] Collecting also nurtures a sense of home. "If you don't have a family, or are trying to break away from them, creating your own environment is really important," a cohort of Powers says (195).

The danger is solipsism. Despite her voluntary poverty, Powers tried daily to "will glamour into being" (58), and with her friends at Planet Records, to "[make] our work lives into a walking theater piece" (163). She admits that one friend's identity is "overshadowed by the aura of her persona," only to assert that in the "thrifting life," fluctuation of identity is not really troubling (197–98). You wear someone else's discarded clothes and play at that identity until you discard it. Over time, playacting becomes the norm, and fixed identity the deviation. Renowned New York City barfly Joe Gould once said that being a bohemian meant making a spectacle of oneself. Powers and her friends "considered everyone else the spectacle, and ourselves their most vocal critics" (58).

Youth itself is a spectacle. "Bastards of Young," a chapter titled after a Replacements song, centers on the extended adolescence Gen Xers regarded as their birthright. Dressing as they did when they were twelve (in Keds sneakers or baby doll dresses), delving into 1970s trivia derived from Afterschool Specials and H.R. Pufnstuf cartoons, Powers and her peers embraced irony as a protective cover for juvenile fantasies and distanced themselves from the previous generation's puerile excesses, cast here as smug and self-serving. Powers shows how rock is a manifestation of those desires, since "rock stars are our avatars of perpetual adolescence" (224). Powers seeks "sustainable youth" but rejects "thoughtless immaturity" (233). She wants a "working definition of 'adult'" that confounds the expectations of her elders:

> What few people have grasped is that the endless adolescence of Generation X was never meant to be taken literally; it is a kind of ritual, the public interrogation of a myth. On one level, this has meant scrambling and unscrambling these images, scrutinizing vintage and contemporary visions of growing up to get at their changing meanings. We are trying to distill some truth from these stories and signs, to see what it might be like to reach adulthood free of habit, without our suits already picked out. (209)

Powers believes that punk and indie rock musicians in particular have evaded the clichés of juvenile fantasy. "As the first generation of rock-and-roll bohemians to watch many of their elders turn sustainable youth into simple vanity," she notes, "American punks were the first to see the negative aspects of perpetual adolescence as well as its promises, and to begin seeking a balance between green impudence and mellow resignation" (211). Wised-up to the pitfalls of hippie self-righteousness and wanting to pursue their "life's work" instead of dreary careers, Generation X musicians, writers, and photographers share with first-generation punks an antipathy toward facile escapism. "Punk rock values are timeless," says Jone, a musician Powers interviews. They include "integrity, a sense of yourself, not being afraid to challenge authority or to question why. Taking an active part in your life, rather than just being a consumer … And to feel really strongly, even if you change your opinion" (230).

It was at age twenty-seven, a fateful time for ill-starred rockers, that Powers decided on another path, crossing the border into "Upper Bohemia." Having completed a master's degree in literature at Berkeley, she opted out of the doctoral program and traded occasional review work for a high-profile job as pop music critic at the *New York Times*. Hence the title of her final chapter, "Selling Out." "Tainted by money, understandable to almost anyone, journalism was a sold-out form," she explains, admitting that her "intense identification with the hidden and the misfit gave way whenever someone or something made me feel as if I'd never be weird enough" (252–53). But at some point you have to say goodbye. You have to admit that you care about the future. Powers's leave-taking is not unlike the one Sleater-Kinney's Carrie Brownstein describes:

> Olympia had been a valuable incubator, but by the time I was in my late twenties, it felt decidedly claustrophobic … At a certain point, I felt too old to hang with the new recruits, too ambivalent toward the quirkiness that small-town DIY life engenders, too young to settle down, too irked by the self-aware preciousness of it all. Art communities and music scenes want to pretend like they don't care, but they will also tell you louder and more frequently that anyone that they DON'T CARE. These self-aware scenes are as cool as a secret handshake and a sly shared gesture of recognition, but at some point I was done living inside the town equivalent of a wink. (2015, 178–79)

Elsewhere, Brownstein has said, "You get in these scenes and you realize, no, I've gone from one set of rules and regulations and codifications of how you should dress and what you should know to another … Am I liking the right song on the right record? Have I picked the right year to stop liking the band?" (quoted in Marcus 2015a, 515). At the *Times*, Powers's role involved splitting the difference between Brownstein's concerns about scenes and trumpeting the music coming out of them.

Powers's rise from the indie underground came at a propitious time. The emergence of niche marketing fooled consumers who believed their purchases represented individual lifestyle choices. Indie music was "the perfect mousetrap for college-aged rock fans," Powers explains (2001, 242), and however much its bohemian ethos railed against material success, people in the industry were dedicated to making money off it. Even before "alternative" became a "corporate-tourist take on indie rock," bands leapt to major labels to see whether indie visions could survive big-budget expectations. The results for Hüsker Dü and the Replacements were "disastrous," Powers recalls, and "their horror stories became fodder for anti-major purists" (243). Granted, some of Paul Westerberg's best songs ("Skyway," "Here Comes a Regular") appeared on the Replacements' major label releases, but the consensus among longtime fans was that he had become too sensitive and that the rest of the band had tamped down their raucous roar in a shameless quest for airplay. In indie circles, the new stuff sounded like treason.

Aware of this trend, Powers sought a comfortable position in corporate journalism that didn't compromise her credibility. She mentions Barbara O'Dair (*Orange County Register*; *Entertainment Weekly*; *Rolling Stone*; *Us*) and Holly George-Warren (Rolling Stone Press) as exemplary in this regard. O'Dair "entered the inner circles of popular media the way a spy-movie heroine infiltrates a foreign embassy" (258), dropping out of Princeton to explore the East Village punk scene, then landing jobs at *High Times* and the *Village Voice*, where unfair labor practices led her to file a sex discrimination lawsuit. Then she took a hairpin turn, choosing to write for apolitical or even conservative publications, bringing a taste of the bohemian life to readers who would otherwise remain unaware or wary of the subject. George-Warren's route to mainstream success is similarly inspiring. A political activist in Chapel Hill frustrated with the post-1960s meltdown of idealism, George-Warren heard Patti Smith sing and decided to move to New York to become a punk rocker. While there, she began writing journalism. Eventually, she traded freelance work for a steady job at *Rolling Stone*, introducing edgier artists like Nick Cave to its aging, affluent readership. For Powers, O'Dair and George-Warren proved that indie spirit could find stability and balance long after the heady days of youthful waywardness had passed. "Rap sheets like [theirs] aren't that rare in Upper Bohemia," Powers maintains. "Some culture-industry insiders are calculating sharks who claw their way to the top on broken promises. But it's just as common to find people who stumbled into their careers while running after some ruling passion" (260). It's a story that gives hope to transitioning adults.

Gen X films of the early 1990s such as *Slacker* or *Singles* made a life of drift seem attractive. O'Dair, George-Warren, and Powers clearly rode that drift to successful careers. But another subset of Gen X youth was not so lucky. Regularly disparaged in mainstream culture, their music, clothing, and politics were also labeled retrograde by trendy underground types. These kids were suburban. They listened to heavy metal. They didn't do well in school or sports. "Who will be king and queen of the outcast teens?" Kurt Cobain asked, addressing no one in particular. Cobain excised that line from "Smells Like Teen Spirit," but the question has been asked since *Blackboard Jungle* and wrapped up with rock and roll all the while.

The teenage alienation on display in John Hughes's film *The Breakfast Club* offers a parallel. Five archetypes of high school society are subjected to Saturday detention and forced for eight hours to co-exist. It's heartwarming, if far-fetched, that they begin to understand one another. As high school upperclassmen in 1985, they are about the same age as Kurt Cobain. Delivering performances that exceeded anything else on their resumes, five Brat Pack actors depict an "athlete," a "princess," a "brain," a "basket case," and a "criminal." Viewers who envision the future of these students might venture that the first three will find some measure of success. The jock will get an athletic scholarship. The brain will attend a prestigious college. The homecoming princess, who comes from money (witness the diamond earrings), will move in privileged society, anchoring herself in a traditional marriage. But the other characters present a conundrum. The "basket case" is so marginalized in high school as to seem mute. She has artistic talent, though, and creative vision. Perhaps, if she can transport herself to the right bohemian enclave or an art school, she has a shot at happiness. Then again, at the end of the film, she receives a fashion makeover from the princess and kisses the jock, so maybe she's headed for white-bread conformity after all.[6] The "criminal" character, John Bender, has the darkest horizon. "You want to see something funny?" the angry principal tells the kids assembled at detention. "You go and visit Bender in five years." Trouble is, a lot of elites do find Bender's story "funny," and that's a shame. Unlike the stories Patti Smith and Ann Powers tell, Bender's brand of rebellion rarely finds traction with intellectuals and tastemakers. Assaulted physically and verbally at home, denied respect at school by teachers and coaches who expect him to toe the line, Bender is misunderstood and dispossessed. In academia, his story is often overlooked.

Fortunately, Donna Gaines's 1991 book *Teenage Wasteland* offers an incisive study of youth like Bender, heavy metal kids forced into each other's company by a society that casts them aside. No matter that Bender's flannel outfit would reappear in the pages of *Vogue* after the grunge movement made sloppy apparel fashionable. No matter that heavy metal, along with hardcore and post-punk, fed the sludgy sound of Seattle stalwarts Mudhoney, Soundgarden, Alice in Chains, and Nirvana. No matter, even, that Bender's musical tastes aren't revealed in the film (he dances to a New Wave soundtrack along with the rest). Most watching *The Breakfast Club* would identify him as a headbanger, one of the wasted. To use Gaines's terminology, Bender is not only a "loser," but also a "burnout," and more likely, due to his surly temperament and style of dress, a "dirtbag."[7] Thus labeled, where can he find empathy? In the film, the kids in detention eventually come around, accepting Bender's stories of abuse when signs (cigar burns) become undeniable, and the effect on viewers is strong. Likewise, on the page Gaines projects as much empathy as expertise when she surveys firsthand the burned out landscape of Bergenfield. "From the beginning," she claims, "I decided I didn't want to dwell too much on the negative. I wanted to understand how alienated kids survived, as well as how they were defeated ... What motivates them to be decent human beings when nobody seems to respect them or take them seriously?" (1998, 12).

Near the end of *Teenage Wasteland*, Gaines reminds her fellow Baby Boomers of the distinct challenges facing young people in Generation X (257–58), but the book is devoted to identifying a sociological split within Gen X itself. In grunge-era Seattle, "Loser" got emblazoned on tee shirts sold at Sub Pop's Lamefest concerts (Cross 2014, 132). In Austin, a character in Richard Linklater's *Slacker* called his band the Ultimate Losers (wouldn't you know it, people always misremembered the name). In Los Angeles, Beck penned "Loser" and launched his ironic postmodern song craft. Across the Atlantic, Radiohead weighed in with "Creep," another song extolling the loser's creed. Weirdly, these paeans to loser status helped artists secure major label deals. But neither Generation X's ironic appropriations of failure nor the pursuit of what Lawrence Lipton termed "dedicated intentional poverty" (quoted in Powers 2001, 57) jibed with the harsh realities faced by John Bender in *The Breakfast Club*, or with the travails faced by "suburbia's dead end kids" in *Teenage Wasteland*. In their situations, it was neither heroic nor humorous to be called a loser; it meant being insulted and forgotten. As a music journalist and street sociologist, Gaines was well-positioned to describe their plight: "I wanted to understand the existential situation they operated in—not simply as hapless losers, helpless victims, or tragic martyrs, but also as *historical actors* determined in their choices, resistant, defiant" (1998, 10).

Unlike Powers, Gaines was not a part of the generation she wrote about. She was about twenty years older than the Bergenfield teens, but her sociological training in "street work" helped her blend in to the scene, disguised as an older cousin visiting from Long Island. When the *Village Voice* assigned the Bergenfield story and linked it with "suicide clusters" affecting teens nationwide, Gaines was reluctant to accept, fearing her reportage would be exploitive. But eventually she saw an opportunity to overturn misperceptions of "troubled losers" (6).

Moving beyond clichéd narratives of failure, Gaines taps an anthropological vocabulary to describe the culture of suburban heavy metal kids. Much as Steven Blush sought a "tribal" understanding of hardcore scenes, Gaines studies "archaeological leavings" in 7-Eleven parking lots and deciphers "cave renderings" inked on nearby walls. "I know from the pose, the clothes, the turf," she says. "Yep, in another age they'd be hitters or greasers or hippies or heads or freaks. On another coast—they'd be stoners. Archenemies of jocks, dexters, rah-rahs, or socs for all eternity" (57). Her classifications suggest a scientific approach, but Gaines lets emotion guide her through various street hassles. At one point she talks of a "transhistorical bond among adventurous girls," claiming she "would never allow young women to be left hung anywhere by guys," whether that meant being abandoned or mistreated, her own research be damned (227). Bonding over the accessories she wore (a Motorhead pin, a skull ring) and exploring the lineage of favorite bands, Gaines earns the trust of the Bergenfield teens and accompanies them to favorite hangouts, including the 7-Eleven (celebrated in many a hardcore song) and the spot where local teens committed suicide. "Soon, this relationship between free space and the recent teen deaths in Bergenfield became overwhelmingly apparent," Gaines says. "Everywhere people partied, they mourned" (52).

Like punks in San Francisco and Los Angeles, heavy metal kids in Jersey appropriated an empty edifice, simply called the Building, as a squat, a free zone where they could make up their own rules and escape tormentors.[8] Yet according to Gaines, these suburban burnouts and dirtbags possessed none of the political impulses driving hardcore kids to live in squats. Neither did they enjoy the reassurances granted Baby Boomer rebels. In *A Misfit's Manifesto*, Gaines shares stories of hanging out with working-class teens at Rockaway Beach in the late 1960s. In *Teenage Wasteland*, she looks back and realizes that despite their aimlessness, she and her peers were riding a cultural groundswell:

> In 1968, there were other choices. If you weren't very spectacular in the eyes of the authorities, it meant nothing and you could care less. Because you knew you were part of something much more grand, you could care less about the bullshitty cliques in your dumb old high school … Intellectuals and activists at the universities stood behind you. They encouraged you to believe that you had a handle on the truth. (1998, 97)

Back in the 1960s, Gaines says, "even marginal affiliation with the subculture gave youth permission to feel their instincts were correct. And because of the ties to the universities, you were intellectually, politically, and morally very cool." By the late 1980s, however, radical chic did not include the white working class. If Bergenfield's kids compared their brand of nihilism with that of the 1960s hippies and 1970s punks, Gaines muses, they would see that they adhered to no political program, no higher principle (99). But that does not mean their lives are without purpose. Indeed, Gaines welcomes their lack of pretense, their suspicion of self-righteousness and "bogus idealism" (197).[9] She admires their humanity and wants to know how they arrived at their predicament.

In *The Breakfast Club*, John Bender has a conversation with the school janitor, Carl. Like many such exchanges in the film, a character's stab at humor exposes his sadness and insecurity. "How does one become a janitor?" Bender asks Carl, with mock seriousness. "You want to be a janitor?" Carl replies. Bender pounces with a stinging rejoinder, meant to impress his peers: "No, I just want to know how one *becomes* a janitor." Introducing *Teenage Wasteland*, Gaines similarly wonders, "How did the kids in Bergenfield become burnouts?" (10). She avoids Bender's sneering tone, maybe because she is on the other end of the age spectrum. Like Carl the janitor, Gaines can recall vividly the spaces teens occupy and the problems they confront. Gaines wants to help the Bergenfield kids, but at moments of intervention she thinks it best to let the kids figure it out for themselves. A boy named Joe tells a story that sounds like it could have come from Bender's mouth: "My dad pulled me out of bed this morning, at 5 a.m., and called me a scumbag" (61).[10] Beaten down by family and "the system," Joe has already given up on life, and he flinches when Gaines tells him he is being too passive, that he is letting his tormentors write history. But then, instead of dispensing further advice or measuring Joe's predicament against Boomer rebellion, Gaines steps back, grows silent, and becomes a kid again:

> This was my moment to explain everything to them, but I couldn't. I couldn't say anything. This is stuff you can never put into words … It is an emptiness, an ache, and it is unspoken. These are the hidden injuries of youth, the scars that don't show. The creepy feelings that will follow you through life. Set up from the start to carry the burdens of your fucked-up family and your stained class, you play a loser's game and then you blame yourself, you're worthless. I wanted to stop them from feeling this way by saying something very real and strong to make them proud of being themselves, rather than ashamed.
>
> I had spent years trying to figure out how to put this into the words that might have made sense to me when I was a teenager and felt like this—like Joe and Nicky do now. But I couldn't say anything. (1998, 61–62)

The Bergenfield kids appreciate Gaines's restraint. For support, they turn to each other, and also, importantly, to music. Their suicide pact demanded that they die together, but prior to that they listened to music together, fighting off the powers that be, assembling their own belief system with the help of meaningful lyrics. "When kids in America learned anything about right and wrong in the brutal 1980s, they learned it from their bands," Gaines asserts. Musicians talked frankly about "the real things that threatened kids: drug pushers, Army recruiters, spiritual isolation, nuclear holocaust, child sexual abuse, mental hospitals" (202–3). Clearly, Gaines's tale has a soundtrack strikingly different from the one Powers offers: Ozzy Osbourne, Twisted Sister, Mötley Crüe, and king of them all, Metallica. The upshot for Gaines: "Heavy metal is white suburban soul music" (181). As journalist Charles Young explained in an otherwise tone-deaf *20/20* feature, hosted by Stone Phillips, about teenage suicide and its link to music:

> Heavy metal speaks to the anger and despair of teenagers today, the way the blues used to speak to the despair and anger of black people in the south. Without heavy metal there would be—there would probably be a lot more suicides, because metal and certain other forms of rock give

teenagers something to believe in that they get no place else. (quoted in Gaines 1998, 209)

As a music journalist, Gaines knows how to digest such information. "To the college/radio-trained ear looking for socially progressive rock product, heavy metal has always meant bad politics." Gaines knows that critics dismiss metal as "mindless" and "vulgar," as "bread and circuses for turnpike trash" (196). Hardcore punk, by contrast, is praised for its positive, political vibe, its DIY self-sufficiency. Rough, rowdy, and rigidly factionalized, hardcore kids intrigued Boomer leftists in a way heavy metal youth never did. At the same time, hardcore enthusiasts separated themselves from 1960s leftist culture, and they rarely admitted adults into their circles. Among kids, thrash metal—a harsh combination of social outrage and personal remorse—went partway toward bridging the divide, fusing elements of heavy metal and hardcore. Metallica, for instance, brought diverse groups together, but usually hardcore devotees and metal fans lived by their own codes.

Gaines ran up against these barriers. She learned that a lot of music she thought spoke to teenage alienation (by DIY trailblazers such as Butthole Surfers, Sonic Youth, and Big Black) simply does not apply in turnpike suburbia. When they listened to Gaines's mix tape of indie bands, the Bergenfield kids heard "droney" noise (66).[11] The stud rock posturing of metal did more for their self-image and spoke more directly to their everyday realities. Early in their career, indie heroes the Replacements paid homage to convenience stores ("Customer," a much funnier version of the Clash's "Lost in the Supermarket"), cheap marijuana ("I Bought a Headache"; "Dope Smoking Moron"), traffic violations ("Run It"), dumb household chores (*Sorry Ma, Forgot to Take Out the Trash*), and bad working conditions ("Goddamn Job"). But by and large, the college radio crowd left this subject matter to hardcore and heavy metal groups, who forged a bond with burnouts by singing about common troubles, including suicide (Metallica's "Fade to Black"). When the suicide pact carried out by four Bergenfield teens brought nationwide attention to a population the locals had done their best to ignore, parents and other "concerned" adults (like Tipper Gore of Parents Music Resource Center) were quick to blame heavy metal music.[12] But as local rocker Billy Milano noted, "The suicide rate would be higher if kids didn't have music" (quoted in Gaines 1998, 213).

The story of Kurt Cobain, one of rock's most famous suicides, parallels that of the Bergenfield teens. Cobain claimed lineage with punk and hardcore bands, wearing their concert tee shirts and covering their songs even after he garnered fame with Nirvana. But he was a heavy metal fan as a teenager, suffering the same abuse Gaines exposed in *Teenage Wasteland*, the first edition of which was published shortly before Cobain became a star.[13] In his town, he was not considered a trendsetter. On the contrary, he was labeled a loser. As Gaines wrote in an afterword to the 1998 edition of *Teenage Wasteland*, Cobain never forgot where he came from; he gave hope and voice to "kids trapped in bad lives across America's nonurban wastelands." As "lumpenprole hero," he "transformed a kid's private hell into a generation's collective howl" (271–72). But how can rock writers interpret such a howl?

Peter Guralnick told me that when he transitioned from journalism to biography he realized he could no longer use the present tense to capture the immediacy of a story (2010, 8/14 interview). History had invaded his writing, bringing with it responsibility and the necessity of reflection. Guralnick found a good balance, elevating discourse on rock and soul from the inside out. As young rock journalists seeking to retain their indie credibility, Kurt Cobain's biographers faced similar challenges.

With his 2001 book *Our Band Could Be Your Life*, Michael Azerrad fashioned a classic, profiling thirteen bands that precipitated the rise of alternative rock (before it became known as such) from 1981 to 1991. Azerrad gained prominence at *Rolling Stone*, and it was there, in April 1992, that he scored a major scoop: an interview with Kurt Cobain. Up to that point, Cobain had acceded only to fanzines and niche publications like *Sassy*, resolutely avoiding the mainstream press. In the cover photograph, Cobain reminded *Rolling Stone* readers of his underlying distrust, wearing beneath his trademark cardigan a tee shirt emblazoned (DIY style, in permanent marker) with the words "Corporate Magazines Still Suck."[14] Cobain's reasoning went beyond usual Boomer/Gen X tensions. When Britain's *Melody Maker* profiled Seattle bands in 1989, Everett True, a future Nirvana biographer, expressed classist bias. "You're talking about four guys … who, if they weren't doing this, would be working in a supermarket, or lumber yard, or fixing cars" (quoted in Cross 2014, 133). No matter that Cobain's father had held two of those jobs, or that his friend Buzz Osborne, leader of the Melvins, held the third, it was True's speculative tone that hurt. We see here the condescension affecting Bergenfield's teens. True probably believed he was honoring Nirvana's authenticity. But as a compliment, his was backhanded at best.

Azerrad's 1993 book, *Come As You Are: The Story of Nirvana*, contains a different set of flaws. Published while Cobain's fame was at its pinnacle, *Come As You Are* misses its chance, valorizing the outrageous aspects of rock star behavior (drug use, profligate spending, rude banter) and offering insipid analyses from Cobain himself as to what his songs really mean. Azerrad was granted interviews and allowed access to personal materials, with the presumption (some have said) that he would portray Cobain in a positive light. As he admits in an afterword to the 2001 edition, "My being a journalist and my friendship with Kurt were on an inevitable collision course." Azerrad reveals that when he talked to CNN following Cobain's suicide attempt in Rome in March 1994, he angered Courtney Love and lost contact with Kurt during his few remaining weeks (2001, 344). But that did not affect *Come As You Are*, published six months prior; it reads like a commissioned portrait.

Everett True, meanwhile, did not publish *Nirvana: The Biography* until almost twenty years after his *Melody Maker* dispatch. Sadly, his book reads like a sour grapes riposte to Cobain's "official biographer," Charles Cross, who is never mentioned by name. In *Heavier Than Heaven* (originally published in 2001), Cross splits the difference between the Azerrad and True books, both in terms of publication dates and in overall tone. Unlike the books by Azerrad and True, *Heavier Than Heaven* is a biography of Cobain rather than a story of the band, and that may account for its gravitas. Cross has his roots in journalism, having edited *The Rocket* during the grunge heyday, but like Guralnick, he transitioned well to biography, offering an empathetic analysis of an influential musician, his social circumstances, and his cultural importance.

In "Serve the Servants," a track from *In Utero* (1993). Cobain alludes facetiously to the lucrative success of "Smells Like Teen Spirit." Cross shows that the singer's "teenage angst" was in truth deeply seated. In rural Washington State, teenagers like Cobain found the pitfalls of poverty difficult to escape. Nirvana's second drummer, Chad Channing, grew up on affluent Bainbridge Island, near Seattle. When he was summoned to Aberdeen for band rehearsals, he registered shock over what he encountered. "I was like stepping into the south side of the Bronx," Channing told Cross. "All of a sudden you have this instant slum" (quoted in Cross 2014, 108). Cobain's social structure mirrored his environment. His parents divorced when he was young. His relationship with his father had always been fractious, and in time relations with his mother and stepfather deteriorated as well. As a teen, Cobain was periodically homeless, spending time under the Young Street Bridge, his travails embellished and mythologized in "Something in the Way," the brooding closing track on *Nevermind* (1991). Bandmate and high school friend Krist Novoselic is pretty sure Cobain never actually slept under the bridge (Cross 2014, 58–59), but Azerrad fails to question any of Cobain's autobiographical enhancements (2001, 37), which included being beaten up by local teenagers and pawning his stepfather's gun to buy his first guitar (or was it an amplifier?). Excoriated by True for getting the latter story wrong, Cross at least recognizes the purpose of the anecdote.[15] "In this one story," Cross says, "were all the elements of how [Cobain] wished to be perceived as an artist—someone who turned redneck swords into punk rock plowshares" (2014, 53).[16]

Cobain was the ultimate outsider. His mother kicked him out of the house once he dropped out of school and failed to get a job. Parents of friends likewise sent him packing after he violated house rules one too many times. Cobain proceeded to collect food stamps. Before long, he was working as a janitor in his old high school, like Carl in *The Breakfast Club*, which came out that year, except that Cobain was the same age as the students.[17] Yet thanks to new trends in mainstream media, especially MTV, being an outsider no longer carried such a stigma. Outsiders developed a sense of humor that was by turns self-deprecatory, defiantly proud, and highly marketable.

In Cobain's time, TV shows such as "Wayne's World" and *Beavis and Butt-Head* made basement-banished suburban offspring the ironic arbiters of cool (because they were so clearly, and refreshingly, *not* cool). "Wayne's World" debuted on *Saturday Night Live* in 1988 and rode the coattails of Aerosmith, which endorsed the show amid their unlikely comeback. The hard rock comedy sketch was still popular when Nirvana broke. In a 1992 sketch reminiscent of MTV's *Headbangers Ball* (which welcomed Pearl Jam as well as Metallica), Wayne and Garth perform Garth's minimalist power chord composition, "Pain Cave," with Garth shouting out at the break, "Eat your heart out, Nirvana!" Garth was well aware that Nirvana had recently played on *SNL* in an appearance that rivaled Elvis and the Beatles in terms of cultural impact, and now here he was, a basement bum, humorously aiming for that same pedestal. Nor was Garth alone. *Beavis and Butt-Head* debuted on MTV a year later as an animated version of Wayne and Garth's hard-rocking buddyhood. The teenage Everyman was having his day in the sun. "I know Beavis and Butt-Head," Cobain told MTV. "I grew up with people like that." So did I, along with people like Garth and John Bender. They may not have listened to the most sophisticated music, nor did they speak in the most elevated language, but Cobain knew they deserved recognition.

Nirvana's sound emerged out of a punk/metal fusion. Grunge made that fusion popular, but at first the band was on the outside looking in. They were too hip for hard rock parties in Raymond, Washington, but not nearly hip enough for the twee indie crowd in Olympia, led by Beat Happening musician and K Records impresario Calvin Johnson, who galvanized the faux-naif kids on the scene (dubbed "Calvinists"), as well as Riot Grrrl bands like Bikini Kill (Cross 2014, 101). Bravado was worn on (record) sleeves: "OLYMPIA, the birthplace of rock" read the back cover of a Kill Rock Stars release (Marcus 2014, 26). The music in Olympia was experimental and politically invested, worlds away from the culture of Aberdeen. When Cobain dated Bikini Kill's Tobi Vail, he felt intimidated by her level of education and her self-confidence (Cross 2014, 157). In an important passage, Cross shows how Cobain negotiated such stratification, especially when he left Olympia for Seattle:

> It wasn't an easy transition, because he had believed in the Calvinist indie ideals and they had served him when he needed an ideology to break out of Aberdeen. "Punk rock is freedom," he had learned, a line he would continue to repeat to any journalist who would listen. But he always knew that punk rock was a different freedom for kids who had grown up privileged. To him, punk rock was a class struggle, but that was always secondary to the struggle to pay the rent, or find a place to sleep other than in the backseat of a car. Music was more than just a fad for Kurt—it had become his only career option. (2014, 197)

The bitter irony is that in the autumn of 1991, Cobain was still sleeping in his old Plymouth Valiant, even as *Nevermind* began its famous climb up the album charts. Near the end, in the spring of 1994, when he owned a million-dollar house, he opted to stay in $18-a-night motels on Seattle's seedy Aurora Avenue. He was looking for a safe place to use heroin after Courtney Love, in a cry for help, barred drugs from their mansion. In the weeks leading up to his death, Cobain clung tight to the run-down aspects of his upbringing. The world's most famous rock star still owned the Valiant. In fact, his Seattle drug companions put him inside the vehicle after an overdose and left him to die. As Cross explains, "He had spent many nights in this car—it was as reliable and cozy a home as he ever had" (213, 327, 336).

Like Elvis Presley and Michael Jackson, Cobain sought protection from the ravages of fame. Actually, the story was cyclical. In 1992, *Nevermind* knocked Jackson's *Dangerous* from the #1 spot. Back in 1969, the Jackson 5's first #1 single arrived shortly after Presley scored his last #1 with "Suspicious Minds." In each case, a torch was passed. Presley dominated the late 1950s and, despite his missteps, had some hits and a fabled comeback in the 1960s. Jackson, the new King (of Pop), was a superstar throughout the 1970s and 1980s. After *Nevermind*, Cobain seemed primed to dominate the 1990s. But his choice of drugs was harder, his demons more intense, and his fans more invested in his addictions ("Kurt! Smack!" fans shouted on his final European tour) (320). Elvis survived twenty years in the limelight; MJ nearly forty. Kurt didn't even last three. As his suicide note declared, he chose to burn out rather than fade away.

Although Cobain's music spoke to alienated teenagers and wayward twenty-somethings, the singer himself seemed motivated to reach back further, into childhood, to work through the trauma visited upon him. At age seven, Cobain was put on Ritalin for ADHD, a less common diagnosis in the mid-1970s than it is today (21). When he was twelve, his parents divorced. It was then he decided to become an artist, withdrawing into his imagination (Azerrad 2001, 18). At age fourteen, Cobain bought a guitar, began using LSD, and informed peers of his plans for suicide (Cross 2014, 34–35). He also began deconstructing dolls, turning them into a mishmash of hurt body parts. Cobain seems never to have abandoned an adolescent mindset. Indeed, Cross shows that when Cobain cashed his first publishing check in 1990, a year before *Nevermind*'s release, he sated his juvenile fantasies with a combination of vengefulness and innocence:

> Kurt spent almost $1000 in Toys 'R' Us on a Nintendo system, two Pixelvision video cameras, two automatic BB guns that looked like M16 rifles, and several Evel Knieval plastic models. He also bought fake dog feces, fake vomit, and rubber severed hands. "He threw it all in a basket," remembered [his friend Joe] Preston. "It was just a bunch of junk he could destroy." It was if an eight-year-old boy had been set loose in the store and told he could have anything he wanted. Kurt used the BB gun to immediately shoot out the windows on the Washington State Lottery

building across the street. He also bought, for $20, a used child's Swinger bicycle, a style that at the time was remarkably unhip: It was so tiny that pedaling it required him to scrunch over with his knees to his shoulders. Kurt gleefully rode the bike until it was dark. (174)

There would be no Jungle Room, and no Bubbles the Chimp, but Cobain's escapist impulse was the same as Presley's and Jackson's. He was a child, through and through. His suicide note was addressed "To Boddah," his imaginary childhood friend, and written by the light of MTV, the life source of teenagers nationwide (351). On that fateful night in 1994, as in the years leading up to the tragedy, Cobain could not let go of adolescence, as painful as it was the first time around.

Cobain also remained tied to the poor white culture of Aberdeen, which he never fully disavowed, despite his public grievances. Everett True was not the first to denigrate Cobain's hometown. Trendsetters in the Olympia scene castigated Nirvana's first drummer, Dave Foster, for looking too much like a redneck. Sub Pop Records took a somewhat different tack; its publicity shots of Nirvana cast a fluorescent glare on Cobain's acne in order to capture his backwoods credibility. Throughout the 1990s, there existed a condescending attitude about Cobain's roots that, while it amused critics and fans, haunted the singer until the bitter end.

And it is very near the end, five months before his death, on a live MTV performance captured on *Unplugged in New York*, that Cobain expressed his pain most poignantly. "Smells Like Teen Spirit" was conspicuously absent on the set list. The "stupid and contagious" feelings Cobain expressed in Nirvana's biggest radio hit and displayed in a video that stood as Gen X's answer to *Carrie*'s vengeful prom scene had morphed by the time of 1993's *In Utero* into the damning introspection of "Dumb" and "All Apologies." On a funereal set MTV designed to his specifications (lilies, candles), the frail-looking Cobain delivered what some critics have deemed his definitive performance. For Greil Marcus, MTV producer Alex Coletti, and Cobain himself, the high-water mark of *Unplugged* is the Leadbelly cover "Where Did You Sleep Last Night?" (Marcus 2000b, 98).[18] Charles Cross maintains that the best song is "Pennyroyal Tea," which refers to an herbal abortion remedy as well as to Cobain's chronic stomach pain (2014, 280). Cobain's solo performance of the song makes him a DIY hero. "Am I doing this myself, or what?" Cobain bewilderingly asks his bandmates, who had not yet rehearsed an acoustic version. "Do it yourself," Dave Grohl responds. "And Kurt did," Cross remembers,

> though halfway through the song he seemed to stall. He breathed a very short breath, and as he exhaled, he let his voice crack on the line "warm milk and laxatives," and it was in that decision—to let his voice break—where he found the strength to forge ahead. The effect was remarkable: It was like watching a great opera singer battling illness complete an aria by letting emotion sell a song, rather than [relying on] the accuracy of the notes. At several times it seemed as if the weight of an angel's wing could cause him to fold, yet the songs aided him: These words and riffs were so much a part of him he could sing them half dead and they'd still be potent. It was Kurt's single greatest moment onstage, and like all the high-water marks of his career, it came at a time when he seemed destined to fail. (2014, 304–5).

In this passage Cross sounds like Greil Marcus on one of his dizzying riffs, or Peter Guralnick, who briefly let his objectivity drop as a frail Elvis, during his final concert, summoned a final burst of energy while performing "Unchained Melody." Success and failure hang in the balance when a vulnerable musician is up on the stage, each performance a remedy, a reenactment of the humble beginnings and painful circumstances from which fame and adoration somehow sprang. Only rock and roll? Suicide up on the stage? Cobain's performance on *Unplugged* is hardly that. It is something I cannot easily define. But I can appreciate it nonetheless, and find in it traces of my own roots.

In the *Unplugged* song that affects me most, Cobain extrapolates from the pendulum of failure and success an autobiographical statement fusing stupidity and joy. In "Dumb," the singer seems not only to be remembering his adolescence, including his adventures with cheap drugs (sniffing glue), but also to be recalling a less complicated time, inhaling on a journey that had him exhaling during "Pennyroyal Tea," losing consciousness during two heroin overdoses, then ceasing to breathe altogether after a self-inflicted shotgun blast. Can you mend a broken heart with glue? It depends on how, and with whom, you use it. Teens from broken homes, deemed "losers" by unknowing or uncaring adults, know how to pick up the pieces. Brought low by personal heartbreak, Cobain and his friends float high amid the clouds, knowing they can share the hangover, too. At song's end, Cobain repeats the phrase "I think I'm dumb" multiple times, accepting the stinging insult, incorporating it, making it a comforting mantra. Like the songs on Hüsker Dü's *Zen Arcade* ("Broken Home, Broken Heart"), "Dumb" helps me reevaluate the roller-coaster experience of lower middle-class teenagers in contemporary America.

Cross does not offer an analysis of "Dumb," or even an explanation other than Cobain's liner notes.[19] Instead, *Heavier Than Heaven* details the situations out of which such cries of pain emerged. "Dumb" is pure Aberdeen, Washington, and for me, pure Penn Yan, New York. Perhaps it is your hometown, too. If you can recall any teenager browbeaten by authority figures, stigmatized as slow, mediocre, or recalcitrant, and subsequently abandoned, the song's twisted escapism makes sense. Okay, Cobain says, I will be who you think I am. I will embrace your derisive labels. But from chemically induced heights, above authority's reach, I will emerge as an incisive critic of your whole community. "Dumb" has always been my favorite Nirvana song. But it wasn't until I read Cross's description of Cobain's upbringing in conjunction with Donna Gaines's portrait of the Bergenfield teens and Judd Nelson's portrayal of John Bender in *The Breakfast Club* that I understood why.[20]

Like Kurt Cobain, Alex Chilton was a high school dropout. He lacked motivation when it came to basic practicalities. He ran into trouble with drugs, mostly downers and alcohol. He even made a few suicide attempts. But few called Chilton dumb. Instead, Generation X kids hailed this Boomer musician as a genius, despite his crippling artistic disappointments. He didn't die young, like Cobain, but after the demise of his band Big Star in the mid-1970s, Chilton became basically unknowable, a recluse in plain sight. As curious indie rockers attended his shows, shared his recordings, and sought him out as a producer, his legend evolved. Chilton deserved a good biographer, but he put many writers (including Barney Hoskyns) off his trail. Holly George-Warren managed to break through his veil of privacy.

In the author's note to *Heavier Than Heaven*, Charles Cross recalls his dual feelings of elation and grief when he was granted three days alone with Cobain's private papers and personal effects. Secured in his subject's inner sanctum, the biographer sorted through his own emotions and prepared to re-create another's life. It was a solemn effort. By contrast, Holly George-Warren conveys a punk rock attitude in her epilogue to *A Man Called Destruction*: "The first time I met Alex Chilton, I threw up in his sink" (2014, 310). It was 1982.

Chilton was thirty-one years old, living in New Orleans, virtually destitute, having burned through money, personal relationships, and business options in Memphis and New York. He moved to New Orleans, he said, to save his life. He could not have known at the time that the young woman vomiting in his sink would be the one writing his life story.

Chilton became influential in the world of indie rock because he mixed cynicism with sincerity. He was enigmatic. When he was just sixteen, he affected a bluesman's gravelly growl in the Box Tops' #1 smash, "The Letter." People who heard the song envisioned an older black man, not a white youngster with a mop top. In his twenties, Chilton wrote and performed "Thirteen," a song of budding romanticism and painful adolescent longing, poignant and immediate, its lyrics set in the present tense. Like Chuck Berry and Brian Wilson before him, Chilton assumed the viewpoint of a teenager to fit the circumstances of his song, and the transformation seemed achingly believable. What's more, it was in Memphis, the cradle of the Delta Blues, during the early 1970s, when R&B labels like Stax and Hi held sway, that Chilton's band Big Star perfected an Anglo pop sound reminiscent of mid-1960s Kinks or Beatles. In each case, it was hard to know who Alex Chilton was, or where he was coming from.

The only study of Big Star prior to *A Man Called Destruction* was Rob Jovanovic's titular volume, originally published in 2004, when Chilton and drummer Jody Stephens, together with two members of the Posies, reunited for an album. Jovanovic's book is good, particularly on *Sister Lovers*, the band's controversial third album. But just as *Heavier Than Heaven* did for Cobain, George-Warren's biography of Chilton digs deeper, exploring the conditions motivating the bandleader's independent spirit.

George-Warren explains that when Alex Chilton was six years old, his mother found his teenage brother drowned in the family bathtub following a seizure. Alex was home at the time, and the memory terrorized him for years. Chilton's parents, meantime, overcompensated for their grief by adopting a freewheeling, bohemian lifestyle. They used a downstairs parlor in their Memphis house as a salon. Chilton's mother ran a small art gallery, and his father invited local and traveling musicians for impromptu jam sessions. Young Alex heard the commotion as he drifted off to sleep. Soon, he began escaping out his bedroom window to enjoy Memphis nightlife for himself. He made the right connections, and under the tutelage of songwriter and producer Dan Penn, he enjoyed commercial success astonishingly fast. Yet some uneasiness remained. Chilton flunked tenth grade. Jilted by a girlfriend shortly before "The Letter" got released, he made a suicide attempt, cutting his wrists then running to his parents for help (47). Another attempt followed in 1976, when Chilton was suffering career doldrums. Both times, he slashed himself in the bathtub where his brother died, only to be rescued, as his brother was not, by his parents (190).

The decade between suicide attempts was for Chilton an uneven experience of fame and rejection. After "The Letter" catapulted the Box Tops to national prominence, the band enjoyed six other Top Forty singles. But frustration mounted. Like many pop acts of the day, the Box Tops were managed from the top down, and Chilton craved artistic freedom. Quitting the Box Tops in 1970, he spent a year holed up in New York City, honing his craft as a singer-songwriter. When he returned to Memphis and formed Big Star with Chris Bell, his ambitions were strong, and the music he produced with his new band, a winning brand of jangly pop, proved equal to his expectations. Big Star's album titles were tellingly ironic. *#1 Record* (1972) was a first record, but not a smash (#1) record. It was also a great record, even if few got to hear it owing to distribution problems at the label. Similar issues arose with *Radio City* (1974). It was classic American power pop, a radio-ready charmer, "catchy and twisted at the same time" (Christgau, quoted in George-Warren 2014, 152), but it missed big radio markets and went largely unheard, except by indie rockers who passed around rare copies, sharing their best musical secret. Chilton didn't help his case. He refused most interviews on Big Star's brief *Radio City* tour and acted petulant during others, telling a WLIR deejay that life on the road was "pretty scummy." Big Star's music was pure and shimmery, but when a pop band gets to the threshold and almost makes it, we are left in disbelief. There's something about pop that isn't supposed to fail.[21]

Absent sales, airplay, and other recognition, frustrations grew insurmountable for Bell and bassist Andy Hummel, who left Big Star after the first and second albums, respectively. Chilton, just as dispirited, soldiered on with darker material he recorded with producer Jim Dickinson in late 1974. The result was *3rd*, commonly known as *Sister Lovers*, another great album few got to hear. *Sister Lovers* circulated only as a white-label promo record until 1978, when it received a proper, albeit limited, release. If it was true what was said of the *Velvet Underground and Nico*—that it only sold 1,000 copies but that everyone who bought it started a band—history repeated itself with *Sister*

Lovers. The album was depressing, haphazard, and spare, musical heir to Sly and the Family Stone's *There's a Riot Goin' On* (which, as Marcus noted in *Mystery Train*, alienated white listeners but enjoyed a big budget release and hit #1, heralding a new wave of politically aware black music). *Sister Lovers* is a messy masterpiece, a cry in the wilderness. It took longer than *Riot* to get heard, but it seems just as influential.

Chilton's fortunes sank even lower in the late 1970s, yet there remained about him an air of misunderstood genius. Rock writers wrung their hands. As the singer became more reticent, the thrill of the chase became the main story line. One of rock's most perceptive scribes, Robert Gordon, situated Big Star among other eccentric local acts in his 1995 book, *It Came from Memphis*. This quirky book does not just collate facts; it conveys a uniquely bawdy Memphis atmosphere where artists had free rein to cross generic barriers and befuddle expectations.[22] The Olympia and Seattle scenes from which Nirvana emerged seem bland in comparison. Gordon pays special heed to Chilton's *Like Flies on Sherbert*, a shambling 1979 solo disc regarded as a disaster by many fans and mainstream rock critics. After *Sister Lovers* went nowhere, Chilton rejected his status as consummate pop stylist. The songwriter who composed "Thirteen" back in 1970 adopted a whole new approach to adolescent expression. "He was trying to play note for note what somebody who doesn't play the guitar would play like," Sid Selvidge recalled (quoted in Gordon 2001, 224–25). Chilton's playing on *Flies* was not so different from what Thelonious Monk tried with piano. As Tom Waits, divorcing himself from L.A.'s singer-songwriters, once said of Monk: "There is no wrong note, it has to do with how you resolve it. He almost sounded like a kid taking piano lessons" (quoted in Hoskyns 2009, 40).

As Gordon shows, Chilton's demolition job on *Flies* paid long-term dividends, for how often does an album with an initial pressing of 500 copies on an obscure label garner so much notoriety? In terms of sheer debauchery, *Flies* fit perfectly with *Stranded in Canton*, a montage of cinema vérité that William Eggleston recorded with a portable Sony camera throughout midtown Memphis. From Gordon's vantage point, the warts-and-all nature of Eggleston's documentary film had its aural equivalent in *Flies*: shoddy, incomplete takes were accepted without a second thought. Little wonder, then, that Eggleston films Chilton playing (with Selvidge) "My Rival," one of the tracks on *Flies*, the musician sitting droopy-eyed amid overflowing ashtrays and sheet music for

"The Saint Louis Blues." In Memphis, Chilton could self-destruct as he damn well pleased, and since Eggleston was an expert at chronicling decadence, the match worked.[23]

As years passed, this pattern of destruction cemented Chilton's cult status among a rising generation of indie rockers, as Gordon explains:

> Flies is an epitome of Memphis music—a complete rejection of the industry norm. It embraces what traditional studio set-ups reject. It is sloppy, often indecipherable, and very, very alive. "Like Flies on Sherbert," a critic has written, "painfully confirmed the degradation of a once-major talent." Such a statement reveals a dickhead writer with a bad record collection. On the album we hear Chilton bumping into the microphone and then laughing about it—where else but Memphis goddamn rock and fucking roll are you going to hear that allowed onto the finished product? "Fixing" that would have made a super alive moment into stone dead rock. Flies presaged the wave of American punk, foretold the return of roots rock, and once again sent out a trend from Memphis that the city itself couldn't swallow until, like a baby bird, it was given predigested versions. (2001, 244)

Keith Richards refers to such imperfections as "hair in the gate," and Chilton admirer Tom Waits explains that if music is "too beautiful, too produced, I back off a little, start getting intimidated" (quoted in Hoskyns 2009, 349). Robert Gordon likewise champions perceptive listeners "who thrive on a little chaos [and] live for beauty in the flaw of the grain" (2001, 201). But tastes dictate whether one prefers Chilton shedding tears on the way down or laughing as he scrapes the bottom. So while Gordon loves Flies, I always go back to Sister Lovers, which was planned as Chilton's first solo effort, even if it clearly benefited from Jody Stephens's musicianship, John Fry's engineering, and Jim Dickinson's production.

Sister Lovers is pure melancholia. In place of the renowned Memphis Horns, we hear the so-called Memphis Strings providing a forlorn wash of sound behind Chilton's plaintive singing (and Stephens's on "For You"). The cowbell punctuating "Kanga Roo" is as forlorn as that instrument has ever sounded. Written by Chilton as a lullaby for his lover, Lesa Aldridge, "Blue Moon" emerges as a pendant piece to British folkie Nick Drake's "Pink Moon," composed that same year: the titular object is a cold but colorful orb of private emotions released by the singer and sent skyward. "Holocaust" is probably the most haunting look-in-the-mirror committed to vinyl: it is Chilton's condemnation of Lesa, himself, or anybody who considers himself a tear-stained fraud. *Sister Lovers* is cynical and ironic, yet strangely lovely, and I wonder whether it took a sustained effort by Chilton to sound this languid and hurt. I suspect that it did not, that personal and professional disappointments led him straight to these harrowing performances.

Over the years, listening to Big Star's third album has become a litmus test. Robert Gordon said it was "almost like a Fellini record" (2001, 235). Chris Stamey, a North Carolina musician who collaborated with Chilton in New York during the late 1970s, recognized *Sister Lovers* as "modern classical music" (quoted in George-Warren 2014, 197).[24] Along with Peter Holsapple and other Chapel Hill musicians, Stamey dedicated himself to preserving Big Star's legacy at a time when Chilton was in a downward spiral. On the other side of the fence were mainstream tastemakers such as Atlantic Records' Jerry Wexler, who heard *Sister Lovers* and lamented Chilton's wasted pop career, telling Jim Dickinson, "Baby, listening to this record made me feel very uncomfortable" (quoted in George-Warren 2014, 181).

Shortly after Stamey and Holsapple began flying the Big Star banner, the band's studio albums and their live performance on WLIR got reissued. Interestingly, the "lost" music struck a chord with Gen X kids. L.A.'s Paisley Underground musicians, led by David Roback, included "Holocaust" on their collaboration *Rainy Day* (1984). REM and the Replacements cited Big Star as an influence, the latter including the song "Alex Chilton" on *Pleased to Meet Me* (1987), recorded in Memphis, aided by Jim Dickinson. When Paul Westerberg claimed that youngsters sang Chilton "by the million," were are tempted to hear that as ironic, or wishful. But twenty years earlier, that was actually true. If Chilton didn't turn his back on his 1960s success, as Sly Stone did, neither did he shrink from failure when it came. With *Sister Lovers* and *Like Flies on Sherbert*, Chilton embraced disappointment and defeat, articulating what it is like to linger in a dark place. Whether we numbered in the millions is hard to say, but a sizeable portion of Gen X music fans, tired of playing stepchild to grandiose Boomers, found in Chilton's 1970s offerings a voice we could trust. It was as though Greil Marcus's famous formulation had been reversed. Marcus asked in his edited collection *Stranded* what album you'd take with you to a desert island. Back then, nobody picked Chilton's albums; in truth they were already stranded. In time they would come to wow a new generation heeding their siren's call of sweet despair.

In the 1980s, Chilton tried different roles, playing guitar for Panther Burns, a Memphis combo fronted by his inept disciple Tav Falco, and producing albums for "shockabilly" heroes the Cramps.[25] In 1982, Chilton moved to New Orleans, reportedly to shun toxic influences. He worked as a dishwasher, a tree cutter, a janitor, and a sideman in a Bourbon Street cover band. He lived in a shotgun shack in Treme, a black section of town. He no longer had Box Tops fans screaming along with the hits or hip rock critics praising his Big Star albums, yet he found happiness as a "tireless journeyman," playing music for its own sake (George-Warren 2014, 309). A 1985 MTV interview depicts Chilton talking offhandedly while playing blues, pop, and classical pieces on an acoustic guitar in a New Orleans graveyard. The pale, skeletal singer, wearing dark shades, looks like he has come back from the dead. He seems relaxed and revitalized, though, or as he says, "freer," content to play roots music in informal situations with local musicians whose names we'll never know. It's one of my favorite interviews of a musician, unpretentious and pure. There was something undeniably soulful in Chilton's story.

Gen X related to Chilton because he bridged hippie idealism and punk negativity, ping-ponging back and forth between lightness and darkness. "I'm a nihilistic jerk half the time and the other times I'm so vulnerable and sincere … That's how most people my age are. They're sarcastic one minute and then caring the next. It's a hard line to follow." Kurt Cobain said that (quoted in Azerrad 2001, 211), but it could just as well have been Chilton talking. Listening to *Sister Lovers*, you can decipher songs like "Take Care," "Jesus Christ," or "Thank You Friends" in drastically different ways, as earnest or ironic by turns. "Take Care" is a slow waltz, the lachrymose strings and Chilton's plaintive valediction suggesting that it's the singer himself who needs caretaking after waving goodbye to rock and roll success. In "Thank You Friends," the music is more upbeat, but the message bitter and ironic, Chilton "thanking" everyone whose lukewarm support made his predicament probable.

As George-Warren's biography shows, self-preservation depends on the balance you strike. Like Hendrix, Joplin, and Morrison before him, and like Cobain and Amy Winehouse after him, Big Star co-founder Chris Bell died at twenty-seven, still seeking the breakthrough that never came. Bell possessed little of Chilton's sense of irony, and thus "I Am the Cosmos," the title track of his solo album, is not so much boast as lonely complaint. That Bell died at twenty-seven, rock's death year, is sadly ironic, for he never achieved the prominence of Hendrix and company. Meantime, Chilton at age twenty-seven was a decade removed from a Top Ten hit and barely surviving. He recorded *Like Flies on Sherbert*, saw the belated release of *Sister Lovers*, and tooled around New York City looking for gigs, mostly in dives catering to the punk crowd. The cover shot of *A Man Called Destruction* shows the "big star" looking like death warmed over. But Chilton got resurrected, ever so gradually and on his own terms, spending the next three decades as a spectral figure, a shadowy sage who may have failed by traditional standards yet became an icon for a generation he didn't even belong to. If it's possible to stand Pyrrhic victory on its head and create a Pyrrich defeat, Chilton did exactly that. As Gordon put it, Alex Chilton was "a presence so strong that his absences are influential" (2001, 154).

Arguably, it's the mainlined injection of personal pain that Chilton fed his late-arriving admirers. At a 2000 Town Hall concert, moping Generation X folkie Elliott Smith distractedly tuned his guitar as the audience callously shouted out their requests for hits. Smith trumped the masses by covering "Nighttime," a spare and gorgeous track from *Sister Lovers*. With its lilting refrain about escaping a hurtful situation, the song is desperate enough to make one want to jump off a cliff, which Smith actually did, in an apparent suicide attempt in 1997 (a tree broke his fall) (Gowing 2004, 84). On another level, "Nighttime" represents a blissful free fall into memory, a slow-motion capture of beauty in unlikely locations, reminiscent of William Eggleston's photography. Chilton's lyrics fasten on the sweet people passing him by in the Memphis night, the kitten-like tenderness of his lover's visage when she is in the mood, and the unfurling scarf that whips behind him as he hurries down freezing streets. The details are mundane, but they are lovely and haunting. "Nighttime" is a minor song on a lost album, but Smith had the song in his memory, and by performing it during the height of his own fame, in front of a clueless audience, he tapped its power.[26] As Tom Waits said in the film *Down by Law*, "It's a sad and beautiful world." Though George-Warren doesn't consider Waits's line or Smith's Town Hall performance in her biography of Chilton, I think she'd agree.

In her Fulton Street apartment in San Francisco, Ann Powers and her Gen X cohorts created art while listening to a soundtrack of doomed Baby Boomer singers: Gram Parsons, Nick Drake, and, of course, Alex Chilton (2001, 50). A more insular listening experience emerges in Dana Spiotta's 2006 novel, *Eat the Document*. A teenager named Jason is the only child of Louise Barrot (formerly known as Caroline Sherman, that name itself an alias of Mary Whittaker), an early 1970s radical who is still on the lam and using an alias. Jason stays mostly in his bedroom, obsessing over the Beach Boys albums he has collected, homing in on Brian Wilson compositions that feature teenagers alone in their rooms, or at least alone with their thoughts. Like his idol Wilson, who on the 1966 album *Pet Sounds* sang "I Just Wasn't Made for These Times," or like his fugitive mother, whose fake hometown is the same as the Beach Boys' (Hawthorne) and whose first alias derives from another *Pet Sounds* track ("Caroline, No"), Jason regards himself as a fish out of water, a brooding romantic hiding out in suburban housing tracts. Just fifteen, Jason is already an old soul, staying indoors, blotting out the sunshine, entering the dream world pop music makes possible.

Jason is "in love with his own youth" (212), but only if youth is mediated by the previous generation's underappreciated rock and roll talents. Jason's journal contains all the ephemera and exuberance you'd expect in a fanzine, but the tone is reflective and analytical. Jason regards his bedroom as his laboratory, and in this he is not alone. In his own journals, Kurt Cobain writes of revisiting his bedroom in Aberdeen and witnessing the scars and stains he left behind in adolescent anger (Cross 2014, 53–54). In a *20/20* television broadcast, a Bergenfield teen tells Stone Phillips, "If anything's on my mind, I just go and sit in my room and play some music, and just sit down and think," only to be admonished by Phillips for "shutting out the world" (Gaines 1998, 208). Huddled in his room, listening to albums and jotting his thoughts in his journal, Jason faces similar adolescent urges, but Spiotta presents his writing as a highly articulate commentary on American culture, a narrative he has woven out of old song lyrics. Mina, the main character in *Lightning Field*, Spiotta's debut novel, listens to her friend Lorene describe her teenage fantasies about country rocker Gram Parsons and comes to believe that "to articulate something, if it gets at all at the thing, if it makes some narrative cohesion of it, even if it's not the truth but the 'truth,' is the only way to escape the things that bind your life" (2002, 177–78). Lorene's "alternate fictions" (200) may sound like New Age doublespeak, and it's true that in *Lightning Field* Spiotta usually skewers such talk. But in *Eat the Document*, alternate fictions are regarded less satirically, especially where rock music is concerned. Jason may locate his version of truth while sorting through another generation's discards, yet Spiotta so effectively captures the voice of this teenager that I am convinced she's playing it straight. In Jason's journals, the endangered innocence of the Beach Boys' "In My Room" or of the unreleased *Smile* gets filtered through a precocious voice of experience, as though Wilson's "teenage symphony to God" had met Walter Benjamin's "Theses on the Philosophy of History." I, for one, don't mind getting my history this way.

In his most intriguing journals, Jason calibrates success and failure in contemporary American society. Although they are responsible for the music providing Jason his theories, the Boomers lack the boy's retrospective powers. A character like Louise, for instance, remembers feeling at the time of her radical activities not quite in control of her thoughts, swayed as she was by the "whoosh of history, the somersault of dialectic rather than the firm step of will" (2006, 14). Meanwhile, her former boyfriend and co-conspirator Nash Davis prefers not to look back on those days, at least not directly. He tries instead to facilitate anarchist revolution among the Gen X set, with middling results. Seattle's post-grunge youngsters mostly ignore him, preferring to steal merchandise from the independent bookstore he manages. Nash lauds doomed Native Americans for trying to "make persuasive and powerful the beauty of their opposition," but the kids regard such talk as silly. Obviously, his hippie idealism is "beside the point" (39, 65–66).

From his suburban remove, the ever-quirky Jason equates Boomer failure with success, provided the failure is noble enough. Besides the Beach Boys, he gravitates toward Badfinger's Pete Ham, Big Star's Chris Bell, and other doomed artists (Skip Spence, Syd Barrett, Nick Drake, Dennis Wilson) with so-called lost albums. Silence has a chance to speak. "In Big Star's history fans confront the fear of having something important to say that no one will hear," Robert Gordon has written. "The band's cult status helps listeners realize their lives are not in vain" (2001, 247). So it is with Jason, whose journal explores the gaps of countercultural history. Jason's own "lost writing" shows the child to be wiser, or at least more reflective, than Boomers flailing about in their middle years. Still, that doesn't make him feel accepted. Writing private journals, listening to lost albums like Bell's *I Am the Cosmos*, and wiling away endless suburban afternoons, he hardly meets the criteria of a well-adjusted teenager; instead, he is made to feel "singular, freakish, alone" (Spiotta 2006, 124).

At the same time, Jason regards himself as the cosmos, or at least "the center of America," prey for advertisers and "cool hunters" targeting a lucrative demographic (123–24). We know that in the 1990s, failure, or "loserdom," gained some status; labeled "alternative," it sold. Yet by 1998, when Jason's journals begin, alternative rock's moment had passed. Taking its place was an ironic nostalgia Simon Reynolds explored in *Retromania*. The early 1970s in particular proved a popular touchstone among Gen Xers. Tellingly, *That '70s Show* used a Big Star track in its opening credits (in a cover version done by Cheap Trick, a once-successful 1970s power pop band paying homage to a failed power pop band that they, and almost everyone else, considered superior). It makes sense. In both the early 1970s and the late 1990s there existed a hangover from the prior era's burst of renegade energy: a deflation of idealism, a dispersal of scenes, a creeping sense of cynicism and distrust (Woodstock '99, anyone? True, it wasn't Altamont, but then no one went into the festival with high expectations, which made it worse). *Eat the Document* confronts this rewind moment, this repetition with a difference. Pop cycles infuse nearly every page, but it is in Jason's journals that they find fullest expression.

In his next-door neighbor Gage, Jason finds a burned-out Boomer who is, strangely, a kindred spirit. Gage is pushing forty and has recently returned to live with his parents. Like Jason, he spends his days obsessing over records and holding forth on their merits and defects. He is a "loser," Jason admits, but also, "in all his dissipated glory … someone I would call a pal" (71). Jason's relationship with Gage recalls the friendship between young Cameron Crowe and Lester Bangs depicted in *Almost Famous*, except that in Spiotta's novel the teenager has the keener cultural perspective and the adult none of Bangs's linguistic gifts. Jason sees Gage "drowning in the circular mess of relativity, the mindfuck of repeated listening, the loss of perspective that comes with looking at something too closely." Still, it takes one to know one. As Jason admits, "I've been there" (75).

During their "listening jags" (74), Jason and Gage hew to an aesthetic so contrarian it cancels out, or at least exposes, the pretentious evaluations put forth by rock journalists and a growing number of amateur commentators. The geeks who work in record stores, edit fanzines, and staff college radio stations have nothing on Jason and Gage, as the former implies in his journal:

My friends—what few friends I have—are the types of guys who will argue about whether the rare RCA single version of "Eight Miles High" is superior to the track issued on *Fifth Dimension*, the Byrds' album release. It isn't, but it is cool to ask the question because it proves you know there are two versions and you are conversant with both. It is even cooler to maintain that the album—a common, reissued object—does have the superior version, and not the rare, hard-to-find single. (This is true, despite the fact, perhaps inconsequential, that the LP version *is* actually the superior version.) It is perverse, and very sophisticated, in these circles, to maintain the common, popular object is the better object. Only a neophyte or a real expert would argue such a thing. So are you getting the picture on my pals, here? I knew instantly that Gage was one of us. Or should I say, given his seniority agewise, we were one of him. We who live for bonus tracks, alternate versions, reissues, demos, bootlegs. Cover versions. Obscure European or Japanese reissues in 180-gram vinyl. Or original issue, original packaging. Authenticity. We like the inside story, the secrets. We constantly feel the best, coolest stuff is being withheld from us. In other words: there is never enough information. There is always more stuff to be had. A new master unearthed, a track unnoticed at the end of a long silence on a master tape. In a safety deposit box, in a basement. Someone didn't notice it! (71–72)

Inconsistencies abound in Jason's journal, and that's precisely the point Spiotta emphasizes throughout her novel. Intellectually inflected mood-swings and brief but fierce investments in objects are indicative not only of a precocious teenager's mindset but also of the pop culture fueling his obsessions. If, as Greil Marcus opined, "the boy's voice is too intense for it not to claim its own story" (2015a, 380), the hidden gems Jason unearths suggest that much of the past has been withheld from Gen X kids.

Jason's journal represents a different way of conceiving Gen X's relationship to rock music. Geographically and temporally removed from the ground zero of Seattle grunge, Jason does what Gina Arnold did in her book on Liz Phair, which was, in Greil Marcus's words, to analyze "the idea of an imagined community that the past leaves behind" (Marcus 2015a, 515). Who needs scenes? Who needs the city? Jason says you can be as weird as you want right now, right where you are, hidden in plain sight:

Suburbia is a freak's dreamworld, a world of extra rooms upstairs and long, lazy afternoons with no interference. A place where you can listen to your LPs for hours on end … You can burn CDs and download music, catalog and repeat, buy and trade, all sitting on your ass in the rec room. The recreation room—in suburbia there are whole rooms dedicated to leisure and play and recreation. There is space and time here, and comfort and ease. Just look at me. Just look at Gage. (73–74)

Whereas in their past life Louise and Nash joined a leftist political collective in an effort to reform American society, and whereas kids of his own generation flocked to Seattle, Austin, and Brooklyn to imbibe the culture that sprang up around homegrown music scenes, Jason cocoons himself in order to hear clearly a distinctive American voice, broad and isolated all at once:

I am at home only in *my own personal* loneliness. The thing of it is I don't necessarily feel connected to Brian Wilson or any of the Beach Boys. But I do, I guess, feel connected to all the other people, alone in a room somewhere, who listen to *Pet Sounds* on their headphones and who feel the way I feel. I just don't really want to talk to them or hang out with them. But maybe it is enough to know they exist. We identify ourselves by what moves us … I think that if you wonder about other people's loneliness, or contemplate it at all, you've got a real leg up on being comfortable in your own. (76–77)

Remember, the setting of this novel predates social media. Today, one's feelings about *Pet Sounds* can be shared instantly with an online community, whereas Jason, circa 1998, is able to ruminate without distraction. In that regard, his connections seem more virtual than those that exist among teenagers today.

Spiotta is adept in setting up contrasts, and hence a sizeable portion of the novel takes place in Seattle, still full of naïve kids arriving from the hinterlands, flailing in a millennial dystopia that does not know itself to be so. Seattle is home to Nash, who like Louise remains on the run from a revolutionary bombing plot that left a housekeeper dead back in 1972. Nash manages Prairie Fire, an independent bookstore owned by Henry Quinn, another Boomer casualty, who suffers from PTSD and manifests symptoms of Agent Orange exposure despite not having served in Vietnam. The kids frequenting the store are of a different worldview. They are skateboarders and crackpot anarchists who are

in love with subversion without having in mind any particular social investment or political cause. If they do have a cause, it is hopelessly obscure and
inevitably abandoned by the next week's consciousness-raising meeting. Nash
and Henry learn the hard way that Gen X kids have absorbed the lessons of
the 1960s and 1970s counterculture contingently and ironically, embracing the
folly of their forbears and adopting only those slogans or actions that seem
useful to their private situations on a given day. Their "tester" activism is "brat
refusal," and nothing more (44).

Nash is perplexed that the pleading signs he has placed on bookstore shelves
("Prairie Fire is not the 'man,' so why are you stealing?") have not decreased
petty thievery. Henry thinks the notes actually entice Gen X kids to steal
expensive imported skateboard magazines, whereas Nash fashions a more
reflective historical analysis:

> "Punk city," Nash said. "Have you noticed they all use that word again,
> *punk*. And *punk rock*. But it seems to mean generally rebellious rather
> than specifically 1977. As in 'You closed down traffic on I-5 during rush
> hour? Punk rock.' Although they tend to say it in a sneering tone, so
> perhaps it is sort of ironic. Or both, everything is both earnest and
> ironic at the same time with them. Which is either a total dodge or some
> attempt at a new way to be."
> "Those signs just don't work," Henry said.
> "But they would never use *city* as an intensifying suffix. Not yet, that is.
> But it will be back eventually, in some mangled retread. Count on it." (28).

Back in 1973, Big Star's second album, *Radio City*, capitalized on that inten-
sifying suffix, drummer Jody Stephens recalls (George-Warren 2014, 143), and
now Nash speculates that Gen X will cycle it through. But do the Seattle kids
believe what they say? Will those who use the term "city" prove as ambiguously
earnest and ironic as Chilton in 1973, or Cobain in 1993?

The answer, for Spiotta, centers on Miranda Diaz, a young woman who piques
Nash's interest when she enters Prairie Fire to attend consciousness-raising
meetings. Miranda listens warily to the latest left-wing rhetoric, agreeing with
some of it but otherwise casting suspicion on the motives of "reggae-listen-
ing, green-panther, righteous rich kids" (60). Impressed by Miranda's ability
to hold opposing views in her head simultaneously, Nash fears that her own
"retromania" is causing her to combine the worst aspects of 1960s and 1990s

counterculture: "She had already made her point, but that didn't stop her because, well, sometimes she couldn't stop. That was one of her problems. She would start out trying to be provocative but end up completely earnest about what she was saying. She would start out being cynical and aloof and end up with an embarrassing catch in her voice" (61).

Apparently, straddling the line between irony and sincerity is effective in art or music but proves more difficult in daily life, unless one is passive-aggressive, which Miranda is not. She is just confused, or in the purest sense of the word, conflicted. She fails to realize that her little attempts at subversion, like writing phrases on her sneakers, are now outdated (Cobain made sneaker doodling popular years before) and maybe even conformist. Yet Miranda is sure she has the best way of navigating postmodern society, telling Nash, "It's more subversive than capitulation or straight opposition to have deliberate, conscious contradictions" (132). Like Jason back in his bedroom, Miranda is self-conscious about every move she makes, and more than a little self-righteous. "I just hate people who have the wrong analysis," she tells Nash (61). As someone who is out there in the world, not just lollygagging inside a suburban house with a turntable and headphones, Miranda confronts contradiction head-on, without the ameliorating effects of music. This is her downfall.

While still a teenager, Miranda left the suburbs to live the bohemian life in Seattle. Her movement toward self-discovery reveals whatever Generation X regards as truth, which is not much. People who appear earnest eventually seem jaded. Political causes lack traction. Communal situations are shells of former living experiments. In Spiotta's depiction, the Black House, a Seattle quasi-squat, splits the difference between the condemned buildings Steven Blush describes in *American Hardcore* and the group houses Ann Powers recalls in *Weird Like Us*. Simply put, the Black House is a sad replica of an older bohemian dream. Miranda thinks the squat looks like paradise the first night as she surveys her room (candles, beads, a futon on the floor), but the next morning the house resembles the Haight-Ashbury crash pads Joan Didion famously lambasted. Fleas bite Miranda's neck and sniffling methamphetamine addicts hover near an oven, trying to keep warm on their way down from a trip (45, 57).

When Miranda ditches Nash for a lover her own age, an unassuming computer hacker named Josh, she realizes that she can no more follow her new beau's headlong immersion into irony (and the late capitalism that feeds on it) than she could accept the washed-out earnestness Nash displayed when facilitating tester kids in the bookstore. The upshot? No one really buys the 1960s dream anymore, unless one is *literally* buying it. When Nash tells Miranda, "Only someone your age gets away with, you know, being so instinctual" (60), he is dead wrong, and he knows it. Miranda's enslavement to recycled history has erased most of her instinct; she is merely acting out someone else's radical script, farcically, and in Nash's opinion, tragically. Walking through a vintage boutique that offers New Left playing cards and premade DIY patches, Miranda balks, but neo-capitalist Josh talks glowingly of the Gruen effect, a "dissociative state in which you will be vulnerable to suggestion" (256). Maybe that explains their mutual attraction, for Miranda seems the most dissociated and vulnerable character of the entire novel. Nash tells her that Josh is "more cynical than he could possibly have a right to be," and that he doesn't like him, but he admits that Josh is "sharp" (218). Josh doesn't get played; he appreciates the irony of fake vintage dresses with bohemian patches, puka shell necklaces, lacquered faux milk crates, and of course, the New Left playing cards, which he offers to buy for Miranda. Miranda does not get the jokey aspect of this gift, and indeed, when she notices Nash's face on one of the cards, the reader suspects that a cosmic joke has been played on her. She realizes too late that Nash is preferable to Josh, a mercenary who goes from hacking big business websites to writing advertising copy for a corporate real estate venture, a "radiant posturbia" modeled deceitfully on the women's commune "Caroline" inhabited while in hiding (237–39).

Influenced by Greil Marcus and other rock journalists, Spiotta spices her narrative of postmodern American culture with knowing musical references, even when music ceases to play. Nash listens to Monk and Coltrane, exhibiting his sophisticated tastes. Josh and Miranda, by contrast, hardly listen to anything. Indeed, the weird thing about the Seattle narrative is the absence of music in the lives of young people (except when Miranda meets her future housemate in a record store, or puts down reggae listeners). Grunge had died out by 1998, but surely kids in Seattle wanted something other than anarchist plots whispered in their ears. And what about Henry? He is haunted by his past, but no music arrives to soothe his soul or put his inner conflicts into broader context. At the other extreme, Jason and Gage constantly incorporate music into their lives as a salve for suburban loneliness.

Louise, too, is attuned to music's power, bonding with Jason over their mutual admiration for the Beach Boys. When she speaks of having bought drinks for Dennis Wilson in a Venice Beach bar back in 1980, she earns her son's respect. As Caroline, Louise displayed her musical knowledge years earlier in the upstate commune she joined. She was affected by the wrenching loneliness and sadness of Funkadelic's 1971 instrumental "Maggot Brain" ("It's not Joni Mitchell, is it?" a communard tells Caroline's earthy-crunchy friend, Berry), even if she responded better to mainstream pop displaying the same feelings. Moreover, when "Good Vibrations" comes on the radio, Berry pronounces it a "cool song." But Caroline seizes on "the sadness that leaks through all that enforced sunny cheer," telling Berry, "It's in the sound, not the words. It's the way you feel, or rather the feeling you get. Like slightly off, rancid America, you know?" (179). *Slightly off, rancid America.* It's a phrase worthy of novelist Rick Moody, even if it's just Louise/Caroline's offhand remark about a song on the radio. Jason's critical acumen does not come out of nowhere, apparently.[27]

Louise's true identity is revealed when Jason sees her on VH1's *Lost Videos*, in a snippet of independent film documenting the 1960s L.A. rock band Love. Importantly, readers learn that the film's director, Bobby De Soto, is now known as Nash Davis. By the power of VH1, the separated radical couple is (virtually) reunited and music remains the common thread after all the years of subterfuge. It's weird, but kind of charming, that a housebound teenager solves the mystery of his mother's identity through his extensive knowledge of "lost" rock music. But in this novel Jason, even more than Chris Bell, is the cosmos; he sits in his bedroom and lets recent American history spin around him like an LP. Keeping his ears and mind open, locating Mary Whittaker, he seems as smart as any professor or FBI operative, even as he retains his adolescent wonder.

Meanwhile, in the cradle of grunge, Seattle testers flit aimlessly, with little investment in music or culture. Prairie Fire bookstore has become "a sanctuary of subversion for misfits and scragglers," entitled kids whose "sarcasm and easy, shallow irony" occasions an "ungenerous righteousness, as if merely being young was somehow to your credit" (35–37). Ultimately, Jason's languor seems more effective than the testers' manic activity, and his journal jottings weightier than the sparse mention of 1990s alternative rock, the real "lost" music in this novel. Through music, Jason unlocks all he needs to know about the troubled Boomers masquerading in his midst: "When you finally figure it out, it seems like you knew it all along" (245).

Teenage sages also figure prominently in Eleanor Henderson's debut novel *Ten Thousand Saints* (originally published in 2011), even if their wisdom is slower in coming and their behavior unconventional in ways their still-unconventional Boomer parents have a hard time fathoming. Teddy McNicholas and Jude Keffy-Horn do not reside in the turnpike suburbia Donna Gaines visited in Bergenfield, nor in a depressed logging town like Kurt Cobain's Aberdeen, but in the small city of Lintonburg, Vermont (based on Burlington), which feels just as claustrophobic and closed off to possibility. Like the Jersey teens Gaines befriended, Teddy and Jude, age fifteen and sixteen, have been regarded as burnouts or dirtbags and cast aside. Like Cobain, they were put on Ritalin for attention deficit disorder and labeled "dumb." They are each looking forward to dropping out of high school and moving to New York City to join Teddy's half brother, Johnny, who works as a tattoo artist and plays in a hardcore band. Initially, the boys do not plan to locate their biological fathers, who have absconded there. Teddy has some curiosity about his dad, whom he has never met, but Jude couldn't care less about his own.

Throughout Henderson's novel, generational barriers loom large. In *Eat the Document*, Jason eventually locates common ground with Louise and other Boomers. "At least you did something," Jason tells his mother. "What a world that must have been where ordinary people actually did things. Things that affected, however tangentially, history" (274). Teddy and Jude hold no such feelings toward their parents, whom they view as irresponsible waste cases, perpetually high on drugs and empowered by no cause other than themselves. Teddy's mother, Queen Bea, is a drunk who abandons him on New Year's Eve 1987 after he inquires about his dad. Approaching forty and living in the East Village, Jude's father works as a high-volume marijuana dealer. When Jude was nine, Lester Keffy was fired from his lab job at Vermont State for growing pot hydroponically. That same year, Jude learned that he was adopted, that he had fetal alcohol syndrome, and that his adoptive parents would be separating in the wake of Lester's extramarital affair. Jude's adoptive mother, Harriet, still works in Lintonburg as a glassblower and artist. She has proved slightly more reliable than Les, and outwardly more loving, although like Queen Bea she is described by townspeople as a "piece of work" (205, 345).

Neglected by their respective parents, Jude and Teddy remain bound to each other, no more so than while "tangled up in some stupid, trivial danger" (7). Their ambition: "to start a band, and to get fucked, and to get the fuck out of Vermont" (12). Wrestling and gouging each other like puppies, they urge each other to action and then sit there wondering who will be first to act, resembling Wayne and Garth during their most inane arguments. Jude and Teddy might feel awkward about their intimacy, but they have no place else to turn: "They'd done the blood brothers thing when they were twelve, cut open their fingertips with a paring knife and made them kiss, the hands of God and Adam, E.T. phone home, almost as faggy as last night ... when they'd shared a mouthful of pot smoke—a *shotgun* was what it was called, a word Jude had taught him—one breathing it into the other's mouth like a secret" (39).

Jude and Teddy do not fit in. The novel opens with them lurking underneath grandstands during a college football game. The teens could not be further removed from the glamour and public acceptance accorded athletes; they hang out beneath the stands to steal pocketbooks they can see through the slats. "They abstained from all things football, and all things college" (5).

Nineteen eighty-seven is a pivotal year in the lives of Jude and Teddy. Coincidentally, it is the year of the Bergenfield suicide pact. In *Teenage Wasteland*, Gaines asserts the importance of Metallica and lesser-known thrash metal bands for 1980s teens dismissed by adult authorities. In Lintonburg, Jude and Teddy hold similar allegiances. Taking turns on guitar, they listen to "hard rock, heavy metal, hair metal, black metal, death metal, thrash metal, metal core, hardcore, grindcore, punk—Black Sabbath and Whitesnake and Black Flag—and then methodically, with ears tilted to the speakers, they'd copy them" (11–12). The boys want a soundtrack reflecting their predicament.

In 1987–1988, the tides of music were changing. "College rock" had its breakthrough. R.E.M. scored with *Document* and was set to release its major label debut, *Green*. Sonic Youth made noise with *Daydream Nation* and followed R.E.M., the Replacements, and Hüsker Dü to a major label. After enjoying huge success with *The Joshua Tree*, U2 looked as though they might be the new Beatles, until *Rattle and Hum* took them down a peg. To the delight of Boomers, the classic rock radio format gained in popularity, and the Grateful Dead scored a Top Ten hit two decades after the Summer of Love. Aerosmith forged an unlikely partnership with Run-DMC. Springsteen, entering a period of marital woes, was losing sales, and Dylan was just plain lost. Rap was becoming more political as Public Enemy hit its stride and as NWA roared straight out of Compton. Under the radar, hardcore punk still attracted a subset of alienated teens, even as it splintered into rival camps, including the "straight edge" style Henderson explores in *Ten Thousand Saints*.[28]

Rhythm Pigs musician Ed Ivey once described hardcore as folk music, complete with its own forms and expectations (Blush 2001, 43). But just as Dylan overturned folk traditions, hardcore bands were as likely as other musicians to stake claims on originality. Jude gets hooked up with hardcore music early on, leaving pop metal to the town jocks (Def Leppard's "Pour Some Sugar on Me" blares at Tory Ventura's New Year's Eve party, where Jude and Teddy meet Eliza, a privileged prep school teen who is the daughter of Lester Keffy's New York City girlfriend). Jude sports a devil lock hairstyle made fashionable by hardcore heroes the Misfits, he has a Bad Brains poster in his bedroom, and he plays Black Flag when his father returns for a surprise visit (Henderson 2012, 3–4, 88). Listening to hardcore, Jude not only runs afoul of Tory and the jocks, he also announces a clear generational break from his parents, who have named him and his sister Prudence after Beatles songs.[29] Jude especially hates a character named Hippie, not only for his predatory drug dealing and his empty talk of peace but also for the Boomer burnout he represents. It doesn't help Jude to know that "by the end of 1987, at Ira Allen High School, the hippie thrived again, enjoying with the jock a marriage of tolerance, if only for sheer numbers. Metalheads and punks, though, were few and far between, and they knew how to watch their backs" (36). Here we grasp the tension driving Henderson's plot.

Jude initially appears as a drug-addled dropout in an out-of-the-way town, listening to Metallica, Slayer, and Megadeth, stealing pot, and "huffing" turpentine, gas, glue, and nail polish remover. He lives out the lyrics of Cobain's "Dumb." On a frigid New Year's Eve, after Teddy impregnates Eliza at Tory's party and Jude gets beat up by the jocks, Jude convinces Teddy to inhale Freon fumes from an air-conditioning unit. Teddy envisions himself floating above Lake Champlain. He passes out and is found unresponsive the next morning, presumably frozen to death (actually, drugs killed him first). Jude survives despite having a body temperature of 87 degrees, but during treatment doctors realize he has fetal alcohol syndrome, an addiction that spans generations. Blame has shifted.[30] Jude is glad the police let him off the hook—"No foul play had taken place, just an accumulation of poor choices" (74)—but Teddy's death haunts him. Reacting to the tragedy and his role within it, Jude spends long hours in his room, sleeping or smoking pot with his buddies, who arrive and leave via the fire escape. Eventually, the self-acknowledged "burnout" (132) shaves his head (whether in an act of mourning or newfound resolve, it's unclear) and flees to New York City, discovering the straight edge, no-drugs lifestyle introduced to him by Teddy's brother, Johnny (who is comforted, oddly enough, by his East Village neighbor, Lester Keffy).

In New York, Jude runs away from Lintonburg's "suicide trap" (labeled by Les, citing Springsteen's "Born to Run"), from Vermont's outworn hippie ethos, and from the foreclosed future that awaits him there as burnout or dirtbag. Differentiating these social groupings, Donna Gaines noted that

> where some of their equally alienated but more politically motivated peers—rads, skins, and punk/hardcore kids—shunned drugs, and practiced nihilism with a purpose, the "burnouts" and the "dirts" didn't ascribe their actions to some higher principle. As stereotyped by their peers, "burnouts" are in the zombie zone of existence. Their main activity is getting high, being oblivious. It is this, not their clothing or music, that sets them apart as a clique. (1998, 99)

The difference is that eventually, music and style *do* matter to Jude. Once he enters hardcore's orbit, he moves beyond burnout categorization and the condescension it brings down upon him as "hallway prey" (Henderson 2012, 37). The origin of his Misfits haircut is a mystery in Lintonburg, and few kids in town know about the Bad Brains. But for Jude these bands signify everything. Like Cobain, Jude uses punk music to transcend his backwater community without betraying his hometown origins. That Jude named his straight edge group the Green Mountain Boys and headlined an all-ages show back in Lintonburg speaks to the lasting influence of his home geography. His is just a different brand of roots music.

Most commentators agree that the DIY vibe ran stronger in the hardcore subgenre than it did in other punk rock categories, college rock, or their aboveground offspring, alternative. "The punk vibe was urbane, elitist and exclusive," Steven Blush maintains. "Everyone preached DIY but few practiced it" (2001, 51). Mike Watt concurs: "The punk thing … was safety pins and writing the names of bands on clothes, but making a label and getting in a van and touring, actually playing other towns? … Maybe it was [Black Flag founder Greg Ginn's] experience with ham radios, but he believed if you try, you can get things beyond your little group" (quoted in Blush 2001, 53). Youthful energy was there, and hardcore channeled it most efficiently. "We were impeccably honest people," Ian MacKaye recalled (quoted in Blush 2001, 23), and while his evaluation may sound self-righteous, honesty brought bands like Minor Threat or Fugazi close to their fan base with minimal cost or interference. Once upon a time, Nirvana recorded *Bleach* for $606.17 (Azerrad 2001, 91). But they traded hardcore roots for the melodic sound producer Butch Vig and Geffen Records were able to provide, and the rest is history. Most hardcore bands could not dream of Nirvana's success, and just as important, they preferred not to. Their DIY roots held firm.

And so it is with Johnny McNicholas and Jude Keffy-Horn in *Ten Thousand Saints*. Johnny's straight edge band may be called Army of One, but his messages about individual responsibility are keyed to a community of fans. When Eliza heads back to New York to search for Teddy's half brother, she finds a muscular, tattooed specimen with a prohibitive X inked on each hand and a motto emblazoned across his chest: TRUE TILL DEATH. It turns out that Johnny, too, had grown up a stoner back in Lintonburg, which is why he empathizes with Jude despite Jude's role in Teddy's fatal overdose. Johnny also knows what it's like to feel abandoned, having had money stolen by his deadbeat father, an ex-con living in Staten Island. At loose ends in the big city, Johnny took the straight edge path, aided by a hardcore drummer named Rooster DeLuca. "Rooster had him hooked on the drug that was no drugs. Fuck the dealers, Rooster said, fuck the drunk drivers, fuck the frail-ass gutter punks with marks up their arms, fuck Robert Chambers and the prep school jocks with coke up their noses and their dicks up some crying girl" (107). It might seem difficult, with so many enemies, to stay positive. Yet Johnny "liked to think of his own role in the neighborhood as a force of benevolence. Not a missionary but a monk. He led by example" (108). Such is the case when Jude comes over to Johnny's to sit in on band rehearsal.

> After they covered Minor Threat's "Straight Edge," the song that spawned the phrase, Johnny told Jude that Ian MacKaye had written it for a friend who died of an overdose, and that was the closest they got to talking about what happened to Teddy. Johnny could see it sinking in, though, the dots connecting before Jude's frozen eyes, the straight edge constellation. Any day now, he'd be taking the plunge. (127)

And Jude does, making a vow to abstain from drugs when he sees an ambulance loading an overdose victim and inscribing an X on each hand to mark his straight edge status (132). At first, Jude would vacillate when it came to drug use, buying mushrooms in Tompkins Square Park, but the music pushes him to the edge, quite literally, at an Army of One matinee at CBGB's:

> The stage wasn't a stage but a knee-high platform, and Jude was drawn to it, as if tied to a rope. Was it fame? The band was glowing. It was the yellow lights, the vibration of the speakers through the concrete floor, but it was also just the band, it was Johnny, the loops in his ears shining like real gold. It wasn't fame. Famous people were untouchable, unknowable. Jude could see the pores glistening on Johnny's scalp … Jude fought through the field of bouncing bodies. A dance had started up in front of the stage, a boisterous, good-natured ritual that involved hurling one's body, like a sack of flour, at other bodies. Arms windmilled, shoes flew. Everything within an inch of stage diving. Jude was close enough to the band to feel the radiance of their sweat, their spit. (134)

Ann Powers recalls Gina Arnold saying that in the indie rock scene of the 1980s and 1990s, fans could imagine having a beer after the show with the ordinary-looking musicians up on stage, and then go have one (2001, 242). The Army of One show Jude attends takes this intimate dynamic to a more extreme level, minus the beer, of course. Henderson writes of Jude, "He was in hell. It was wonderful" (2012, 135).

Henderson clearly absorbed the stories that abound in Azerrad's *Our Band Could Be Your Life* and Blush's *American Hardcore*, and learned even more from the firsthand accounts of her husband, Aaron Squadrilli, to whom *Ten Thousand Saints* is dedicated. Like Spiotta, she brings a novelist's touch to rock writing. Setting and character development are crucial. In Henderson's descriptions of the clubs, the sweat and spit shine. Moreover, we know exactly what Jude lacks when he looks up at the stage, and when he goes with Johnny to the Hare Krishna temple looking for salvation. "Jude wanted to be devoted. He had never been this clean before, and he only wanted to be cleaner" (147).

Burnout, loser, orphan, retard: those oft-hurled insults no longer apply to Jude once he becomes part of a hardcore tribe. Kids with "broken homes and broken hearts" (Hüsker Dü) find positive messages and cooperative arrangements, dispatching the irony that runs rampant in other indie camps, fostering families stronger than those they have escaped. Johnny claims fatherhood and agrees to marry Eliza in an effort to raise the baby Teddy sired, while also shepherding Jude through the hardcore scene and caring for his boyfriend Rooster as he dies from AIDS. It's a low-key, nonjudgmental haven Johnny provides these lost souls. "*Just* friends?" he tells Jude. "None of us are just friends anymore" (163).

The Boomers, for their part, seem bewildered. Lester Keffy recognizes in Johnny an underground businessman adept at taking care of young people, yet he thinks that "behind the competent, tattooed façade was a kid who needed a swift kick in the ass" (152). Eliza's mother, the wealthy Diane Urbanski, voices similar concerns about Johnny's group while sipping wine at her daughter's birthday dinner: "Listen to you three, with your secret codes. You're all very busy together, aren't you?" (174). Jude and Eliza, having been let down by Les and Diane, have no such reservations about the new family they have joined. "You could live without most things most people depended on, according to Johnny: a family, a phone, a furnace, a taxable income, a high school diploma. And he was sort of right. Here they were, three teenagers, planning for a baby, and the sky was still high above them, winter blue; it hadn't fallen" (150). Here and elsewhere, Henderson describes what it meant to live on your own in the pre-Internet age, when introductions by mail and band tours by Econoline van brought Gen X wayfarers together.

Johnny's group heads up to Vermont, in part to shield Eliza from her mother (who had suggested abortion). In a heartwarming turn, Harriet accepts Eliza like a daughter, nurturing her through her pregnancy and making an earnest attempt to understand the new filial ties she, Jude, and Johnny have forged. One clue comes from the music made in her basement:

> Harriet asked Eliza to translate the lyrics for her, but even she could make out only a handful of words. If Jude were to name his own children after the songs of his youth, they might be named Truth, Strength, or Justice. Purity, Brotherhood, Loyalty, Trust. The words filled Harriet with a measure of gratification—her son was singing the merits of purity!—but they also amused her, embarrassed her, and concerned her. What kind of teenage boys sang songs about purity? What happened to songs about getting stoned? Getting laid? And if one had to sing songs about purity (she didn't mind songs about purity!), why did they have to be so hard on the ears? They were awfully *angry*, these songs. The classics of her own youth, about getting stoned and getting laid, were

strummed on the guitar, they were hummed in the shower, there were harmonicas. (219–20)

In Henderson's hands, generational differences are not played for laughs, even if there is a trace of humor in the above passage. Neither are they fodder for preachy earnestness, fiction's death knell. Her characters simply play the hands they've been dealt, using music as their guide. Like the novelist herself, Harriet is adept at "life drawing," erasing her mistakes when they become painfully evident, doing her best to get it right next time. Jude faces his own challenges. Like Jason in *Eat the Document*, he is a teenager searching for purity, but his historical moment is different and his socioeconomic situation such that disconnection from parents and other authority figures puts him in a more perilous bind. His situation begs the familiar question: What can a poor boy do, except sing in a rock and roll band?

In Vermont, Jude and Johnny's past and future collide in an all-ages show their new band performs at the town recreation center, recently host to Spaghetti Dinner Family Night. Jude makes light of that fact from the stage, but Henderson indicates throughout her novel just how much Jude and Johnny would have liked to attend such a dinner with attentive, loving parents. The hardcore show becomes, in effect, a substitute for the family gatherings the boys never got to enjoy. The show also marks the debut of the Green Mountain Boys, Jude aptly recalling when he stood on this stage in a tricornered hat, performing his role in a school play about colonial Vermont's ad hoc gang of "guerilla citizens" (222). A couple centuries down the line, the name and the cause remain the same. From behind his stage prop, a Ronald Reagan mask, Jude notices that the audience itself resembles a ragtag militia. "In the dark of the gymnasium, it was hard to tell who was from New York, who was from Lintonburg, and who was from the periphery—Rutland, Montpelier, the far-flung farms of Linton County." Regardless, the crowd symbolizes resilience and strength. "Where did these people come from? And where were they last year when Jude was getting locker-slammed by Tory Ventura for sporting a devil lock?" (223). Later, a small army of hardcore kids aid Jude in revenge beatings of Hippie and Tory Ventura.

For Jude, solidarity is late in arriving, but he gets to pay it forward once kids flock to Harriet's house, which has become Green Mountain Boys' headquarters. "One by one the kids would sidle in and say, 'Eaten nothing but plants for three days, man!' And they'd get noogies and ass slaps from Jude and Delph and Kram, more approval than they'd gotten all year for their mediocre performances as students and athletes and sons, and they'd come in the next day as though they had no other place to be" (245–46). These kids are hardly as cerebral or talented as Chilton, Cobain, or the fictional Jason, but thanks to the straight edge network a few Vermonters have fostered, they find a cure for their isolation and low self-esteem. "They were all Green Mountain Boys now; the name had bled beyond the band to its crew of scouts, its brethren" (247). The promise of indie rock solidarity had reared its head in Seattle, but we know from Cobain's story, and from Spiotta's novel, that it never fully arrived. It simply couldn't on such a large scale. But in Vermont, for a moment, it has.

All in all, I prefer Jason and Alex Chilton's lonely, poignant musings, and Cobain's late-career reenactments of personal failure, to the aggressive music Jude and Johnny play. But as a writer Henderson proves deft in capturing the raw emotion and physical desire causing hardcore communities to form, evolve, and splinter. She splices into her narrative an interview with Jude and Johnny as it appeared in the (fictional) *On the Edge* fanzine, replete with misspellings, followed by the fanzine editor's "How I Spent My Summer Vacation" essay, written for his third-period high school class, in which he tells of "a truley [*sic*] musical experience" (263–67). Henderson's description of the Green Mountain Boys' tour of the I-95 corridor in the halcyon days of 1988 abounds with period details: "five or six-dollar covers split among five or six bands of five or six guys each"; tee shirt sales in dank, sticky clubs; endless rides in the van past highway billboards; and collect calls dialed from phone booths (295). And in place of sex, there was the show itself: "It was carnal, it was communal, it was religious" (296). Full of little victories, Henderson's novel is as evocative of the indie rock scene as any book I've read.

"Who can know the heart of youth but youth itself?" Patti Smith asks in *Just Kids* (135). There are many who wish to stay forever young, as Smith has, through rock music. Good writing provides necessary reflection on this process. In the epilogue to *Ten Thousand Saints*, Jude revisits CBGB's on its closing weekend in 2006. He looks for Johnny in the crowd, and also for Teddy's son, who would be eighteen now, older than Teddy ever got to be. He sees neither, only hundreds of kids who could be them. Meantime, the neighborhood has gentrified. In Tompkins Square Park, the stroller set has arrived. Luxury condos have gone up. Punk rock is still in fashion, but sadly, it's to the tune of fifty-dollar Misfits tee shirts. Rock and roll will never die, and it will not fade away. No, it will just get cycled through, again and again.

Millions have gravitated to rock music because of its immediacy, because it enlivens the present moment. But as the writers featured in this chapter demonstrate, music also serves as a memory bank, its capital as cultural as it is personal. But when it comes to growing up in DIY America, I cannot help but be subjective. I think back to the mix tape. Then I do more than think. I go to the basement, pull the tape out of storage, find a working tape deck (it's in my minivan), and wait for the Mekons' "Learning to Live on Your Own." I could cue up this song on iTunes, but that wouldn't be the same. I was twenty-six when it arrived in the mail from San Francisco. It centered me and cemented a lasting friendship. The tape itself is now twenty-six years old, and very fragile, rather like Kurt Cobain and Alex Chilton were when, at that age, they made their most affecting music. Despite the background hiss, the music plays: not just the Mekons but also the Meat Puppets, Dinosaur Jr, X-tal, the Silos, the Velvet Underground, and others. It helps to hear from those who faced tough predicaments and lived to tell the tale. And it hurts to know that some, like Cobain, the Bergenfield teens, and Teddy from *Ten Thousand Saints*, didn't survive very long. Rock is there to tell their tales, too. Great rock writers take up the story from there.

Epilogue

In *It's Just the Normal Noises*, I've attempted to underscore the connection between rock music and serious thought in an American context, and to showcase writers who have put that connection on the page. The impulse to write can be mysterious. "Somewheres back I took the time to start writin,'" Bob Dylan confessed in a 1963 Town Hall program, "but I never did take the time to find out why" (2004, "My Life in a Stolen Moment"). "I started writing about music as soon as anyone would listen," Peter Guralnick wrote in 1971, introducing *Feel Like Going Home* (8). Today, American rock writing looks quite different. The Internet abounds with professional and amateur scribes enamored with music, and commentary there can range from the ridiculous to the sublime. I have tapped the digitalized archives of *No Depression* and an occasional Internet article, but I have pretty much left online music writing to other commentators. Happily, trade houses and university presses continue to publish books on rock: not just instant, cheesy bios, but cogent appreciations of popular music in historical and cultural contexts. Preston Lauterbach's recent volumes on rhythm and blues music in the mid-South, cited previously, are prime examples.

In truth, there are a number of great books, *favorite* books, I haven't even mentioned in *It's Just the Normal Noises*. Volumes on British popular music did not fit my American theme, yet I regard Rob Young's *Electric Eden: Unearthing Britain's Visionary Music* (2010) and Simon Reynolds's *Rip It Up and Start Again, Postpunk 1978–1984* (2005) as two of the most valuable books on my shelf. My love of Fairport Convention's folk rock blend grew stronger once Young situated it alongside Romantic historiography and contemporary folk revivalists like Bert Jansch and Vashti Bunyan. So too did Reynolds elicit my admiration for bands I'd heard but never fully explored: the Fall, Public Image Ltd., Joy Division. The aspects of (pre-Brexit) "Britishness" Young and Reynolds revealed in their work influenced me as I explored "Americana" in my own.

There are also some great books on American music I didn't include, even though they shed light on important cultural trends. Ken Emerson's *Always Magic in the Air: The Bomp and Brilliance of the Brill Building Era* (2005) and Sheila Weller's *Girls Like Us: Carole King, Joni Mitchell, Carly Simon—and the Journey of a Generation* (2008) have changed the way I regard AM pop of the 1960s and 1970s. All that heartbreak hiding behind the sunny melodies! Jeff Chang's history of hip-hop and Stanley Booth's memoir of the Rolling Stones' 1969 tour, mentioned briefly in *It's Just the Normal Noises*, also deserve more attention. I'd take either of these books to a desert island (but not if it meant abandoning *Mystery Train* or *Sweet Soul Music*).

Greil Marcus and Peter Guralnick, who have received a lot of my attention, remain America's most influential rock writers. Their friendly rivalry, marked by divergent styles of writing and different areas of focus, continues to pay dividends half a century after they helped launch serious rock journalism. Both men issued substantial books in 2015 as I was putting the finishing touches on my own. At key times, these writers shared their thoughts in lengthy sit-down interviews (Marcus at his Princeton office, Guralnick in his Massachusetts home), fielding follow-ups by phone and e-mail. Inspired by their honesty and acumen, fortified by their expert analyses, I realized early on that *It's Just the Normal Noises* would use their work as its baseline, and that my project would either succeed or fail depending on how well I established its importance. Theirs is not just music writing, it's national narrative. What Marcus says about David Lynch's films describes their focus: "America emerges not as a place, a history of deeds or a set of ideas. Instead it's a story people tell each other: a fable about how people can be expected to act, about how events can be expected to unfold" (Marcus 2015a, 176). Those are high stakes, and yet we encounter them almost every time the radio plays.

Turning to *No Depression* magazine in chapter 3 and to a select group of novelists, memoirists, and biographers in chapter 4, I revisited my formative years in the Generation X heyday. The roots rock writing of Marcus and Guralnick was newly contextualized, since I was now locating my own roots. I noticed *No Depression*'s writers and novelists like Eleanor Henderson doing the same while maintaining an American focus. *No Depression's* Kurt Reighley introduced me to Americana trends existing under the radar: homemade ricotta cheese makers, old-school cobblers, and embroidery craftswomen who eschewed machines in "Zen-like" devotion to "repurposing" (Reighley 2010, 35, 208). According to craftswoman Callie Janoff, empowerment emanated from creative decisions rather than high-profile professional contacts, and ultimately, through the "sharing [of] community while making choices" (quoted in Reighley, 209). Alt-country music thrived in the same grassroots atmosphere, at least for a while, and as I composed *It's Just the Normal Noises*, I found myself recapturing that DIY spirit.

There ensued for me some introspective thought about generational differences. Hearing my contemporaries discourse freely on Americana made me reconsider my attitude toward the past, including the legacy of "classic rock." I noticed, however, that Peter Blackstock and Grant Alden announced in the first issue of *No Depression* their allegiance to long-standing roots heroes: not just Hank Williams but relevant Boomer forebears. "We claim Gram Parsons as our unholy ghost, minister of the shotgun wedding of country and rock 'n' roll long before the Eagles crashed the reception," the editors said, right out front (*ND* #1 1995). I, too, had high regard for the hippie-era country rocker. Back in 1987, in my Berkshire Street apartment, my housemate Chris put Parsons albums in heavy rotation. He grew his hair long and posed in our rocking chair, replicating the portrait of Parsons on the *GP* album. Like a lot of literary-minded fans, Chris tried to make it new by honoring the past, in this case, a fallen angel.

Composed chronologically, *It's Just the Normal Noises* also reflects my growing distance from academia, with its politics, its jargon, and its obsession with assessment, which comes at the expense of experimentation and exploration. Hence my affinity for *Weird Like Us*, Ann Powers's memoir of living in group houses, going to rock shows, working bookstore jobs, and entering graduate school (but feeling ambivalent about what one found there). Beyond mere nostalgia, I recognized in *Weird Like Us*, and in myself, "personal epiphanies and battles still raging, meaningless if you think only in terms of an impossible revolution, but crucial to the incremental process through which society actually changes" (287). In a university setting, I've sometimes been made to feel insufficiently political. But Powers suggests that I've been revolutionary all along. Simply by absorbing the ethics of a Bob Dylan or Mavis Staples song, memorizing Chuck D's lyrics, or attending Camper Van Beethoven shows, where progressive politics were leavened by humor, I've been part of "incremental" changes in American culture.

More important, I've reminded myself throughout this project that reading, writing, and listening to music have shaped my person. I love the freedom of American music, but I also love how it helps me make sense of my limitations and failures, "life's little ups and downs," as the incomparable Charlie Rich put it. *It's Just the Normal Noises* is unique because it moves beyond that music to explore journalism, memoir, and fiction. Yes, I trace my own roots when I listen to roots rock (including punk), just as I am able to explore other aspects of American culture, but that process has been facilitated mightily by those who have written about this music. Happily, we're *all* free to take the leap, to write about what we're hearing, digging, or dancing to.

For proof, recall that Dana Spiotta gives final word in *Eat the Document* to a teenager jotting his reflections in a journal. After his mother's radical past has been revealed, Jason retreats to his room and considers how his listening habits have changed. His obsession with the Beach Boys has waned, and yet he knows their records comprise an important chapter of his life. For Jason, as for me, music and writing come together to shape personal history:

> I need these records because some day, years from now, I will listen to this music and I will remember exactly what it was like to be me now, or me a year ago, at fifteen, totally inhabited by this work, in this very specific place and time. My Beach Boys records sit there, an aural time capsule wired directly to my soul. Something in that music will recall not just what happened but all of what I felt, all of what I longed for, all of who I used to be. And that will be something, don't you think? (289–90)

I feel the same when I hold my Sly and the Family Stone LPs, stare transfixed at the Gerhard Richter candle on the cover of Sonic Youth's *Daydream Nation*, play the mix tapes that guided me through certain transitional moments, or look at the volumes of rock writing arranged on my bookshelf. Maybe I will feel that way, years from now, when I glance back at *It's Just the Normal Noises*. And so, perhaps, will you.

Notes

Introduction

1. Consider Greil Marcus on Don Henley: "While it's well known that as one gets older, one tends to find changes in the world at large unsettling, confusing, fucking irritating, *a rebuke to one's very existence*, it's generally not a good idea to make a career out of saying so" (*Real* 206).

2. Elvis was "too well-suited for success," Guralnick posited, for he showed an "almost total lack of taste" once "Colonel Tom" Parker transformed his million dollars' worth of talent into millions of dollars (*Lost Highway* 1989, 133–34). Margaret Rich said that Charlie Rich's late-arriving success in the 1970s coincided with his growing lack of enthusiasm (156).

3. See Howard Sounes's *27* for the long list.

4. Even though Marcus is regarded as one of the "academic" rock critics, his investigations are infused with the same enthusiasm he had reviewing records for *Rolling Stone*. "Mainly I'm having fun," Marcus told Simon Reynolds when describing his early journalism assignments. "'Isn't this great? Don't you want to talk about this? Is there anything better to talk about? This is the best conversation we can have right now'" (Reynolds 2012, part 1).

5. Sadly, these symbols have been excised from the sixth edition of *Mystery Train* (2015).

6. See Dave Markey's film *1991: The Year Punk Broke*.

7. *The Anthology of American Folk Music* impacted musicians from the start. In *Chronicles*, Dylan recalls its influence, and Patti Smith says she felt a "kinship" with the voices Smith anthologized (2010, 114).

8. For more on Willis and Robinson, see Rhodes, *Electric Ladyland*, especially the chapter "Rock Women Who Wrote."

9. See Dwight Garner's praise for *Mystery Train* in Virgin Eyes, a column in which *New York Times* critics recall work they wish they could experience again for the first time (2015).

10. "I've never met anybody who doesn't want to tell their own story," Peter Guralnick said prior to the release of his Sam Phillips biography. "They may not tell you the story you want to hear—but I'll take whatever I can get, because it's *their* story I'm looking for" (2015). "To Sam his life was epic, mythic, intimate, and instructive by turns," Guralnick says in the biography, and it took him decades to describe that life (2015a, xii).

Chapter 1

1. By the 1970s, Jim DeRogatis explains in *Let It Blurt*, Marcus and Christgau were regarded as the "academic" critics, yet Marcus was friend and champion of their rambunctious competitors, the "noise boys" (Bangs, Marsh, Nick Tosches), based at Detroit's *Creem* magazine.

2. Book-length studies of rock by Nik Cohn, Charlie Gillett, Richard Meltzer, Richard Goldstein, and Michael Lydon preceded *Mystery Train* by a few years.

3. Stephen Paul Miller reminds us that the bizarre events in *The Rocky Horror Picture Show* take place on August 8, 1974, the night of Nixon's resignation speech, another example of how Nixon became America's "secret self" in this decade (1999, 39, 91).

4. For Marcus's debt to myth-symbol scholars, see Mazullo 1997.

5. For the link between New Historicism and 1960s college campuses, see Liu 1989 and Gallagher 1989.

6. Erich Auerbach and Theodor Adorno, fleeing totalitarian regimes in Europe in the 1930s and 1940s, also prefaced theoretical studies with personal stories describing the situation of their writing.

7. In 2000, Marcus conveyed another car radio anecdote, recalling a time when he drove around Berkeley in circles, "transfixed," trying to regain reception of the pirate radio station that played a Moby song (2015a, 205).

8. Because myth-symbol scholars were unabashed fans of the literature they studied, they were asked to defend what Leo Marx admitted was an "unscientific method" reliant on emotion and consensus. Their fusion of concept and emotion

into an image conveniently effaced ideological intentions, Bruce Kuklick explains (1999, 72, 78). Their "paradigm dramas" may have been "passionately intense and personal books," Gene Wise says, but they glossed over a deceptive and "wholly unorganized" framework built more on appreciation than intellectual rigor (1979, 183). Brian Attebery, by contrast, defends their "unscientific" methods (1996).

9. Marcus talks here and there about the reception of Elvis in the African American community, but never with any sustenance or momentum. Perhaps he is more comfortable letting African Americans speak for themselves so as not to perpetuate the issue at hand: white theft of black culture. Reviewing "Elvis: A Cultural and Legendary Phenomenon," an exhibition at UC Berkeley in 1994, Marcus simply reprints the anonymously penned invective scrawled in the exhibition's visitors book ("Elvis is a racist, doesn't anybody remember?" "WHAT'S UP NEGRÉ?" "Was it *he* who was racist or the society he lived in?" "Why do you choose to glorify the memory & life of a man who did nothing but steal the rhythms of African American blues singers & destroy himself?" "SUCK MY BIG BLACK DICK ELVIS PELVIS" "We are a nation of Elvis fans, a nation who can't hear James Brown") with no attendant commentary (2000b, 80–82). None is needed.

10. "The controlling reason why it is so hard to think about Elvis aesthetically rather than sociologically," Marcus says in *Dead Elvis*, "is that his achievement—his cultural conquest—was seemingly so out of proportion to his means" (193). Throughout *Double Trouble*, Marcus implies that the same holds true for Bill Clinton.

11. In 1991, a sermon announcement Marcus saw in Ohio mirrored his thesis: "What kind of country is it in which people believe God is dead but Elvis is alive?" (Marcus 2015a, 91).

12. Marcus told Simon Reynolds he prefers modernism (in English punk) to postmodernism (in New York punk) because of its commitment to changing the world (Reynolds 2012, part 3).

13. Although this Elvis was British, he was "an acrid rockabilly with a punk point of view" (Marcus 1993, 25). *King of America* (1986), one of the "quietist punk records ever made" (7), placed Costello firmly in an American tradition, and *Taking Liberties* (1980) presented itself as a new Bill of Rights (135). In a 1982 interview with Marcus for *Rolling Stone* ("Elvis Costello Repents"), the British singer, made to answer for the disparaging racial remarks he had made about Ray Charles and James Brown, joins the ranks of Jerry Lee Lewis, Jimmy Swaggart, and others whose foibles and ensuing apologies have shaped the gothic landscape of the American South

(Marcus 1993, 221–34). For more on the connection between Lewis and Swaggart (and between religion and the seamier side of rock and country music) see Tosches, *Hellfire* and "Pentecostals in Heat."

14. Calling him "the greatest rock lyricist this side of Bob Dylan" (2000, 45), Robert Christgau lauds Berry for having "achieved an optimism that was cultural as well as personal" without stooping to the level of "tomming" that plagued other black musicians in the American public eye (47). Compare this to Christgau's put-down of Jimi Hendrix, whom he ignominiously referred to as an Uncle Tom in a January 1968 *Esquire* review of the Monterey Pop Festival (1973, 31). Although Christgau later atoned for his sin (2000, 92; 2015, 180), I cannot help but notice how as one of the "academic" rock journalists, he analyzes black performativity by reference to a classic literary text, the result, perhaps, of his American studies training at Dartmouth (see 2000, 117).

15. Reviewing Springsteen's *Nebraska* (1982), Marcus said that any separation of Springsteen and Reagan "would be a fraud." This stark album of acoustic murder ballads and hard-luck stories was critically acclaimed, yet it failed to find much of an audience in the early Reagan years, probably because its bleak message did not jibe with the spirit of optimism the newly elected president was trying to instill. Perhaps *Nebraska*'s indictment of American hypocrisy was too subtle for the American masses to understand, or perhaps, considering the fate of "Born in the U.S.A.," too subtle for them to *misunderstand*. One thing was clear: the singer was not going to provide any help. "Because Springsteen is an artist and not a politician," Marcus says, "his resistance is couched in terms of the bleakest acceptance, his refusal presented as a no that doesn't know itself. There isn't a trace of rhetoric, not a moment of polemic" (1993, 236–37).

16. Recently, Marcus recounted Paul McCartney's proto-punk threat, made in 1967, to repeatedly record "God Save the Queen" and to sing it off key each time if Brian Epstein sold management of the Beatles to Robert Stigwood (2014, 51n).

17. Marcus traces "ruins" ideology from Dadaist Richard Huelsenbeck (whose art seized upon an advertisement for a tour of the battlefield at Verdun), to Lettrist Michel Mourre (who said his co-optation of Notre-Dame cathedral was meant "to indulge in a romantic taste for ruins and dead glory"), to the graffiti artists of May 1968 (who spray painted "Soon to be Picturesque Ruins" on an advertisement for Club Med vacations), to the Sex Pistols (whose illustrator, Jamie Reid, painted "Believe in the Ruins" on jackets, and whose "Holidays in the Sun" was an effective updating of the situationists' anti–Club Med graffito) (1990, 228–29, 284–86). Curiously, Marcus

fails to mention Walter Benjamin's "Theses on the Philosophy of History," a famous meditation in which the "angel of history" looks back into the past to see the pile of ruins left behind by the "progress" of Western civilization (Benjamin 1968, 257–58). Nor does Marcus cite the pronouncement put forth by William Carlos Williams in his foundational study of Americana, *In the American Grain*: "The terrible beauty of the New World attracts men to their ruin" (1956, 155).

18. The impulse that drove Smith, Dylan, and Springsteen enters our own lives when we reach out to others to combat feelings of alienation or restlessness. In my twenties, whenever I was running low on funds (which was often), I hit up one of my far-flung friends for a mix tape of songs from their private record collections. What I received in the mail a week or so later was a snapshot of the local scene in San Francisco or Boston, and an indirect but stunningly articulate registry of the emotions my friends were experiencing at the time. I repaid them in kind, and we established a coterie project, an anthology of American voices: some of them our own, but most not; some of them well-known, but most of them obscure; most emanating from a particular region, but all of them emblematic of an imagined community we professed to share across the miles. A similar dynamic held sway in 1983, in Aberdeen, Washington—a redneck town where not much was happening—when a young grocery clerk named Buzz Osborne gave his friend Kurt Cobain a compilation tape of punk songs. Eight years later, with the release of Nirvana's *Nevermind*, the world discovered en masse what this gift had wrought. But what happened in 1983 is even more telling, for it restages a drama that played itself out time and again before social media took hold. Our real hometowns might not welcome us in the way we would like them to—a fact duly noted by Marcus in his discussions of Dylan's "I'm Not There" (1997, 199) and Presley's "Stranger in My Own Hometown" (44) (both of them unreleased bootlegs)—but we are free to roam the rest of America, at least in our imaginations, searching for stories and spaces that accurately reflect our desires. "The story was always the same," Marcus says, reflecting on Osborne's gift to Cobain. "The music made a promise that things did not have to be as they seemed, and some brave people set out to keep that promise for themselves. The story was always different: each version left behind its own local legends, heroes, casualties, a few precious documents, a tale to tell" (1993, 4).

19. Liu claims that the short-lived revolution of May 1968 and the despair of May 1970 brought forth a painful memory of the "carnival-tragedy" atmosphere to intellectuals "embarrassed" by their failure to effect radical political change (1989, 747). While the New Historicism of the 1970s and 1980s marked a "renascence" of

historiography on one level, on another it functioned as a belated form of compensation, assuaging intellectuals whose political revolutions never got off the ground.

20. Along with T. J. Clark's *Farewell to an Idea* and Robert Cantwell's *When We Were Good*, *The Basement Tapes* suggest for Marcus the "life and death feeling of a world vanishing. The question then becomes, 'Are you going to save it? Or, like Crusoe going back to the ship, will you just turn around and wave goodbye?'" (2000a, conversation). As Cantwell put it, "The folk song has created a whole new man, a whole new culture, a whole new world in which to live—a world which, like the dreams of Andersen's match girl, exists only when it is going out of existence, one which as a consequence we can never really come to know" (1991, 388).

21. Several musicians have taken the Fourth of July as their frame of reference. Elvis had his first jam session with Scotty Moore and Bill Black on July 4, 1954 (Guralnick 1994, 91–93). Forty years later, Marcus reports, Martina McBride's "Independence Day," a Nashville tear-jerker about family abuse and uneasy redemption, "joined Van Morrison's 'Almost Independence Day' and X's cover of Dave Alvin's '4th of July' in the thin folio of recordings that expose a legacy nearly too distant and demanding to think about. It's a legacy that still carries an echo of Herman Melville's version: 'The Declaration of Independence makes a difference'" (2000b, 83). Consider, too, Marcus's analysis of a Meat Puppets song that Nirvana transformed into a prophetic utterance on *Unplugged in New York*:

> The Meat Puppets' "Lake of Fire" feels as if it's been retrieved from a cave, not borrowed from another punk band. With its lyric constructed like an authorless folk-ballad—each line, each prophecy or joke, at once a literal non-sequitur and a poetic link to every other line—the out-of-nowhere reference to "the Fourth of July" suggests that here, as in "The Coo Coo," in America the type case for this kind of song, the Fourth of July is a predestined date, waiting, deep in the unknown traditions, to be found and used. In other words, the feeling the music gives off is that, as a talisman, the Fourth of July not only preceded the Declaration of Independence but called it into being. Or as if the song could call it back. (2000b, 99)

22. As he sang his proto-grunge jeremiad, "Rockin' in the Free World," on *Saturday Night Live* in 1989, Neil Young wore an Elvis tee shirt. According to Marcus, the face on the shirt "seemed to take on the cast of the busts of Abraham Lincoln that dot the interiors in *The Manchurian Candidate*: saddened, betrayed, forced to witness every treason" (1991, 196). In *Almost Famous* (2000), Cameron Crowe's achingly

sweet memoir of his precocious start in rock journalism, a portrait of Lincoln peers out from beneath the posters of Led Zeppelin and the Allman Brothers in young Cameron's bedroom, providing wry commentary on his fall into experience.

23. Ashley Kahn's books on Miles Davis's *Kind of Blue* and John Coltrane's *A Love Supreme*, published in 2001 and 2002, safeguarded the legacy of albums in an era of file sharing and digital downloading. Continuum Press's 33 1/3 series on influential albums (each title was shaped and illustrated like a CD cover) followed in 2003.

24. In *The Seventies Now*, Stephen Paul Miller links "pop cycles" with the popsicles Wolfman Jack offered Richard Dreyfuss in *American Graffiti*, a nostalgic film that recaptured American innocence through rock and roll "oldies."

25. The ten songs: "Shake Some Action"; "Transmission"; "In the Still of the Nite"; "All I Could Do Was Cry"; "Crying, Waiting, Hoping"; "Money (That's What I Want)"; "Money Changes Everything"; "This Magic Moment"; "Guitar Drag"; "To Know Him Is to Love Him."

Chapter Two

1. Marcus Gray faced a similar situation when writing *Route 19 Revisited*, his book on *London Calling*. Joe Strummer was already dead. Other members and associates of the Clash refused interviews, probably in reaction to Gray's previous book, *Last Gang in Town*, which cast suspicion on their political commitments. In *Route 19*, Gray's scramble for information becomes its own fascinating drama.

2. Because Hoskyns has deep knowledge of Los Angeles singer-songwriters (see *Hotel California*), he's able to fill in the gaps of Waits's story. But it's the difficulty of tracking down his elusive subject that remains his book's defining feature.

3. See Robert Gordon's contention that most writers and documentary filmmakers stole from blues musicians the "only thing exclusively their own," their "presence," refusing to pay or sufficiently honor them for interviews conducted and access granted (2001, 126–27). At Newport especially, that presence was put up on display. In 1964, Skip James was clearly nonplussed performing in front of the well-heeled crowd. In 1966, Howlin' Wolf changed from his traditional stage suit to bib overalls and a straw hat to feed the appetite of white liberals for southern authenticity: call it sharecropper chic (Gioia 2009, 302).

4. Musing on Nick Tosches's biography of Sonny Liston, Greil Marcus said, "The biographer's subject has no inner life. No matter how many letters, diaries, or suicide notes the subject leaves behind, all you have are lies. You can't know what goes on in

someone else's head—unless you are a novelist, and are willing to imagine another's inner life, at which point biography ceases and fiction begins" (2015a, 197).

5. In jacket copy, Bob Dylan praised *Last Train to Memphis* using similar language: "Elvis steps from the pages, you can feel him breathe."

6. In his Walker Art Center talk, Marcus uses his broad-brush approach to emphasize American myths embedded in radio favorites, parsing "Thunder Road" in a way that makes it seem archetypal. Guralnick, meanwhile, regards a song as something that's written once then performed countless times by musicians whose livelihood depends on it.

7. Guralnick told me he was drawn to longer biographies after writing a profile on Johnny Shines and thinking about how much more he wanted to say (2010, 8/14 interview).

8. See similar mention of Gavin's book in Marcus (2011a, 164n).

9. In *Last Train*, Guralnick writes that Elvis was "literally spent" after the performance (315). At a 2002 conference, Guralnick shared the randy connotations of his euphemism, shocking Camille Paglia (Marcus 2015a, 297).

10. As Marcus told Simon Reynolds in 2012, "I'm *not* interested in [musicans] as people. I'm interested in Elvis's story as he enacted it. And it was a mythic story: he stepped into a myth, or many myths, that were there before he was. And I was interested in the way he transformed those stories, those roles, those personae, and how he made them new, something they never were before. But I wasn't interested in his inner demons or the particulars of his upbringing. I was interested in him as the person that existed in the music that he made. And I think that's true for anybody I write about. Just as I'm not really interested in myself. I don't care what anybody I write about wanted to accomplish. I hear certain ambitions and desires and demands in the work itself" (quoted in Reynolds 2012, part 4).

11. See Lauterbach, *Beale Street Dynasty*.

12. See Guralnick's early profile: "Elvis, I think, changed forever the whole concept of the popular hero, grown bigger than life and smaller at the same time, through the process of media magnification" (1989, 94).

13. "It's clear from both [Presley] volumes that Guralnick is as much passionate fan as cool scholar," Mitchell Moore wrote in alt-country magazine *No Depression* in 1999. "But it couldn't have been much fun, as a fan, to write *Careless Love*, and as a scholar it must have been equally difficult. It's a story of decadence and inexorable decline, of tragic self-destruction, and the temptations to despair and moral judgment must have been great. He avoids both with grace and ease."

14. Yet farcical anecdotes abound. We are talking about a man who was asked to sing to a bull in the movies, who sang "Do the Clam," and who, in his stage patter, likened his jump-suited persona to the NBC peacock, splitting his pants while leaning over to kiss a fan. Elvis was not groovy. His sole trip on LSD failed to move him off his routine (he watched a science fiction movie and ate pizza). And then there were the corny jokes. A politician sizing up a potential office holder once asked Elvis what he might run for. "The city limits," the King replied (1994, 341–42). Asked his opinion of his GI haircut in 1958, Elvis quipped, "Hair today, gone tomorrow" (463). Elvis's down-home ways didn't resonate with the elite. They couldn't understand where he was coming from when he complained at a formal dinner about the undercooked meat, or when he greeted an RCA executive with an electric buzzer handshake (242, 249). After his initial run in Vegas clubs, at that time fairly upscale venues, *Newsweek* likened Elvis to "a jug of corn liquor at a champagne party" (274). Then, as now, laughs at this entertainer's expense expose rifts in American demographics and class structure.

15. The passion for blues was strong. Charters wrote *The Country Blues* (1959) in just thirty-six days. Gauging the success of the Robert Johnson LP, Origin Jazz Library reissued old blues 78s in the early 1960s. In 1964, white blues fans, including Nick Perls, Stephen Calt, John Fahey, David Evans, William Ferris, Phil Spiro, and Alan Wilson, traveled to remote regions of the South to locate their lost musical heroes (Gioia 2009, 349, 351, 354, 362–64, 372–74).

16. For an opposing viewpoint, see Preston Lauterbach's *The Chitlin' Circuit*, which reclaims the blues as a "vital" genre with "spry wit," played for black audiences for entertainment, not as a "dark soundtrack of our national drama," analyzed by middle-aged white men (2011, 4).

17. The Upsetters were Little Richard's first big group, but hardly anyone remembers that, and it's interesting how the term never took on the same resonance outside black culture.

18. Guralnick introduced Burke to another of his heroes, Sam Phillips, at the publication party for *Sweet Soul Music*, only to have the men stare each other down (2015a, 545).

19. Compare William C. Rhoden's obituary of boxer Joe Frazier, remembered by most as Muhammad Ali's great rival and unwilling foil. Rhoden reminded readers of Coretta Scott King's funeral, when speaker after speaker used the occasion for sermons on civil rights. Bill Clinton, who followed them, gestured toward King's coffin and said, "I don't want us to forget that there's a woman in there. Not a symbol, a

real woman who lived and breathed and got angry and got hurt and had dreams and disappointments" (quoted in Rhoden 2011). Joe Frazier was a man, not a symbol, Rhoden asserts. And so too, Guralnick shows, were Redding, Cooke, and Presley simply men.

20. Stax, the famous Memphis recording studio and record label located in an old theater on East McLemore, also housed a record store. Stax was a safe haven, a hangout for R&B and soul fans resisting Jim Crow culture, a physical extension of the invisible integrationist space southern radio provided. Booker T. Jones described the record store as a "magical place," and label co-owner Jim Stewart said, "I think a lot of these ivory tower executives, if they spent a few weeks behind the counter, might put out some better records" (quoted in Guralnick 1999b, 108, 110). Stax's "open-door policy" clearly benefited the white musicians. According to co-owner Estelle Axton, "Our kids [Packy Axton, Charlie Freeman, Duck Dunn, Chips Moman, Steve Cropper] just picked up so much technique and soul—up until then it had been mainly rock 'n' roll, just twang-twanging the guitars and the drummer going wild, but when it really got down to feeling, they were just taken with black musicians. They learned how to write. They picked up the feel. And they became great at it" (quoted in Guranlick 1999b, 111). For Guralnick, they were "kids dreaming of some kind of transcendence, partly slumming, partly looking for an edge, but mostly looking for a nameless kind of beatitude, a future they couldn't quite envision but that was different from anything they knew" (115). Duck Dunn recalls, "I think I was the first white guy to play in a black band in Memphis, and that was where I really started to learn something" (quoted in Guralnick 1999b, 157).

21. Deejays on high-wattage stations did the same: Hoss Allen in Nashville, Bill Cook in Newark, Zenas Sears in Atlanta, Poppa Stoppa in New Orleans, and Butterball in Philadelphia (George 2004, 15–59).

22. Atlantic Records producer Jerry Wexler is best known for his work with Aretha Franklin, but his interventions in the world of black music are manifold. Once, Wexler stepped from behind the studio glass to show Wilson Pickett how to dance the Jerk, with accents on beats two and four, so he could nail his recording of "In the Midnight Hour" (Guralnick 1999b, 155). Lieber, who joined Mike Stoller to write R&B hits for the Coasters and other black groups in the 1950s, was known to adopt black vernacular in everyday speech: "Aretha is suffering from upward mobility. We all does it" (quoted in Guralnick 1999b, 338). In the 1970s, Tom Waits and Rickie Lee Jones fashioned themselves "White Spades" as they gallivanted around the seedy side of Los Angeles, putting on "jazzbo" airs to counter the fey excesses of the lily-

white singer-songwriter scene based in Laurel Canyon (Hoskyns 2009, 195).

23. The trend went national in 1954, when Ray Charles's "I Got a Woman" and Little Walter's "My Babe" borrowed from The Southern Tones' "It Must Be Jesus" and Sister Rosetta Tharpe's "This Train," respectively. Secular R&B replaced gospel for singers like Sam Cooke (Guralnick, *Dream* 113) and Clyde McPhatter. Yet, as Lauterbach reveals in *The Chitlin' Circuit*, the R&B movement was spearheaded earlier with Roy Brown's "Good Rockin' Tonight," one of several "rockin'" hits performed exclusively for black audiences. Recording "Good Rockin' Tonight" and Big Mama Thornton's "Hound Dog" (written by Lieber and Stoller) in the mid-1950s, Elvis gave white musicians the impetus to join traditions that had flourished out of their earshot.

24. "Before he met me, Elvis had a million dollars' worth of talent," Colonel Tom crowed after signing him to RCA. "Now he has a million dollars" (quoted in Guralnick 1992, 30).

25. In his 2015 biography, Guralnick rationalizes Phillips's decision to abandon Thomas: "With the great blues singers—Howlin' Wolf for example—[Phillips] found himself in a state closer to awestruck wonder than the cool sense of control he was now able to adopt in his mentoring role [with white artists]" (2015a, 300).

26. Stewart told Guralnick, "I had scarcely seen a black till I was grown" (quoted in 1999b, 99). Yet as a young man he played fiddle on black-owned WDIA, which played country music on occasion even as it emerged as one of the most important soul outlets in the nation.

27. In Washington, where he performed the next night, Brown toured ghetto streets at Hubert Humphrey's bequest, to keep things "cool."

28. Redding died three days after recording his transcendent single "Dock of the Bay" and nearly three years to the day Sam Cooke passed. "Who knows what would have happened if Otis had lived," Guralnick muses, "any more than one can guess what would have happened if the Kennedys or Dr. King had survived" (1999b, 340). A comment offered by Johnny Jenkins reveals conspiracy theories circulating in the black community: That's "what happens to a nigger with ideas." Muhammad Ali weighed in similarly on Cooke's death: "If it had been someone like Elvis Presley or one of the Beatles, the FBI would still be investigating and someone would be in jail" (quoted in Guralnick 2006, 630). Elvis himself seemed to believe there was a conspiracy against Cooke, a black man who, in his words, "got out of line and … was taken care of" (quoted in Guralnick 2006, 643). David Henderson expressed the same uneasiness about Jimi Hendrix's death in *'Scuze Me While I Kiss the Sky* (2009).

29. "They'd always send me out there to tempt the niggers," Penn remembers; "you know, 'Go out there and stir 'em up, Penn.' 'Cause I would just go out there and squeal, and they'd say, 'Aw, shit, I can beat that'" (quoted in Guralnick 1999b, 341).

30. Wexler left Memphis for Muscle Shoals after a six-month experiment with Stax. He came to exploit Rick Hall the same way he did Jim Stewart. When he wore out his welcome in Alabama, Wexler returned to Memphis, this time landing at American Studios with Chips Moman. Each time, Wexler brought Wilson Pickett and recorded a hit with studio heads the others considered their enemies (Guralnick 1999b, 176, 215, 296).

31. For more on NATRA as "old boys network" for black deejays, see George (2004, 112–15).

32. After the King assassination, a number of Hi studio musicians led by Willie Mitchell were allowed by Memphis police to break curfew and go to work. Their quiet determination to keep working in the wake of tragedy stood in stark relief to the racial strife going on down the street at Stax.

33. Describing Elvis's return to Vegas in 1969, Priscilla Presley speaks of a "proudness that you only see in an animal" (quoted in Guralnick 1999, 351).

34. In 1957, black communities were buzzing about a comment Elvis reportedly made: "The only thing Negroes can do for me is buy my records and shine my shoes" (Guralnick 1994, 426). Elvis flatly denied issuing the barb, but bad vibes lingered and rumors held sway. During a 1975 show in Norfolk, according to a UPI account, Elvis announced on stage that "he smelled green peppers and onions" and that his backup singers, the Sweet Inspirations, "had probably been eating catfish," embarrassing the singers and causing two to leave the stage (Guralnick 1999, 570). But as Guralnick pointed out to me recently, Louie Robinson had discredited the shoeshine story in the pages of Jet in 1957, saying that the quote was out of character and that Elvis never played the venues where the remarks were purported to have been made. Regarding the 1975 Norfolk event, Guralnick says that the singers heard the remarks as "hostile," but that "none of them thought it was racial" (570). Guralnick says that to accuse Elvis of racism or "cultural theft" is not only to misunderstand him but also to misunderstand popular culture, which has engaged in "polyglot borrowings" since before the phonograph was introduced (xiv–xv). Even so, borrowing is not always the same as showing respect.

35. Presley's mindset changed in the mid-1960s, when he became enamored of Larry Gellar, a pseudo-intellectual self-help counselor who recommended New Age literature, sending the Memphis Mafia into a tizzy.

36. Guralnick shows that sex infiltrated the gospel world in mischievous ways. Little Richard's Bible doubled as his sex diary (2006, 427). In gospel nightclubs, waitresses dressed like Playboy Bunnies sported angel wings (521).

37. In 1997, *Life* ranked the discovery of Elvis #99 in the most influential events of the past thousand years (Guralnick 2015a, 610).

38. Phillips was not present at Sun Studios when Jerry Lee Lewis auditioned (Lewis and his father sold all the eggs on their Ferriday, Louisiana, farm to finance their trip to Memphis). But his lieutenant Jack Clement rolled tape. "Where in *hell* did this man come from?" Phillips told Clement after hearing Lewis play piano (quoted in Guralnick 2015a, 324). Well, you could say he came from the same place as Ike Turner, Howlin' Wolf, Elvis Presley, and Carl Perkins. Happily, these American "originals" found a man in Memphis willing to give them a chance.

Chapter Three

1. Newer alt-country labels included Little Dog, Yep Roc, Freedom, Back Porch, and Lost Highway, supplementing pioneers like Blind Pig (1977), Sugar Hill (1978), and High Tone (1983).

2. In front of the wrong audience, that admixture could ruffle feathers. Bill Friskics-Warren reported that Jason and the Scorchers were treated rudely at Vanderbilt because students thought the band was mocking country music (*ND* #6 1996).

3. Judy Zimola's *No Depression* feature on the International Musical Saw Association's festival held at Roaring Camp, California, described the assortment of folks the Americana movement brought together: "The crowd is what one would expect if one were to give any thought to musical saw enthusiasts: fans of old-timey music (distinct by their vintage outfits), cowboys, geezers of every age. But peppering the audience are beret-wearing Frenchmen, Japanese families, and kids who look like they just left a Strokes concert. Betty Page look-alikes wearing baby doll dresses and Doc Martens compare mallet techniques with sunburned ranchers in gimme caps" ("A Place to Be," *ND* #54 2004).

4. Blackstock writes in his album review of *Uncle Tupelo 89/93: An Anthology*: "More than a decade, now, since an old friend at Waterloo Records started raving about a new album they'd just gotten at the store. Roscoe was probably the world's biggest Replacements fan (that was his bootleg cassette they swiped and disseminated as *The Shit Hits the Fans*), and so it was no surprise that the garage-rock abandon of this young Illinois trio called Uncle Tupelo caught his ear from the git-go. Me, I

dug the Replacements too, along with such long gone heroes as Scruffy the Cat and Doctors' Mob; but I was just as likely to seek out songwriters such as Peter Case and Butch Hancock when I ventured into Waterloo or out on the town. It didn't seem such a stretch for those worlds to co-exist, or maybe even occupy the same plane. Enter *No Depression*" (*ND* #38 2002). Blackstock's dual affection for punk and alt-country bands extended to similarly coined nicknames: the "Mats" were replaced in alt-country circles by the "Tupes" and the "B'Rox" (Bottle Rockets).

5. "Part of me suspects I'm a loser, and part of me thinks I'm God almighty," Lennon once said, summing up the posture alt-country slackers later adopted (quoted in Elborough 2009, 225). In the 1960s and 1970s, Edd Hurt noted in *ND* #71 (2007), "Memphis artists such as Alex Chilton, Bobby Womack, and Jim Dickinson acted as archaeologists of their own demise, searching pop detritus like dopers trying to find a buried stash." If the Memphis musicians never found the commercial success they deserved, their failure cemented their status as cult figures. Townes Van Zandt, who penned "Waiting Around to Die," played the role of beautiful loser to the extreme, dying on January 1, 1997, the anniversary of the death of his role model, Hank Williams. The trick, Bob Seger sang, was not to play the game too long. Even if you did, it was best to disarm anybody who treated you as a god. Steve Earle once said, "Townes Van Zandt's the best songwriter in the world, and I'll stand on Bob Dylan's coffee table in cowboy boots and say that." Van Zandt's deflective reply was priceless: "I've met Bob Dylan's bodyguards, and if Steve Earle thinks he can stand on Bob Dylan's coffee table, he's sadly mistaken" (quoted in Kruth 2007, 7–8).

6. David Pichaske asserts that Bob Dylan's childhood trainspotting resulted in the machine-in-the-garden musings he included in liner notes to *Joan Baez in Concert, Part 2* (2010, 129). *The Machine in the Garden*, Leo Marx's study of American pastoral, comes to life on the cover of Uncle Tupelo's *89/93: An Anthology*, which shows power lines framing a desert highway.

7. In a memorable dig, one reader referred to Whiskeytown as "the Stone Temple Pilots of Alternative Country" ("Box Full of Letters," *ND* #4 1996). Gillian Welch was constantly chided for being the daughter of film industry parents and for faking her Appalachian style of dressing and singing. A profile of Diana Jones in *ND* #65 (2006) refers to the singer's "Gillian Welch type dress," shorthand, by that juncture, for an affected "homespun" look.

8. Years after the Beatles split, the Lennon-McCartney rivalry remained a touchstone. Hüsker Dü bassist Greg Norton submits that Grant Hart and Bob Mould filled these roles in his band (Azerrad 2002, 177–78). Fans tended to ally themselves

either with Hart's melodic sensibility or Mould's grating angst. Just the same, enthusiasts of Uncle Tupelo preferred either the melodic bassist (Tweedy) or the fiery guitarist (Farrar). The songwriting team in Throwing Muses (Tanya Donelly and Kristin Hersh) inspired similar debates. The Lennon-McCartney dynamic could even be glimpsed in the divergent stances of *No Depression* editors Peter Blackstock (McCartney) and Grant Alden (Lennon). "Truth be known," Blackstock admitted in one "Hello Stranger" column, "there's not a whole lot of artists that Grant and I see eye-to-eye on" (*ND* #63 2006).

9. As this title implies, humor regularly affected the editorial process. A typical correction: "The Shel Silverstein poem mentioned in a live review of Bobby Bare Jr. in *ND* #43 is called 'True Story,' not 'I lied.' (Sorry, we lied)" (*ND* #44 2003). The taglines of feature writers also contained some gems: "Like Fidel Castro, ND contributing editor Geoffrey Himes learned his theology at a Jesuit high school" (*ND* #33 2001). In a later issue, readers learned that "Himes has written for such now-defunct music magazines as Musician, Crawdaddy, Country Music, New Country, Fi, Request and Replay. And don't even ask him about the now-vanished websites he's written for" (*ND* #47 2003). Pithy titles were another specialty. When the Carter-Cash estate was auctioning family heirlooms, *No Depression* added a "Sittin' and Thinkin'" essay inspired by the Louvin Brothers' "Cash on the Barrelhead," now titled "That'll Be Cash on the Auction Block, Son" (*ND* #54 2004).

10. Occasionally, a bookend column went missing. "Hello Stranger" was absent in *ND* #19 (1999) and *ND* #37 (2002). There was no "Screen Door" in *ND* #42 (2002), *ND* #45 (2003), *ND* #48 (2003), and *ND* #58 (2005).

11. Himes points out that a formidable roster of musicians emerged from Texas social circles at key junctures of country rock and alt-country: Townes Van Zandt, Jerry Jeff Walker, and Mickey Newbury gathered in Houston in 1968; Jimmie Dale Gilmore, Joe Ely, Butch Hancock, and Terry Allen in Lubbock in 1972; Lyle Lovett, Robert Earl Keen, Nanci Griffith, and Eric Taylor in Houston in 1977; Ray Wylie Hubbard, Patty Griffin, Jimmy LaFave, Gurf Morlix, and Troy Campbell in Austin in 1999.

12. See also Alden's "A Late Meditation on the Oral History of Grunge," his review of Mark Yarm's *Everybody Loves Our Town* (2011): "The very last thing I wished to be a part of was mythologizing somebody else's demons to the point where kids would move to town and seek to embrace those demons."

13. Introducing *ND* #59, Alden proclaimed "our formal retirement of the phrase 'alt.country (whatever that is)," which had "confounded academics, annoyed musicians, and proved less and less descriptive of *No Depression* as it evolved." A

new subtitle, he argued, would allow the magazine to "settle into being what we have become—an American music magazine … surveying the best of the various musics rooted in the disparate traditions of this continent." Alden's writings from this point forward echoed this serious tone, even as Back Porch Records took out a two-page ad congratulating *No Depression* on "10 years of 'Whatever.'" An ad for the compilation CD *No Depression: What It Sounds Like, Vol. 2* also reverted to familiar language: "If, in fact, alternative-country music actually exists, this is what it sounds like. More or less" (*ND* #63 2006). If that weren't enough, readers hungry for more could buy copies of *ND* contributor Linda Ray's *Original Alt.Country Community (Whatever That Is) Cookbook*.

14. "The Original Harmony Ridge Creek Dippers wasn't initially meant for the public," Alden explains in *ND* #13 after interviewing Olson and his wife/bandmate Victoria Williams (herself a refugee from David Geffen's label) at their Joshua Tree home. In the same issue, Don McLeese heralds Butch Hancock's latest release on his Rainlight label: "After a flirtation with national distribution through Sugar Hill, Hancock has returned to self-imposed obscurity, the sort of obscurity that comes when the process of writing a song is its own reward, the recording of the song a spontaneous lark, the selling of the song an afterthought." The woodshedding aura imbuing profiles of Olson and Hancock struck a nerve with a *No Depression* community enamored with lo-fi approaches. "It is tempting to ask Mark about the Jayhawks, and his leaving," Alden wrote, "but one need simply compare the rough-hewn glory of his solo debut to the pop sheen of the Jayhawks' new *Sound of Lies* for the only answer that matters."

15. Instead, Marcus championed Iris DeMent, who was considered "too country" for Real Country radio (2015a, 150).

16. "Old Hank" received honorifics from the Replacements, who played "Hey Good Lookin'" in their shows, and Bob Dylan, whose backstage renditions of Williams numbers (in duets with Joan Baez and Johnny Cash) were captured in his 1967 and 1972 documentary films *Dont Look Back* and *Eat the Document*.

17. Patty Griffin remembered when PolyGram executives handed her a copy of U2's "Beautiful Day" and asked her for ten such singles (*ND* #39 2002).

18. Tom Morello of Rage Against the Machine has called *Nebraska* his "gateway drug" to acoustic music.

19. Compare these with two other public radio outlets: Garrison Keillor's *Prairie Home Companion*, dismissed as "affable Americana" in one *No Depression* review (*ND* #64), and *Mountain Stage*, hosted by Larry Groce in West Virginia.

20. An early Web source was the creatively titled "Modern Sounds in Country and wwWestern Music" ("Screen Door," *ND* #18 1998).

21. Abstractly examining suburbia's "unexamined lives," the rock ensemble Arcade Fire fashioned a masterpiece on "the sprawl" and its disaffected youth on *The Suburbs* (2010).

22. Professor Tichi had already moved beyond literary criticism, publishing *High Lonesome: The American Culture of Country Music* in 1994, at age fifty-two (my current age). I've sometimes thought about the coincidence as I've assembled *It's Just the Normal Noises*.

23. After Larry Brown died, Algonquin Books of Chapel Hill advertised his books in *No Depression*. A musical tribute to Brown, performed by various alt-country artists and issued by Bloodshot Records, was reviewed in *ND* #70 (2007).

Chapter Four

1. "We made the rules; you have to live with them," a Boomer friend told Powers. "Although his arrogance made me flinch," she recalls, "I knew on one level he was right" (2001. 35).

2. Carrie Brownstein likewise complained about academia's insularity during her brief MFA stint (2015, 201).

3. A vision shared in my Rochester apartment was a photo on Fairport Convention's 1969 album *Unhalfbricking*, which showed band members sharing a simple meal around a wooden table.

4. Smith says, "Robert and I were irrevocably entwined, like Paul and Elisabeth, the sister and brother in Cocteau's *Les Enfants Terribles*. We played similar games, declared the most obscure object treasure, and often puzzled friends and acquaintances by our indefinable devotion" (2010, 200). Their relationship took on new dimensions once Mapplethorpe photographed Smith. "He saw more in me than I could see in myself," Smith remembers. "Whenever he peeled the image from the Polaroid negative, he would say, 'With you I can't miss'" (192). The most famous example is the iconic photo gracing the cover of Smith's debut album, *Horses*.

5. Before digitalization, I noticed what books or albums friends displayed on shelves. A row of Faulkner paperbacks told you one thing, a Duncan Sheik CD quite another.

6. Ann Powers identified as an "arty girl" in her high school, derided by jocks and shoved around by stoners (2001, 252).

7. Gaines says burnouts listen to the Grateful Dead and dirtbags to heavy metal. Burnouts are spaced out on drugs, whereas dirtbags tend toward violence.

8. Ironically, the Building was once a production center for *Parents* magazine (Gaines 1998, 82).

9. Accordingly, Gaines emphasizes the harder edges of the 1960s. She dates the birth of the burnout from Jimi Hendrix's "Star Spangled Banner," the crash-and-burn anthem used as background music in the *Woodstock* film as the festival wound down. Gaines also mentions the Shangri-Las, whose tough-girl posturing ("it was very high status to have a boyfriend in serious trouble with the law") was adopted by teens in Bergenfield (1998, 120). Amy Winehouse was also smitten. "I didn't want to just wake up drinking, and crying, and listening to the Shangri-Las," Winehouse said, but she did exactly that, putting snippets of "Remember (Walking in the Sand)" into her own "Back to Black" in 2006 (Marcus 2014, 248).

10. In another parallel with *The Breakfast Club*, Bergenfield teen Ruthie wears Joe's leather jacket and he wears her earring, just as Claire (the "princess") and Bender exchange accessories at the end of the film.

11. Similarly, Bruce Springsteen's songs were dismissed as "whiny" music for "college kids" (Gaines 1998, 166).

12. Gaines describes Tipper Gore as "a woman about my age with young children and not a clue about how music works in kids' lives" (1998, 207).

13. Cobain liked to say that his first concert was Black Flag, but it was actually a Sammy Hagar show at the Seattle Center Coliseum. Everett True comments: "Journalists would attempt to make something out of the fact that Kurt Cobain—like 99 per cent of his peers in small town America—saw some butt rock band at his first ever show; and even caught UK hard rock/metal outfit Judas Priest at the Tacoma Dome the same summer. Kurt also once owned an REO Speedwagon album. So what? Doesn't mean he'd found his calling: just that he didn't know where to look" (2007, 16).

14. In an alternate photograph *Rolling Stone* decided not to use, Cobain's tee shirt reads Kill the Grateful Dead (Azerrad 2001, 253).

15. "There's an apocryphal story about how Kurt claimed he bought his first guitar in return for the proceeds of some recovered guns," True writes in *Nirvana: The Biography*. "The strange thing is, Kurt never actually claimed this—but the falsity proved a useful stopping-off point for one journalist to pontificate about Kurt's story-telling abilities. And now, because it's been written that Kurt made the claim, the supposition that he was lying about that moment is itself part of the myth. Confusion is layered upon confusion. In reality, Kurt pawned the guns and spent

the cash on an amplifier." Then, in a knife-twisting maneuver, True repeats Cross's words: "Never let the truth get in the way of a good story" (27, 28).

16. Like Dana Spiotta's fictional rocker Nik Worth in *Stone Arabia*, Cobain was known to compose and archive fake reviews of his songs and performances before he actually hit the big time with Nirvana (Cross 2014, 70, 114). Weirdly, Nik ends up committing suicide, too. Or at least he writes his own obituary, mentioning suicide, before disappearing into Topanga Canyon with his favorite guitars. After she wrote *Stone Arabia*, Spiotta says she "discovered … that there are a lot of people that do not just do the basement recordings, which you can imagine is very common, but [are] also keeping fake liner notes and doing a journal and creating a sort of alternative reality. That seems to be less unusual than you would imagine" (2011a).

17. Paul Westerberg of the Replacements also worked as a janitor after dropping out of school.

18. Marcus calls the Leadbelly cover "shattering, one of those performances where you can't imagine the singer escaping from the song" (2000b, 98). Coletti calls the song's ending, replete with Cobain's loaded pauses and his "rubbery, hillbilly-ish face," "possibly the most memorable moment in *Unplugged* history." Asked by Coletti whether he wanted to end the concert right then, Cobain replied, "How do I top that last song?" (quoted in Yarm 2011, 436).

19. Cobain's liner notes for "Dumb": "All that pot. All that supposedly, unaddictive, harmless, safe reefer that damaged my nerves, and ruined my memory, and made me feel like blowing up the prom. It just wasn't ever strong enough, so I climbed the ladder to the poppy" (quoted in Cross 2014, 280).

20. See also Nick Soulsby's *I Found My Friends*, an oral biography that focuses on the lesser-known musicians who appreciated Cobain for who he was, not for what he became.

21. See Nik Worth's power pop ensemble, the Fakes, in Spiotta's *Stone Arabia*. Consider, too, the Cavedogs, a talented power pop trio from Boston who seemed primed for success after a 1992 *Rolling Stone* profile, only to be dropped by their label a year later.

22. As Peter Guralnick wrote, "Memphis, always a haven for eccentrics and individualists, is the only locale I know that actually boasts of its craziness" (1989, 337).

23. Eggleston's photography graces the cover of Big Star's *Radio City* and Jovanovic's book.

24. Chilton likewise categorized his 1970s music as classical (George-Warren 2014, 201).

25. According to Jim Dickinson, Falco "could play in one tempo, sing in another tempo, and have them both be wrong" (quoted in George-Warren 2014, 228). The Cramps were better musicians, yet Chilton preferred to keep the sound as raw as possible. In a memorable studio sequence, a hanger-on distracts Cramps front man Lux Interior during the introduction to "I Was a Teenage Werewolf," causing the song to sputter and halt. Lux spends a full minute cursing out the clueless spectator, imploring him to leave, as another band member groans into the microphone "Oh, Jesus Christ!" In true form, Chilton kept tape rolling, capturing both the false start and the ensuing studio kerfuffle (the Cramps 1980; George-Warren 2014, 234–35).

26. Evan Dando performed "Nighttime" at the SXSW festival following Chilton's death in 2010.

27. Caroline is also quick to identify the desperado-outlaw style popularized by the Band ("studiously unscrubbed and unglamorous") when she hears "The Night They Drove Old Dixie Down" in an upstate bar filled with young men affecting that look (Spiotta 2006, 184–85). For Caroline, as for Marcus in *Mystery Train*, the song reflects the state of American identity, which more and more seems based on fantasy. There is no mention of Jason listening to the Band, but he does listen to *Maggot Brain* at Gage's house. Marcus once called the lengthy title track "peace beyond words" (2015a, 126), but Jason doesn't think so. He returns to *Pet Sounds*, trading Funkadelic's "too dark" guitar for the California band's "choir voices," much as his mother had, decades prior (Spiotta 2006, 212).

28. Interviewing Stormtroopers of Death front man Billy Milano, Donna Gaines refers to a "scene fracture" in hardcore, claiming that "by 1987, the dream of a scene was long gone. The clubs were now slime pits of broken bones, vomit, and rudeness" (1998, 214).

29. Les says he also named Jude after the saint, "the loyal apostle" (Henderson 2012, 154), which is exactly what Jude ends up becoming for Johnny.

30. After hearing doctors discuss in clinical terms "the source of your son's behavior," Harriet examines her pocketbook. "In it was the detritus of her slipshod motherhood—keys, Kleenex, aspirin, cigarettes, a Snickers wrapper, an old shopping list, and a dime bag inside an old Altoids tin inside a glove, which she decided then and there to flush the next time she had a chance. She closed her eyes. She could fall asleep right here, disappear. How wonderful it would be to find the source of all this, to blame it on some other mother" (75). It turns out that Jude hides his pot the same way. Harriet, knowing by instinct where to look, confiscates his stash (86).

Works Cited

1991: The Year Punk Broke. 1992. Directed by Dave Markey. Los Angeles: Sonic Life/ We Got Power Films.

Alden, Grant. 2013. "A Late Meditation on the Oral History of Grunge." *No Depression* online, June 1. http://www.nodepression.com.

———. 2010. "Field Notes." *No Depression* online, September. http://www. nodepression.com.

———. 2006. "Q&A with Grant Alden." *Columns: The University of Washington Alumni Magazine*, March. http://www.washington.edu/alumni/columns/ march06.

Alden, Grant, and Peter Blackstock, eds. 2005. *The Best of No Depression: Writing about American Music*. Austin: University of Texas Press.

Almost Famous. 2000. Directed by Cameron Crowe. Culver City, CA: Columbia Pictures.

Ambrose, Stephen E. 2014. *Nixon Volume 1: The Education of a Politician 1913–1962*. New York: Simon and Schuster.

Anthology of American Folk Music. 1997. Compiled by Harry Smith. Washington, DC: Smithsonian Folkways Records.

Arcade Fire. 2010. *The Suburbs*. Durham, NC: Merge Records.

Attebery, Brian. 1996. "American Studies: A Not So Unscientific Method." *American Quarterly* 48 (June): 316–43.

Azerrad, Michael. 2002. *Our Band Could Be Your Life: Scenes from the American Indie Underground, 1981–1991*. Boston: Back Bay.

———. 2001. *Come As You Are: The Story of Nirvana*. New York: Broadway.

———. 1992. "Nirvana: Inside the Heart and Mind of Kurt Cobain." *Rolling Stone*.

April 16, 1992. http://www.rolingstone.com.

Bangs, Lester. 1988. *Psychotic Reactions and Carburetor Dung*. Edited by Greil Marcus. New York: Vintage.

Banta, Martha. 2015. *Failure and Success in America: A Literary Debate*. Princeton: Princeton University Press.

Benjamin, Walter. 1968. "Theses on the Philosophy of History." In *Illuminations: Essays and Reflections*, edited by Hannah Arendt, translated by Harry Zohn, 253–64. New York: Schocken.

Berkhofer, Robert F. 1999. "A New Context for American Studies?" In *Locating American Studies: The Evolution of a Discipline*, edited by Lucy Maddox, 279–304. Baltimore: Johns Hopkins University Press.

The Big Chill. 1983. Directed by Lawrence Kasdan. Culver City, CA: Columbia Pictures.

Big Star. 2006. *3rd/Sister Lovers*. Memphis: Ardent Records.

Blush, Steven. 2001. *American Hardcore*. Los Angeles: Feral House.

Booth, Stanley. 2000. *The True Adventures of the Rolling Stones*. Chicago: A Cappella.

The Breakfast Club. 1985. Directed by John Hughes. Universal City, CA: Universal Pictures.

Brownstein, Carrie. 2015. *Hunger Makes Me a Modern Girl: A Memoir*. New York: Riverhead.

———. 2009. "Blood on the Tracks." In *The Cambridge Companion to Bob Dylan*, edited by Kevin J. H. Dettmar, 155–59. New York: Cambridge University Press.

Cantwell, David. 1997. "Elvis Presley—Fanfare for the Common Man." *No Depression* #11.

Cantwell, Robert. 1996. *When We Were Good: The Folk Revival*. Cambridge: Harvard University Press.

———. 1991. "Smith's Memory Theater: The Folkways Anthology of American Folk Music." *New England Review* Spring/Summer: 364–97.

Chang, Jeffrey. 2005. *Can't Stop, Won't Stop: A History of the Hip-Hop Generation*. New York: Picador.

Chilton, Alex. 1985. Interview on MTV's *The Cutting Edge*. http://www.youtube.com/watch?v=105yeWrjoEc.

Christgau, Robert. 2015. *Going into the City: Portrait of a Critic as a Young Man*. New York: Dey Street.

———. 2000. *Grown Up All Wrong: 75 Great Rock and Pop Artists from Vaudeville to*

Techno. Cambridge: Harvard University Press.

———. 1973. "Anatomy of a Love Festival." *Any Old Way You Choose It: Rock and Other Pop Music, 1967–1973.* Baltimore: Penguin.

Clark, T. J. 1999. *Farewell to an Idea: Episodes from a History of Modernism.* New Haven: Yale University Press.

Costello, Elvis. 1978. "Radio Radio." *This Year's Model.* New York: Radar Records.

Cott, Jonathan, ed. 2006. *Bob Dylan: The Essential Interviews.* New York: Wenner Books.

"The Country and Western Music Portfolio." 2006. *Vanity Fair,* November. http://www.vanityfair.com/culture/photos/2006/11/country_portfolio200611.

The Cramps. 1980. "I Was a Teenage Werewolf." *Songs the Lord Taught Us.* Hollywood, CA: Capitol Records.

Cross, Charles R. 2014. *Heavier Than Heaven: A Biography of Kurt Cobain.* New York: Hyperion.

The Decline of Western Civilization, Part One. 1981. Directed by Penelope Spheeris. Los Angeles: Spheeris Films.

DeCurtis, Anthony, et al., eds. 1992. *The Rolling Stone Illustrated History of Rock and Roll.* Rev. ed. New York: Random House.

DeRogatis, Jim. 2000. *Let It Blurt: The Life and Times of Lester Bangs, America's Greatest Rock Critic.* New York: Broadway.

Dettmar, Kevin J. H. 2009. "Among Schoolchildren: Dylan's Forty Years in the Classroom." In *Highway 61 Revisited: Bob Dylan's Road from Minnesota to the World,* edited by Colleen J. Sheehy and Thomas Swiss, 154–65. Minneapolis: University of Minnesota Press.

Down by Law. 1986. Directed by Jim Jarmusch. Universal City, CA: Island Pictures/Universal Pictures.

Dylan, Bob. 2005. *Chronicles.* New York: Simon and Schuster.

———. 2004. "My Life in a Stolen Moment." In *Studio A: The Bob Dylan Reader,* edited by Benjamin Hedin, 3–7. New York: Norton.

———. 1975. "Tears of Rage." *The Basement Tapes.* New York: Columbia Records.

Easy Rider. 1969. Directed by Dennis Hopper. Culver City, CA: Columbia Pictures.

Elborough, Travis. 2009. *The Vinyl Countdown: The Album from LP to iPod and Back Again.* Brooklyn: Soft Skull.

Fairport Convention. 1969. *Unhalfbricking.* Santa Monica, CA: A&M Records.

Fiedler, Leslie. 1960. *Love and Death in the American Novel.* New York: Crowell.

Fox, Aaron A. 2008. "Beyond Austin's City Limits: Justin Trevino and the

Boundaries of 'Alternative' Country." In *Old Roots, New Routes: The Cultural Politics of Alt.Country Music*, edited by Pamela Fox and Barbara Ching, 83–110. Ann Arbor: University of Michigan Press.

Fox, Pamela. 2008. "Time as 'Revelator': Alt.Country Women's Performance of the Past." In *Old Roots, New Routes: The Cultural Politics of Alt.Country Music*, edited by Pamela Fox and Barbara Ching, 134–53. Ann Arbor: University of Michigan Press.

Fox, Pamela, and Barbara Ching. eds. 2008. *Old Roots, New Routes: The Cultural Politics of Alt.Country Music*. Ann Arbor: University of Michigan Press.

——— 2008a. "Introduction: The Importance of Being Ironic—Toward a Theory and Critique of Alt.Country Music." In *Old Roots, New Routes: The Cultural Politics of Alt.Country Music*, edited by Pamela Fox and Barbara Ching, 1–27. Ann Arbor: University of Michigan Press.

Gaines, Donna. 2007. *A Misfit's Manifesto: The Sociological Memoir of a Rock and Roll Heart*. New Brunswick: Rutgers University Press.

———. 1998. *Teenage Wasteland: Suburbia's Dead End Kids*. Chicago: University of Chicago Press.

Gallagher, Catherine. 1989. "Marxism and the New Historicism." In *The New Historicism*, edited by H. Aram Veeser, 37–48. New York: Routledge.

Garner, Dwight. 2015. "When a Book Became a Trusty Companion." *New York Times*, September 3, C1, 4.

Gear Daddies. 1988. "Statue of Jesus." *Let's Go Scare Al*. Minneapolis: Gark Records.

George, Nelson. 2004. *The Death of Rhythm and Blues*. New York: Penguin.

George-Warren, Holly. 2014. *A Man Called Destruction: The Life and Music of Alex Chilton, From Box Tops to Big Star to Back Door Man*. New York: Viking.

———. 2011. Interview with Kimberly Austin. *The Rock Book Show*, May 1. https://www.youtube.com/watch?v=Z5fRW8XznzE.

Ginsberg, Allen. 1984. "Wichita Vortex Sutra." In *Collected Poems 1947–1980*, 394–411. New York: Harper and Row.

Gioia, Ted. 2009. *Delta Blues: The Life and Times of the Mississippi Masters Who Revolutionized American Music*. New York: Norton.

Goldberg, Michael. 2000. "Greil Marcus, World's Greatest Rock Critic." Interview, September 7. *Addicted to Noise*. http://www.addict.com.

Goodman, Fred. 1997. *The Mansion on the Hill: Dylan, Young, Geffen, Springsteen, and the Head-on Collision of Rock and Commerce*. New York: Times Books.

Gordon, Kim. 2015. *Girl in a Band*. New York: Dey Street.

Gordon, Robert. 2013. *Respect Yourself: Stax Records and the Soul Explosion*. New York: Bloomsbury.

———. 2001. *It Came from Memphis*. New York: Pocket Books.

Gowing, Liam. 2004. "Mister Misery." *Spin* 20 (December): 80–92.

Gray, Marcus. 2010. *Route 19 Revisited: The Clash and London Calling*. New York: Soft Skull.

———. 1997. *Last Gang in Town: The Story and Myth of the Clash*. New York: Holt.

Greenblatt, Stephen J. 1990. *Learning to Curse: Essays in Early Modern Culture*. New York: Routledge.

Guralnick, Peter. 2015. Interview with *Entertainment Weekly*, June 4. http://www.ew.com/article/2015/06/04/peter-guralnick-sam-phillips-biography.

———. 2015a. *Sam Phillips: The Man Who Invented Rock 'n' Roll*. New York: Little, Brown.

———. 2010/2011. Interviews with the author, August 14, 2010; October 14, 2010; December 5, 2011.

———. 2006. *Dream Boogie: The Triumph of Sam Cooke*. Boston: Back Bay.

———. 2005. "Brief Encounter." Interview with James Marcus, October 5. http://housemirth.blogspot.com/2005/10/brief-encounter-peter-guralnick.html.

———. 1999. *Careless Love: The Unmaking of Elvis Presley*. Boston: Little, Brown.

———. 1999a. *Feel Like Going Home: Portraits in Blues and Rock 'n' Roll*. Boston: Back Bay.

———. 1999b. *Sweet Soul Music: Rhythm and Blues and the Southern Dream of Freedom*. Boston: Back Bay.

———. 1994. *Last Train to Memphis: The Rise of Elvis Presley*. Boston: Back Bay.

———. 1992. "Elvis Presley." In *The Rolling Stone Illustrated History of Rock and Roll*, rev. ed., edited by Anthony DeCurtis et al., 21–36. New York: Random House.

———. 1989. *Lost Highway: Journeys and Arrivals of American Musicians*. New York: Harper Perennial.

The Harry Smith Connection: A Live Tribute to the Anthology of American Folk Music. 1998. Washington, DC: Smithsonian Folkways Records.

Hebdige, Dick. 1979. *Subculture: The Meaning of Style*. London: Methuen.

Henderson, David. 2009. *'Scuze Me While I Kiss the Sky: Jimi Hendrix: Voodoo Child*. New York: Atria.

Henderson, Eleanor. 2012. *Ten Thousand Saints*. New York: Ecco.

Henthoff, Nat. 2006. "The Crackin', Shakin', Breakin' Sounds." In *Bob Dylan: The Essential Interviews*, edited by Jonathan Cott, 13–28 New York: Wenner Books.

Heylin, Clinton. 2003. *Bob Dylan: Behind the Shades Revisited*. New York: Harper
Entertainment.

High Fidelity. 2000. Directed by Stephen Frears. Burbank, CA: Buena Vista Pictures.

Holmes, Richard. 1996. *Footsteps: Adventures of a Romantic Biographer*. New York:
Vintage.

Hoskyns, Barney. 2009. *Low Side of the Road: A Life of Tom Waits*. New York:
Broadway.

————.2006. *Across the Great Divide: The Band and America*. New York: Hal
Leonard.

————. 2006a. *Hotel California*. Hoboken, NJ: Wiley.

Hüsker Dü. 1984. "Broken Home, Broken Heart." *Zen Arcade*. Long Beach, CA: SST
Records.

Jameson, Fredric. 1991. *Postmodernism, or, the Cultural Logic of Late Capitalism*.
Durham, NC: Duke University Press.

Johansen, David. 2000. *David Johansen and the Harry Smiths*. New York: Chesky
Records.

Jovanovic. Rob. 2005. *Big Star: The Short Life, Painful Death, and Unexpected
Resurrection of the Kings of Power Pop*. Chicago: A Cappella/Chicago Review
Press.

Kerouac, Jack. 1986. *On the Road*. New York: Penguin.

Khan, Ashley. 2002. *A Love Supreme: The Story of John Coltrane's Signature Album*.
New York: Viking.

————. 2001. *Kind of Blue: The Making of the Miles Davis Masterpiece*. New York:
Granta.

Kot, Greg. 2004. *Wilco: Learning How to Die*. New York: Broadway.

Kruth, John. 2007. *To Live's to Fly: The Ballad of the Late, Great Townes Van Zandt*.
New York: DaCapo.

Kuklick, Bruce. 1999. "Myth and Symbol in American Studies." In *Locating
American Studies: The Evolution of a Discipline*, edited by Lucy Maddox, 71–90.
Baltimore: Johns Hopkins University Press.

Lauterbach, Preston. 2015. *Beale Street Dynasty: Sex, Song, and the Struggle for the
Soul of Memphis*. New York: Norton.

————. 2011. *The Chitlin' Circuit and the Road to Rock 'n' Roll*. New York: Norton.

Lawrence, D. H. 1964. *Studies in Classic American Literature*. New York: Viking.

Liu, Alan. 1989. "The Power of Formalism: The New Historicism." *ELH* 56: 721–71.

Maddox, Lucy, ed. 1999. *Locating American Studies: The Evolution of a Discipline*.

Baltimore: Johns Hopkins University Press.

Mailer, Norman. 1992. "The White Negro." In *The Portable Beat Reader*, edited by Ann Charters, 581–605. New York: Penguin.

Marcus, Greil. 2015. *Mystery Train: Images of America in Rock 'n' Roll Music*. 6th rev. ed. New York: Plume.

———. 2015a. *Real Life Rock: The Complete Top Ten Columns, 1986–2014*. New Haven: Yale University Press.

———. 2014. *The History of Rock 'n' Roll in Ten Songs*. New Haven: Yale University Press.

———. 2011. Review of James Gavin's *Deep in a Dream*. August 30. http://www.barnesandnoble.com/review/deep-in-a-dream.

———. 2011a. *The Doors: A Lifetime of Listening to Five Mean Years*. New York: Public Affairs.

———. 2010. *Bob Dylan by Greil Marcus: Writings 1968–2010*. New York: Public Affairs.

———. 2010a. *When That Rough God Goes Riding: Listening to Van Morrison*. New York: Public Affairs.

———. 2006. *Like a Rolling Stone: Bob Dylan at the Crossroads*. New York: Public Affairs.

———. 2006a. *The Shape of Things to Come: Prophecy and the American Voice*. New York: Farrar, Straus, and Giroux.

———. 2000. "Bruce." Email to Dave Marsh. December 15. Cited with permission.

———. 2000a. Conversation with the author, Princeton University, December 8.

———. 2000b. *Double Trouble: Bill Clinton and Elvis Presley in a Land of No Alternatives*. New York: Holt.

———. 2000c. "Prophecy and the American Voice." Course syllabus. University of California, Berkeley, Spring; Princeton University, Autumn (revised).

———. 1998. "Four Moments of Prophecy." *Threepenny Review* (Winter): 15–19.

———. 1997. *Invisible Republic: Bob Dylan's Basement Tapes*. New York: Holt.

———. 1995. *The Dustbin of History*. Cambridge: Harvard University Press.

———. 1993. *Ranters and Crowd Pleasers: Punk in Pop Music, 1977–1992*. New York: Doubleday.

———. 1992. "Anarchy in the U.K." In *The Rolling Stone Illustrated History of Rock and Roll*, rev. ed., edited by Anthony DeCurtis et al., 594–607. New York: Random House.

———. 1992a. "The Beatles." In *The Rolling Stone Illustrated History of Rock and Roll*, rev. ed., edited by Anthony DeCurtis et al., 209–22. New York: Random House.

———. 1991. *Dead Elvis: A Chronicle of a Cultural Obsession*. New York: Anchor.

———. 1990. *Lipstick Traces: A Secret History of the Twentieth Century*. Cambridge: Harvard University Press.

Marcus, Greil, ed. 2007. *Stranded: Rock and Roll for a Desert Island*. 2nd ed., New York: Da Capo.

Marcus, Greil, and Werner Sollors, eds. 2009. *A New Literary History of America*. Cambridge, MA: Belknap/Harvard University Press.

Marcus, Sara. 2010. *Girls to the Front: The True Story of the Riot Grrrl Revolution*. New York: Harper Perennial.

Marx, Leo. 1969. "American Studies: A Defense of an Unscientific Method." *New Literary History* 1: 75–90.

———. 1964. *The Machine in the Garden: Technology and the Pastoral Ideal in America*. New York: Oxford University Press.

Mather, Olivia Carter. 2008. "'Regressive Country': The Voice of Gram Parsons." In *Old Roots, New Routes: The Cultural Politics of Alt.Country Music*, edited by Pamela Fox and Barbara Ching, 154–74. Ann Arbor: University of Michigan Press.

Mazullo, Mark. 1997. "Fans and Critics: Greil Marcus's *Mystery Train* as Rock 'n' Roll History." *The Musical Quarterly* 81 (Summer): 145–69.

McDonough, Jimmy. 2003. *Shakey: Neil Young's Biography*. New York: Anchor.

McNally, Dennis. 2014. *On Highway 61: Music, Race and the Evolution of Cultural Freedom*. Berkeley: Counterpoint.

The Mekons. 1989. "Learning to Live on Your Own." *The Mekons Rock 'n' Roll*. London: Blast First Records.

Miller, Jim, ed. 1976. *The Rolling Stone Illustrated History of Rock and Roll*. New York: Rolling Stone Press.

Miller, Perry. 1964. *Errand into the Wilderness*. New York: Harper and Row.

Miller, Stephen Paul. 1999. *The Seventies Now: Culture as Surveillance*. Durham. NC: Duke University Press.

Milward, John. 2006. Review of Peter Guralnick's *Dream Boogie*. "Bound." *No Depression* #61.

Moore, Mitchell. 1999. Review of Peter Guralnick's *Careless Love*. "Bound." *No Depression* #19.

Mystery Train. 1989. Directed by Jim Jarmusch. Los Angeles: Orion Classics.

Nirvana. 1994. "Dumb," "Lake of Fire," "Pennyroyal Tea," and "Where Did You Sleep

Last Night?" *Unplugged in New York*. Santa Monica, CA: Geffen Records.

———. 1993. "All Apologies" and "Serve the Servants." *In Utero*. Santa Monica, CA: Geffen Records.

———. 1991. "Smells Like Teen Spirit" and "Something in the Way." *Nevermind*. Santa Monica, CA: Geffen Records.

No Depression. 1995–2008. Print issues #1 to #75, edited by Grant Alden and Peter Blackstock. Digitally archived at http://nodepression.com.

Palmer, Robert. 2009. *Blues and Chaos: The Music Writing of Robert Palmer*, edited by Anthony DeCurtis. New York: Scribner.

Pareles, Jon. 2007. "When It Takes Three People to Make a Duet." *New York Times*, October 21. http://www.nytimes.com/2007/10/21/arts/music/21pare.html.

Pecknold, Diane. 2008. "Selling Out or Buying In? Alt.Country's Cultural Politics of Commercialism." In *Old Roots, New Routes: The Cultural Politics of Alt.Country Music*, edited by Pamela Fox and Barbara Ching, 28–50. Ann Arbor: University of Michigan Press.

Petty, Tom, and the Heartbreakers. 1979. "Even the Losers." *Damn the Torpedoes*. Universal City, CA: Backstreet/MCA Records.

Pichaske, David. 2010. *Song of the North Country: A Midwest Framework to the Songs of Bob Dylan*. New York: Continuum.

Polito, Robert. 2009. "Bob Dylan's Memory Palace." In *Highway 61 Revisited: Bob Dylan's Road from Minnesota to the World*, edited by Colleen J. Sheehy and Thomas Swiss, 140–53. Minneapolis: University of Minnesota Press.

Powers, Ann. 2001. *Weird Like Us: My Bohemian America*. New York: Da Capo.

Pynchon, Thomas. 1973. *V*. New York: Bantam.

Reighley, Kurt B. 2010. *United States of Americana: Backyard Chickens, Burlesque Beauties and Handmade Bitters*. New York: Harper.

The Replacements. 1987. "Alex Chilton." *Pleased to Meet Me*. London: Sire Records.

———. 1981. "Shiftless When Idle." *Sorry Ma, Forgot to Take Out the Trash*. Minneapolis: Twin/Tone Records.

Reynolds, Simon. 2012. "Myths and Depths: Greil Marcus Talks to Simon Reynolds." *Los Angeles Review of Books*. Parts 1–4: April 27, May 4, May 11, May 18. https://lareviewofbooks.org/article/myths-and-depths-greil-marcus-talks-to-simon-reynolds-part-1/.

———. 2011. *Retromania: Pop Culture's Addiction to Its Own Past*. New York: Faber and Faber.

Rhoden, William C. 2011. "At His Essence, Smokin' Joe Was More Than Just a

Symbol." *New York Times*, November 14, D3.

Rhodes, Lisa L. 2005. *Electric Ladyland: Women and Rock Culture*. Philadelphia: University of Pennsylvania Press.

Ross, Andrew. 1989. "Hip, and the Long Front of Color." In *No Respect: Intellectuals and Popular Culture*, 65–101. New York: Routledge.

Salewicz, Chris. 2008. *Redemption Song: The Ballad of Joe Strummer*. 2007. New York: Faber and Faber.

Schaper, Julie, and Steven Horwitz, eds. 2009. *Amplified: Fiction from Leading Alt-Country, Indie Rock, Blues and Folk Musicians*. Brooklyn: Melville House

Seger, Bob, and the Silver Bullet Band. 1976. "Mainstreet," "Night Moves," and "Rock and Roll Never Forgets." *Night Moves*. Hollywood, CA: Capitol Records

Sex Pistols. 1977. "God Save the Queen." *Never Mind the Bollocks Here's the Sex Pistols*. Burbank, CA: Warner Brothers Records

Sheffield, Rob. 2010. "Punk Days." Review of Kristin Hersh's *Rat Girl*. *New York Times Book Review*, October 8, 13.

Sheehy, Colleen J., and Thomas Swiss, eds. 2009. *Highway 61 Revisited: Bob Dylan's Road from Minnesota to the World*. Minneapolis: University of Minnesota Press.

Shepard, Sam. 2004. *The Rolling Thunder Logbook*. New York: Da Capo.

Simkin, Stevie. 2008. "'The Burden Is Passed On': Son Volt, Tradition, and Authenticity." In *Old Roots, New Routes: The Cultural Politics of Alt.Country Music*, edited by Pamela Fox and Barbara Ching, 192–221. Ann Arbor: University of Michigan Press.

Slacker. 1991. Directed by Richard Linklater. Los Angeles: Orion Classics.

Sleater-Kinney, 2000. "You're No Rock and Roll Fun." *All Hands On the Bad One*. Portland, OR: Kill Rock Stars Records.

Smith, Elliott. 2000. "Nighttime." Live performance at Town Hall, New York. https://www.youtube.com/watch?v=mLRPvlvbSD8.

Smith, Henry Nash. 1950. *Virgin Land*. Cambridge: Harvard University Press.

Smith, Jon. 2008. "Growing Up and Out of Alt.Country: On Gen X, Wearing Vintage, and Neko Case." In *Old Roots, New Routes: The Cultural Politics of Alt. Country Music*, edited by Pamela Fox and Barbara Ching, 51–82. Ann Arbor: University of Michigan Press.

Smith, Patti. 2010. *Just Kids*. New York: Ecco.

———. 2002. "Piss Factory." *Land (1975–2002)*. New York: Arista Records

———. 1975. *Horses*. New York: Arista Records

Son Volt. 1995. "Loose String" and "Windfall." *Trace*. Burbank, CA: Warner Brothers

Records.

Sonic Youth. 1988. *Daydream Nation*. Culver City, CA: Enigma Records.

Soulsby, Nick. 2015. *I Found My Friends: The Oral History of Nirvana*. New York: Thomas Dunne/St. Martin's.

Sounes, Howard. 2015. *27: A History of the 27 Club Through the Lives of Brian Jones, Jimi Hendrix, Janis Joplin, Jim Morrison, Kurt Cobain, and Amy Winehouse*. New York: Da Capo.

Spiotta, Dana. 2011. "Interview with Alex Shephard." *Full Stop*, December 11. http://www.fullstop.net/2011/12/11/interviews/alex/dana-spiotta/.

———. 2011a. Interview with Carolyn Kellogg, *LA Times Jacket Copy*, August 3.http://latimesblogs.latimes.com/jacketcopy/2011/08/dana-spiotta-on-living-the-creative-life.html.

———. 2011b. *Stone Arabia*. New York: Scribner.

———. 2006. *Eat the Document*. New York: Scribner.

———. 2002. *Lightning Field*. 2001. New York: Scribner.

Springsteen, Bruce. 1982. *Nebraska*. New York: Columbia Records.

Stranded in Canton. 2008. Directed by William Eggleston. New York: Eggleston Artistic Trust.

Thornton, Sarah. 1996. *Club Cultures: Music, Media, and Subcultural Capital*. Hanover, NH: Wesleyan University Press.

Tichi, Cecelia. 1994. *High Lonesome: The American Culture of Country Music*. Chapel Hill: University of North Carolina Press.

Tosches, Nick. 2000. "Pentecostals in Heat." In *The Nick Tosches Reader*, 276–85. New York: Da Capo.

———. 1998. *Hellfire: The Jerry Lee Lewis Story*. New York: Grove.

True, Everett. 2007. *Nirvana: The Biography*. 2006. Cambridge, MA: Da Capo.

Uncle Tupelo. 2002. "Watch Me Fall." *89/93: An Anthology*. New York: Legacy Records.

———. 1990. "Screen Door," "That Year," and "Whiskey Bottle." *No Depression*. New York: Legacy Records.

Velvet Underground. 1993. "Heroin." *Live MCMXCIII* (recorded in Paris). London: Sire Records.

Waits, Tom. 1999. "What's He Building?" *Mule Variations*. Los Angeles: Anti-Records.

Wareham, Dean. 2009. *Black Postcards: A Memoir*. New York: Penguin.

Whiskeytown. 1998. "Faithless Street." *Faithless Street*. Los Angeles: Outpost

Recordings.

Wilco. 1996. "Sunken Treasure." *Being There*. Burbank, CA: Reprise Records.

Williams, Victoria. 1990. "Summer of Drugs." *Swing the Statue!* London: Rough Trade Records.

Williams, William Carlos. 1985. "To Elsie." In *Selected Poems*, 53–55. New York: New Directions.

——. 1956. *In the American Grain*. New York: New Directions.

Wise, Gene. 1979. "Paradigm Dramas in American Studies: A Cultural and Institutional History of the Movement." In *Locating American Studies: The Evolution of a Discipline*, edited by Lucy Maddox, 166–210. Baltimore: Johns Hopkins University Press.

Woodstock. 1970. Directed by Michael Wadleigh. Burbank, CA: Warner Brothers Pictures.

X. 1981. "We're Desperate." *Wild Gift*. Los Angeles: Slash Records.

Yarm, Mark. 2011. *Everybody Loves Our Town: An Oral History of Grunge*. New York: Crown Archetype.

Zanes, Warren. 2016. *Petty: The Biography*. New York: Holt.

Index

Hersh, Kristin, 96, 139

Heylin, Clinton, 90

High Noon, 107

Hill, Trent, 112

Himes, Geoffrey, 102–3, 114, 122

Holmes, Richard, 52, 56

Holsapple, Peter, 100, 162

Hoskyns, Barney, 7, 52–55, 157

Howlin' Wolf, 59, 69, 88

Hurt, Edd, 111, 122

Hüsker Dü, 143, 179

irony, 26–28, 68, 110–12, 141,
    153, 163, 167, 170–73

Jackson, Mahalia, 85

Jackson, Michael, 66–67, 133, 154–55

Janoff, Callie, 187

Jenkins, Johnny, 71

Jennings, Waylon, 56, 59

Johnson, Robert, 94

Jones, Booker T., 71, 79

Jovanovic, Rob, 158

Joy Division: "Transmission," 46–48

Juanico, June, 65

Kael, Pauline, 7

Keisker, Marion, 87–89

Kerouac, Jack, 86; On the Road, 72, 75

Killing Them Softly (film), 48–49

King, Martin Luther Jr., 38, 79, 81, 85

Klein, Allen, 85

Kot, Greg, 12

Landau, Jon, 71

Lauper, Cyndi, 47

Lauterbach, Preston, 185

Lawrence, D. H., 26–28; Studies in
    Classic American Literature, 20, 42

Lennon, John, 99

Lincoln, Abraham, 37–38

Linklater, Richard, 131. See
    also Slacker (film)

Lipton, Lawrence, 145

Little Miss Cornshucks, 127–28

Liu, Alan, 35

Locke, Dixie, 64–65

"lost albums," 133, 164, 166, 173

Louvin, Ira, 84

Love, 173

Lyon, Randall, 6, 137

MacKaye, Ian, 178

Mailer, Norman, 18; "The
    White Negro," 72

The Manchurian Candidate (film), 38

Mapplethorpe, Robert, 135–36, 138–39

Marcus, Greil, 9–10, 14–50, 58, 60–63,
    69, 74, 112, 119, 130–31, 156, 168,
    186; Bob Dylan by Greil Marcus,
    42–45; Dead Elvis, 25–26, 64; The
    Doors, 45; Double Trouble, 25–26;
    The History of Rock 'n' Roll in Ten
    Songs, 45–49; Invisible Republic,
    30–37, 42, 44; Like a Rolling Stone,
    42; Lipstick Traces, 28–30, 33, 42;
    Mystery Train, 1, 2, 4, 7–8, 19–20, 33,
    42, 94; Real Life Rock, 49; The Shape
    of Things to Come, 41–42; When
    That Rough God Goes Riding, 3

Marcus, Sara, 13

McCullough, David, 60

The New American Canon

Violet America: Regional Cosmopolitanism in U.S. Fiction since the Great Depression
by Jason Arthur

The Meanings of J. Robert Oppenheimer
by Lindsey Michael Banco

Workshops of Empire: Stegner, Engle, and American Creative Writing during the Cold War
by Eric Bennett

Places in the Making: A Cultural Geography of American Poetry
by Jim Cocola

The Legacy of David Foster Wallace
edited by Samuel Cohen and Lee Konstantinou

Postmodern/Postwar—and After: Rethinking American Literature
edited by Jason Gladstone, Andrew Hoberek, and Daniel Worden

After the Program Era: The Past, Present, and Future of Creative Writing in the University
edited by Loren Glass

It's Just the Normal Noises: Marcus, Guralnick, No Depression, *and the Mystery of Americana Music*
by Timothy Gray

American Unexceptionalism: The Everyman and the Suburban Novel after 9/11
by Kathy Knapp

Pynchon's California
edited by Scott McClintock and John Miller

Richard Ford and the Ends of Realism
by Ian McGuire

Reading Capitalist Realism
edited by Alison Shonkwiler and Leigh Claire La Berge

How to Revise a True War Story: Tim O'Brien's Process of Textual Production
by John K. Young